Alister McGrath is the Andre
Religion at Oxford University, ~~Director of the Ian Ramsey~~
Centre for Science and Religion. He holds Oxford doctorates in
the natural sciences, intellectual history and Christian theology.
McGrath has written extensively on the interaction of science
and Christian theology, and is the author of many books, including the international bestseller *The Dawkins Delusion? Atheist
Fundamentalism and the Denial of the Divine* (SPCK, 2007), and
the market-leading textbook *Christian Theology: An Introduction*
(Wiley, 2016). McGrath also serves as the Gresham Professor of
Divinity, a public professorship in the City of London, established in 1597, that promotes the public engagement of theology
with the leading issues of the day.

THE LANDSCAPE OF FAITH

An explorer's guide to the Christian creeds

Alister McGrath

First published in Great Britain in 2018

Society for Promoting Christian Knowledge
36 Causton Street
London SW1P 4ST
www.spck.org.uk

British Library Cataloguing-in-Publication Data
A catalogue record for this book is available from the British Library

ISBN 978–0–281–07625–3
eBook ISBN 978–0–281–07626–0

Typeset by Manila Typesetting Company
First printed in Great Britain by Ashford Colour Press
Subsequently digitally reprinted in Great Britain

eBook by Manila Typesetting Company

Produced on paper from sustainable forests

'We cannot simply eat, sleep, hunt and reproduce – we are meaning-seeking creatures.'

Jeanette Winterson

'My own eyes are not enough for me, I will see through those of others . . . In reading great literature, I become a thousand men and yet remain myself. Like the night sky in the Greek poem, I see with a myriad eyes, but it is still I who see.'

C. S. Lewis

'Of all disciplines theology is the fairest, the one that moves the head and heart most fully, the one that comes closest to human reality, the one that gives the clearest perspective on the truth which every disciple seeks. It is a landscape like those of Umbria and Tuscany with views which are distant and yet clear.'

Karl Barth

'I think the attempt to defend belief can unsettle it, in fact, because there is always an inadequacy in argument about ultimate things.'

Marilynne Robinson

Contents

Part 4
THE THIRD ARTICLE:
THE HOLY SPIRIT AND THE CHRISTIAN LIFE

Preface

The English writer Evelyn Waugh is best known for his novel *Brideshead Revisited*, published in 1945. Some years earlier, Waugh had made the momentous decision to convert to Christianity. Such was his fame at that time that his conversion made the front pages of some British newspapers. He later wrote to a friend describing how his new faith allowed him to see things clearly for the first time. He felt that he had left behind a distorted and illusory realm of shadows, and embraced and entered a strange and wonderful new world. And having stepped into that world, Waugh began 'the delicious process of exploring it limitlessly'.

Like Waugh and many others, I too remember experiencing that sense of anticipation and excitement, mingled with more than a little trepidation, as I hesitantly began to explore the landscape of the Christian faith. As a younger man, I had embraced, perhaps a little uncritically, the intellectual certainties of a rather dogmatic atheism. It was all too easy for someone like me, who loved the natural sciences, to be lured into a bleak and austere metaphysics, in which science determines what is real, rather than illuminating what is observed.

I was woken out of my intellectual complacency during the months before going to Oxford University to study chemistry. I began to read books about the history and philosophy of science, fully expecting these to confirm my scientific atheism. Instead, they undermined its plausibility, forcing me to confront the limits of the scientific method, the provisionality of scientific knowledge, the problem of radical theory change in science, and the simple fact that most scientific theories were corrigible interpretations of evidence, not factual statements. Things were more complicated than I had realized. C. S. Lewis was quite right when he remarked that 'a young man who wishes to remain a sound Atheist cannot be too careful of his reading. There are traps everywhere.' I know, because I fell into them.

My eyes were now opened, and I began to see a more complex world, resistant to the simplifications of those who saw science as a convenient weapon against religion. What I had taken to be certainties suddenly seemed vulnerable and precarious. I had regarded science as factual, and religion as fictional. Perhaps for the first time, I realized that both the natural sciences and religious belief might be rationally motivated and informed interpretations of reality, representing attempts to understand aspects of our world using different methods and approaches. I tried to suppress such disturbing thoughts, realizing that, if this was true, any notion of scientific atheism being intellectually privileged was untenable.

Perhaps it was inevitable that I would experience a crisis of faith during my first year at Oxford University, while I was studying the natural sciences. On the one hand, I finally had to concede that atheism was not as intellectually robust as I had once believed. It was a faith, an interpretation of our world, rather than a set of evidenced certainties. On the other hand, I began (to my surprise) to appreciate that Christianity offered a plausible and winsome 'big picture' of reality that seemed to make more sense than my faltering atheism of what I saw around me and experienced within me.

Reluctantly, I decided to embrace the Christian faith, conscious that I was entering a new universe which I neither knew nor understood. This was not a conclusion I had expected to reach, nor was it one I welcomed. I was a stranger in paradise, unready for the challenging new world of ideas that I had decided to make my home.

As a boy, I took delight in reading books about faraway places, such as R. M. Ballantyne's *Coral Island*, Daniel Defoe's *Robinson Crusoe* and Robert Louis Stevenson's *Treasure Island*. They captured my youthful imagination, setting me alongside people who arrived on mysterious islands with hidden secrets waiting to be discovered. I realized that my discovery of the Christian faith was like being washed up on the shores of one of these mysterious islands, and challenged to explore its landscape.

I began to try to make sense of the strange new world in which I now decided to live, move and have my being. Sometimes

I did this by reading books about Christian theology, sometimes by talking to others who already knew parts of that island well and were able to help me find my way around. Gradually I settled into this new world, shedding my status as a newcomer, and becoming one of the island's long-established residents – someone who knew its landscapes, language and customs well.

This book is an explorer's guide to the landscape of the Christian faith. It is a tool for study, a resource for wisdom in leading an intelligent, reflective and grateful life of Christian discipleship. Having now inhabited this world for more than 40 years, I feel confident enough to write this book, aiming to help others to discover, encounter, appreciate and understand its rich and sumptuous, yet often puzzling, features. My aim is to help my readers develop their own map of the island of the Christian faith by telling them what I have found as I travelled, and how I built this into my own 'big picture' of faith.

At times, you will find yourself disagreeing with me – possibly because you feel I am wrong, but more likely because you feel that there is much more that needs to be said, and that I have not developed certain approaches adequately, or failed to take account of others. These criticisms are entirely fair. You may find it helpful to see me simply as a conversation partner, explaining the approaches that I find helpful (and why), but wanting to help you develop your own vision of the Christian faith, grounded in the creeds, yet reflecting your personal experience and interests. At times, I will touch on connections between faith and the natural sciences, since this is an important part of my own history. Yet you may wish to explore other connections and engagements – with the arts, literature or other areas of life.

The approach I adopt is similar to that of C. S. Lewis's *Mere Christianity* (1952), in that I try to explore a basic consensual Christianity, without engaging with contentious questions of denominational identity. Like Lewis, I write as a member of the Church of England, seeing this as neither a privilege nor a problem. This work sets out a generous consensual Christian orthodoxy, which allows you to make your own decisions about your denominational commitments, and how you fill in the fine detail of the 'big picture' of faith sketched in this volume.

Some will wonder about my decision to organize this book around the statements of the creeds. I can understand this concern. My own first encounters with those creeds were decidedly unpromising. They seemed dry and dull, lacking any sense of vibrancy or excitement. To begin with, I tried to ignore them, despite the fact that they feature so prominently in public worship. Then I gradually began to realize they were best seen as maps of the landscape of faith, helping us to find our way, and telling us what to look out for.

This work tries to be a guidebook to the landscapes mapped by the Christian creeds. As such, it has clear limits. A guidebook's brief description of the location of an island waterfall cannot even begin to express its beauty and splendour, or capture the sound of its rushing water. But that is not what a guidebook is meant to do; its role is to help its readers locate that waterfall, and experience it for themselves, by preparing their imaginations and heightening their attentiveness.

Yet enough has been said by way of introduction. We need to begin our exploration of the strange, fascinating and sometimes overwhelming landscape of the island of faith.

As this work appeals so much to the Apostles' and Nicene Creeds, I have provided my own translations of these important documents as Appendices at the end of the work (pp. 249–50).

Alister McGrath
University of Oxford

Acknowledgements

Apart from a few scattered exceptions in the early chapters, none of the ideas in this work are original. I have gathered them over many years from the rich pasturelands of the Christian tradition. I gladly acknowledge those who have particularly helped me develop and shape the ideas in this book: Anselm of Canterbury, Thomas Aquinas, Athanasius of Alexandria, Augustine of Hippo, Emil Brunner, John Calvin, G. K. Chesterton, Dante Alighieri, Charles Gore, George Herbert, Irenaeus of Lyons, C. S. Lewis, Martin Luther, John Mackay, Stephen Charles Neill, Marilynne Robinson, Dorothy L. Sayers, Rowan Williams and Huldrych Zwingli. Many readers will be able to discern their influence without needing any help from me, but it is still important that I name my sources, and acknowledge their influence. They have become my travelling companions on the Road.

Part 1

MAPPING THE
LANDSCAPE OF FAITH

1

The discipleship of the mind: a journey of exploration

'I believe'. These opening words of the Christian creeds are an invitation to a journey of discovery. To believe is to step through a door – a door that many have failed to notice or find – into the rich pasturelands of the Christian faith, and begin a process of exploration and appreciation. Faith is an attitude to reality, a way of seeing things that helps us grasp how much there is to discover, and its potential to transform our lives. The creeds are not a list of beliefs to be memorized, but a snapshot of a way of thinking and living that has brought intellectual satisfaction and personal fulfilment to countless people down the ages.

This book is an explorer's guide to the landscape of faith. It uses the creeds as tools of discovery which heighten our attentiveness towards some of their leading themes. It is written by someone who discovered that landscape a generation ago, and has inhabited and explored it ever since, trying to work out the best ways of describing that vista of faith, and explaining its relevance.

The island of faith

It's a storyline that has captured many imaginations. A commercial passenger jet flying between Australia and the United States crashes near a mysterious tropical island somewhere in the South Pacific. The survivors find themselves washed up on its shoreline, watching the warm turquoise water lapping the island's silver sands. So what is this strange place? What awaits them in its deeply wooded interior? Where can they find food and water? Are there others already on this island? And how might they escape, and find their way back to their own worlds? Yet while they wait to be found and rescued, they begin to explore the island and uncover its secrets.

Life is about exploring this strange cosmic island on which we find ourselves, and trying to make sense of it. Is this our real home? Or is there another island somewhere else which is where we really belong? And if so, how do we get there? One of the most distinctive features of human beings is that we search for meaning – for an understanding of our world and ourselves that helps us discover who we are, why we are here and what we should be doing. We seem to have been born with an inbuilt longing to understand, not merely how things *work*, but what they *mean*. 'All people by nature desire to know,' as Aristotle once observed. Yet the knowledge he had in mind was not an accumulation of disconnected facts, but a deeper discernment of the patterns underlying our observations, which allowed us to answer questions that begin with the provocative word 'Why?'

Physical survival matters; yet it is not enough for us. We sense that there is more to life than simply getting by from one day to another. We are meant to do more than merely *exist*. The contemplation of beauty in nature, the discernment of meaning in life and the scientific investigation of the world all point to the fact that we are fundamentally meaning-seeking creatures. We want to locate our universe and ourselves on a map of understanding which makes sense of what we see around us and experience within us. That's why we set out on journeys of exploration of the landscape of this world.

We are pilgrims and wayfarers across the face of this world, who try to make sense of it as we pass through. The Acts of the Apostles reports that Christians were initially known as 'followers of the Way' (cf. Acts 9.1–2; 22.4). In the Middle Ages, the Latin term *viator* came to be used in a symbolic sense, meaning a pilgrim or wayfarer who was travelling across the landscape of this world, in transit to the new Jerusalem. This is not where we really belong; it is a landscape through which we pass on our way to somewhere else which is our true homeland. But part of our journey involves discovering more about ourselves and our world, to prepare us better for the journey itself, as well as its final destination.

Two journeys of discovery

Human beings long to make sense of their worlds – both the world they see around themselves, and the interior world that they experience within themselves. The philosopher Immanuel Kant spoke of the two things that filled him with wonder: the starry heavens above him, and the moral sense within him. Kant's words help us see that there are two journeys of discovery that we must make: exploring the world around us, and our deepest intuitions within us.

The first of these human journeys of discovery is found in the natural sciences, which are basically an attempt to make sense of our physical world. We observe the way the planets move against the fixed stars, or the way objects fall to earth, and try to work out what 'big picture' of reality helps us to understand these observations. A scientific theory is really a way of looking at our world which helps us to work out the way in which natural objects and forces are related to one another.

Some scientists see these theories as offering a complete account of our world. There is nothing more that needs to be said, or that can be said. Others, however, see these as offering only a partial insight into our universe. They fill in part of the 'big picture' of reality, yet need supplementation from other sources. As Albert Einstein once observed, the scientific method can disclose little more than how observations are connected to each other. Scientific truth may well be precise and objective; it is, however, also incomplete, filling in only part of the 'big picture' of life. Our universe may be partly revealed by the natural sciences; it remains, however, tantalizingly unexplained by them.

There is, however, another journey of discovery that many undertake, which takes us into a hidden world of value and purpose. It goes beneath the surface of things, and opens up a deeper grasp of reality. When rightly understood, it denies nothing of a scientific understanding of the world, other than its finality. For Einstein, religious faith provided a vision of reality which created space for the natural sciences, while engaging the deeper existential questions about meaning and purpose which are of such fundamental importance to human beings. For Einstein, we need to inhabit both worlds if we are to live authentically.

I began my exploration of the world by inhabiting the realm of the natural sciences. On cold Irish winter nights back in the 1960s, I explored the night sky using a small telescope I had built, marvelling at the rich star-fields of the Milky Way and the silent witness of the orbits of the moons of Jupiter to the regularities of a Newtonian universe. My great-uncle, who had been a pathologist in one of Ireland's leading hospitals, gave me an old brass microscope which allowed me to discover a new world of life in what seemed to be an unpromising drop of pond water. My expanding sense of wonder at nature created a desire to understand its hidden secrets. I knew I wanted to be a scientist, and so specialized in mathematics, physics and chemistry so that I could achieve my boyhood dream of studying science properly at Oxford University.

Yet I can now see that, instead of allowing science to open me up to the wonders of our strange and majestic universe, I restricted reality to what science could disclose. The world I chose to inhabit was limited to the scientifically demonstrable, which I took to be an island of certainty in the midst of a cruel sea of subjectivity and irrationality. I trusted only what could be proved to be true, and saw 'faith' as an intellectual liability, the outcome of a failure to conform our thinking to the secure deliverances of faith and reason. I embraced a confident atheism, partly as a response to the religious tensions I saw around me in my native Ireland, but mainly because of my conviction that the natural sciences both demanded and authorized the principled rejection of any transcendent realm.

This world of certainty was, I soon discovered, rather narrow and bleak. Yet I then saw this, simplistically and not a little smugly, as an intellectual virtue. So deeply was I embedded in this way of thinking that I regarded its obvious lack of appeal as an indicator of its truth. I ridiculed those who believed what they liked, yet failed to see that I had simply inverted their frame of reference. Where some of my friends adopted world views that gave meaning to their lives, I regarded meaninglessness as a guarantor of truth. The unattractiveness of an atheist world view thus became a marker of its validity. It was, I fully concede, a circuitous and flawed way of thinking, perhaps foreshadowing the intellectual upheaval I would later experience as I came to see what is obvious to me now, but was a rational 'blind spot' for me at that time.

Thinking I had achieved intellectual freedom, I had in fact become a captive within a rational cage I had unwittingly created for myself. My attempt to liberate myself from religious dogmatism through embracing a shallow scientific positivism had merely imprisoned me within an anti-religious attitude, framed by a set of assumptions that were just as dogmatic as any proposed by my religious friends. I was marooned on an island of spurious certainty, which I had hoped would be lush and verdant, yet turned out to be a desert landscape, enlivened only by the occasional ball of tumbleweed, blown aimlessly along by a passing breeze. Yet every now and then, something would wash ashore on the beach of this island of failed dreams, like a strange plant, suggesting that there were other habitable islands that I had yet to discover.

Having become an admirer of the atheist philosopher Bertrand Russell, I came across a passage in which he annoyingly called my youthful certainties into question. Philosophy, Russell declared, tries to teach us 'how to live without certainty, and yet without being paralyzed by hesitation'.[1] I began to realize that Russell was really an intellectual agnostic, who believed that we should suspend judgement about metaphysical questions as a matter of intellectual integrity – a judgement that was confirmed when I got round to reading the great 1948 debate about God between Russell and Frederick Copleston, in which Russell clearly and categorically defined himself as an agnostic. His atheism was a personal and pragmatic choice rather than a conclusion forced upon him by the evidence.

Russell's words opened up a rather disturbing question for me. What, I wondered, if only *shallow* truths could be proved? After all, in my heart of hearts I knew that I could not demonstrate that atheism was right, which troublingly implied it was really a working hypothesis rather than a secure truth. If so, I would need to reconsider all the great questions of life which I had hitherto dismissed as deluded fantasies. Perhaps I was like someone surveying the still waters of a beautiful palm-enfolded lagoon, but failing to see the fish darting below the surface.

As for so many before me, Oxford University provided both the opportunity and means to open up questions that I had once thought were settled but knew in my heart were unresolved. I had no intention of abandoning the natural sciences, which I loved. But what if they illuminated only part of a grander vision of life, rather than determining that 'big picture' in its totality? Was there some other 'big picture' which could accommodate the successes of the natural sciences, while at the same time illuminating their limits? And might this other grander vision of things deal with the deeper questions of purpose and meaning that are of such importance to human existence and flourishing?

For a scientist, the ultimate test of a theory is its 'empirical fit' – its capacity to accommodate what we experience and observe. My atheist world view was able to cope with the inconvenient existence of intelligent people who believed in God with admirable simplicity. They were actually deluded and irrational people, incapable of either engaging evidence or coping with the harsh realities of life, who sustained their miserable lives by grasping at consoling illusions. Yet I was never entirely persuaded by this glib response, not least because some of my acquaintances who believed in God performed rather better than I did in school examinations. What if they had seen something that I had missed?

Dorothy L. Sayers once remarked that she wrote her best novel, *Gaudy Night*, to 'exhibit intellectual integrity as the one great permanent value in an emotionally unstable world'. In the end, I decided that this intellectual integrity demanded that I should reconsider my world view. I had, after all, little to lose by doing so. If atheism was right, it had nothing to fear from either my probing of its credentials, or of exploring alternative outlooks.

Yet even then, I was beginning to appreciate that the form of atheism I had espoused was really a faith – a belief that could not be proved to be true, and thus ultimately had to be accepted on trust and had to be publicly sustained by rhetorical denunciation of anyone who pointed out its obvious intellectual deficits. If human beings have to learn to 'live without certainty', the terms of the debate about the rationality of faith shift significantly. No longer could this be framed as a simple contrast between atheist fact and religious faith. Rather, the debate had moved on to the question of which faith or belief system is to be preferred. Atheism, or something else? I realized that if I were to remain an atheist, I would have to come to terms with the fact that my beliefs were not self-evidently true or demonstratively provable. Alternative beliefs would now have to be taken with intellectual seriousness and personal respect.

And so I came to reconsider Christianity. Setting aside my accumulated prejudices about religion in general and Christianity in particular (of which there were many), I focused on its core ideas, and the 'big picture' which lay behind them. How did this make sense of what I observed in the world around me, and experienced within myself? How did it fit in with the natural sciences?

As I explored this strange new world, I gradually began to appreciate its intellectual capaciousness. Although I could only manage to glimpse something of the richness of its vision, I could see that even this imperfectly apprehended Christian 'big picture' gave me a viable framework for understanding the world and opening up deeper questions of meaning, purpose and value. It appeared capable of accommodating everything that seemed to really matter, without intellectual violence or distortion.

 Some are drawn to Christianity because it offers a strong sense of identity and purpose, others because of the beauty of its vision of God and the world. In my own case, I experienced an intellectual conversion, which changed the way I saw and understood things. Both the New Testament and many early Christian writers speak of *metanoia* (e.g., Acts 5.31; 11.18; 20.21; 26.20). Although this Greek term is often translated as 'repentance', this does not adequately convey the full richness of its meaning. *Metanoia* really means something like 'a complete change of mind', a mental about-turn or a fundamental re-orientation of the way in which we think, leading to a new way of seeing or imagining the world and acting within it.

Repentance is certainly part of the meaning of *metanoia*. Yet the term affirms more than turning *away* from a lesser vision of reality that is now seen as inadequate, flawed or impoverishing; it hints at the rational or aesthetic excellence of what the mind is drawn *towards* – in this case, the vision of God. I came to see that Christianity offers an articulated conceptual unity with the capacity to transform individual human lives. Its vision of reality is imaginatively compelling and existentially transformative, reassuring us that there are indeed answers, even if only half glimpsed, to the ultimate questions of life.

I realized that faith is not an intellectual vice, but a simple necessity if we are to live meaningfully within our world. We cannot engage with the complexities of reality without making judgements we cannot prove. Every reflective atheist I know concedes this point, although some understandably prefer to do so in private. There are some more fundamentalist atheists who bristle with anger at being challenged to prove their belief that there is no God. 'I refuse to dignify that question with a response.' It is, however, a perfectly reasonable request. Atheists who demand that religious people prove their core beliefs must be willing to apply the same criterion to their own. The most fundamental and lethal criticism of the New Atheism, a movement which briefly attracted attention in the first decade of the twenty-first century, is that it arrogantly refuses to be judged on the basis of the intellectual criteria by which it judges others.

Reason and imagination

I recall that, while still an atheist, a few months before going to Oxford University, I read Plato's *Republic*, and was challenged by his famous image of a group of people trapped since birth in a dark underground cave, knowing only an austere world of flickering shadows cast by a fire. Having no experience of any other reality, they assume that there is nothing behind or beyond their shadowy cavern. Yet the reader knows that there is another world beyond this smoky cave, waiting to be discovered.

My hardened rationalism was quick to dismiss any such idea. What you see is what you get, and that was the end of the matter.

Yet a still, small voice within me whispered words of doubt. Suppose what we observe and experience is only part of the story? What if this world is only a shadowland of something better and greater? What if there is something more wonderful beyond it? I suppressed those thoughts. Yet looking back, I can now see that my stubborn refusal to take this possibility seriously was really a symptom of a deeper and growing unease with my atheism.

Plato's analogy offered me an alternative way of imagining our world. It is natural for those who feel threatened by these alternative worlds to try to suppress them and ridicule the human imagination for creating them in the first place. For example, the 'Age of Reason' tried to discredit those who challenged its common-sense, taken-for-granted world by dubbing them 'irrational'. This failed attempt to suppress the imagination merely enriched Western culture, giving rise to movements such as Romanticism, which were highly critical of the dull platitudes of rationalism.

Today, few would accept the severely truncated vision of reality commended by the 'Age of Reason' – not because reason has been abandoned, but rather because the critical application of reason shows the obvious failings of this simplistic approach to what can be known. For Pascal, the supreme achievement of reason is to grasp its limits, recognizing the vast array of things that lie beyond its reach. Happily, theologians have now come to see the impoverishing impact of the 'Age of Reason' on the way we think about the Christian understanding of faith. Instead of offering reduced and rationalized accounts of faith, they have rediscovered the importance of imagination in grasping the meaning of life and transforming human existence.

The New Atheism was deeply hostile to any appeal to the imagination. Although this deep prejudice against the imagination was carefully presented as a necessary defence of the rationality of science, it was really driven by a fear that people might discover and inhabit a deeper vision of reality than the diminished account offered by this 'glib and shallow rationalism' (C. S. Lewis).

Although the natural sciences are often portrayed in incorrigibly rationalist terms, in reality the scientific method involves an appeal to the imagination as much as to reason. We are asked to imagine another way of thinking about observations, and check it out against the observational evidence. To suppress the imagination is to compromise one of the most important tools of scientific discovery.

✳ The Christian faith offers us a new way of seeing ourselves and our world. We are invited to re-imagine things, seeing them in a fresh light. *Metanoia* is about the transformation of the human reason and imagination, so that we are no longer condemned to a superficial reading and experience of the world, but are enabled to go deeper. 'Do not be conformed to this world, but be transformed by the renewing of your minds' (Romans 12.2).

Paul's point here is that the way we see ourselves and the world should not be a passive reflection of contemporary cultural norms and transient ideas of values, but should instead arise from a transforming encounter with the living God. For writers such as Augustine of Hippo and Thomas Aquinas, the imagination is a link connecting our deepest intuitions and the unseen depths of our universe, helping us to grasp who we are, and why we matter.

Yet there is a deeper point here. It is not simply that Christianity enables us to see the world in a new way; it is that we come to
✳ see the world *as it really is*. The reason this is 'new' is that we are trapped within materialist ways of looking at the world, shaped by the controlling belief that there is nothing that lies beyond our world of experience. As Ludwig Wittgenstein pointed out, we can easily become trapped within a 'picture', a certain way of thinking, and then find that we cannot extricate ourselves from our self-imposed servitude. We need help to break free from this limiting and limited vision of reality.

It is not surprising that some dismiss this alternative vision of reality as irrational, or resist any attempt to redefine the 'real' in terms which go beyond what we encounter in the physical world. 'Irrational' here means little more than a refusal to conform to the cultural establishment's view of the way things ought to be – which in turn reflects its own vested interests and agendas. The
✳ Christian vision of reality is perceived as a threat only by those who depend on an unthinking acceptance of the ability of science or human reason to determine what is real.

The 'Age of Reason' portrayed itself as the champion of reliable and secure knowledge. Yet, when seen from the standpoint of Christianity's alternative vision of reality, this turns out to be little more than self-imprisonment within a rationalist cage, like those trapped within Plato's cave who refuse to countenance any idea of a world beyond the cave. When seen in this way, the Christian faith offers an empowering and energizing invitation to escape from this austere and inadequate way of thinking about the world. We are invited to leave the shadowy world of a narrow rationalist enclosure, and discover the sunlit uplands of the rich landscape of the Christian faith.

As we prepare to explore the Christian landscape, it will be helpful to reflect on the notion of the 'discipleship of the mind' which arises from the *metanoia* just described. So what is this discipleship, and what form might it take?

The discipleship of the mind

Many motivations can be given for the kind of exploration I set out in this volume. Intellectual curiosity is one of them. Yet for the Christian, the most important is that this pilgrimage of the mind is an act of love for God which promises to deepen the quality of the life of faith. 'You shall love the Lord your God with all your heart, and with all your soul, and with all your mind, and with all your strength' (Mark 12.30). To love God with all our mind is to yearn to understand God as best we can, given the limits placed on human capacities – and to see our world and ourselves in that light.

The discipleship of the mind is the intellectual expression of the faithfulness of the heart's yearning for what has been revealed as the only satisfying object of its desire. It is a passionate and committed quest to grasp our object of desire in all its fullness, using every faculty and capacity that is at our disposal. We throw every resource we possess into our heartfelt desire to know and love God, in the full awareness that such a discipleship of the mind can never be restricted to the mind, but extends to take in every means by which we apprehend the living God.

Inevitably, this involves reflecting on Christian beliefs or doctrines, as these are set out in the creeds. Christian reflection on the place of doctrines in the life of faith generally focuses on

13

three questions. First, what are the reasons for believing that a certain doctrine is true? Second, how can they best be expressed and communicated? And third, if these doctrines are true and trustworthy, what are their implications? What difference does the Christian faith make to the way in which we understand our world, and behave within it? What new or distinctive way of seeing things does it enable, and how does this affect the way in which we live out our lives in the world? And is it rich enough and stable enough to be able to offer something distinctive to the world without being captured by the world? This third task of theology invites us to explore the new way of seeing ourselves and our lives made possible through the core ideas of the Christian faith.

Yet Christianity is about salvation, not merely illumination. The preaching of the risen Christ is not merely an invitation to understand ourselves in a new way, while remaining in an essentially unchanged universe; rather, we are being invited to enter and inhabit a transformed universe which has been renewed through the resurrection of Jesus Christ. Wherever Christ is a living presence, there is a new creation (2 Corinthians 5.21). In Augustine of Hippo's famous words, what we encounter in contemplating God is 'not only to be looked at but to be lived in'. Yes, we see ourselves and our world in a new way as we develop new habits of thought and beholding; yet both we and our world – and hence our relationship with that world – have also been changed. We are observers with a transformed capacity of vision exploring a world which itself is being recreated through God's grace and power.

So how might we think of this journey of exploration? Or, since this journey of discovery is best approached through the imagination, how can we visualize this encounter with the riches of a Christian way of thinking? One of the most helpful approaches is stimulated and informed by the image of an island. Imagine once more that the Christian faith is like an island – perhaps a beautiful tropical island in the South Pacific Ocean, or one of the many Greek islands in the Aegean Sea, such as the Cyclades or Dodecanese. How might we explore and appreciate its landscape?

14

First, we need to *discover* this island. (In my own case, I thought I already knew something about Christianity, and regarded it as moribund and barren. Only later did I realize that I had rejected a caricature, and failed to appreciate what it was really about.) And having discovered this island, we set out to explore its landscape.

Some, of course, will feel they need to *rediscover* this island. Perhaps an over-familiarity with its vistas has led to a loss of interest and erosion of curiosity on their part, so they need to refresh their perceptions of the island. Some returning to the island after many years' absence from its shores may experience a resurgence in their interest and appreciation as they encounter what was once familiar but has become strange through absence. Others may value the literary technique of defamiliarization, by which they intentionally try to see something as if it were for the first time.

This naturally leads to the second phase of our encounter with this island – *exploration*. Having arrived on the island, we want to discover its main features – its mountains, woods, pastures, rivers and towns. Perhaps we might draw a map of the island, both to identify these features and position them. The map is a two-dimensional representation of a rich and complex three-dimensional reality. It can never be a substitute for the island's mountains or rivers. But it helps us to find our way to them, and work out how to get around the island. A map is an essential instrument of exploration that allows us to locate and experience the island's many features.

The creeds are maps of the landscape of faith, helping us to grasp and assimilate its key themes. They set an agenda of discovery, in that they tell us what to look for within the landscape of faith, and invite us to encounter and appreciate it. They are not, and were never intended to be, substitutes for an experience of the love of God, or capturing a glimpse of the glory of God through contemplating the solemn stillness of the night sky. The creeds sketch the territory through which we will travel, and invite us to fill in the detail from our own experience of journeying through that landscape, our conversations with fellow travellers, and our reading of the key resources of faith, such as the Christian Bible. They lay out the direction in which the life of faith is moving towards its fulfilment in God, reassuring us that this journey is meaningful and worthwhile, while mapping out the challenges and obstacles that we must face as we explore.

That process of exploration can take many forms. Others who have lived on that island for some time – such as C. S. Lewis, Dorothy L. Sayers or Thomas Aquinas – might take us on a journey around the island, pointing out its main features, and explaining how they understood and valued them. As I grew in my faith, I came to value mentors or travelling companions, who would help me to understand particular issues or ideas, passing on their wisdom, so that I could in turn pass it on to others.

And finally, we *inhabit* the island, as it becomes the place where we make our home rather than a destination that we merely visit. We learn its language, its customs and its values. The creeds help us to grasp both the grammar and vocabulary of faith through a process of immersion in the community of faith. We come to realize that the language of faith, while at times overlapping with that of everyday life, has its own distinct meaning. The landscape of faith becomes our homeland – not something that we admire as tourists, but a place in which we belong as citizens.

The image of the 'landscape of faith' is deeply embedded within the Christian tradition, and is grounded in the Bible itself. The biblical stories of exodus from Egypt and entry into the promised land, of exile to Babylon and return to Jerusalem, invite us to imagine the people of God journeying through the physical landscapes of the ancient Near East. Yet these descriptions of travelling through the world are to be seen against a deeper landscape of divine presence and action. We are pilgrims and sojourners on earth, who must learn to marry the physical landscapes through which we travel with an imagined – but not *imaginary* – landscape of faith which informs us as we journey, interpreting the situations in which we find ourselves. We undertake a journey which takes us deeper into this landscape of faith ('further up and further in', as C. S. Lewis put it towards the end of his Chronicles of Narnia). The deeper we go, the better we see things.

The framework of consensual Christian orthodoxy, as set out somewhat prosaically in the creeds, gives us a new way of seeing our world. It is no accident that the New Testament frequently uses the imagery of sight to speak of both the spiritual discernment that arises from faith and the failure to see things properly as a distinguishing characteristic of the human condition. We are visually impaired, and cannot see things as they really are. We need to be healed if we are to see properly. A veil needs to be removed from before our eyes if we are to see the world and ourselves as they truly are.

The French novelist Marcel Proust spoke of the 'only true voyage of discovery' being 'not to travel to new landscapes, but to possess other eyes, to behold the universe through the eyes of another, of a hundred others'.[2] Christianity offers us a transformed vision of the landscape of our world, which is articulated and displayed in the New Testament, as well as by the great writers of the Christian tradition. Augustine of Hippo spoke of the Christian gospel in transformative terms: it was about 'healing the eye of the heart so that God might be seen'.[3] Our 'outward eyes' cannot cope with the grandeur of God; they need to be healed if they are to see past the world of experience and appearance, and discern what lies beyond and behind it.

This chapter has introduced the idea that Christianity gives us a way of seeing our world and ourselves, and making sense of the enigmas of experience. We shall develop this idea further in the next chapter, focusing on four images which help us to visualize how this might happen. We have already touched on some of these themes; they deserve fuller discussion.

2

The Christian faith: a map, lens, light and tapestry

The great English Victorian art critic John Ruskin once remarked that 'the greatest thing a human soul ever does in this world is to see something, and tell what it saw in a plain way'.[1] The creeds are the Christian Church's attempt to tell believers and the world what it has *seen* – a transformative and utterly compelling vision of God which resists any attempt to reduce it to plain words.

The casual reader of the creeds could be excused for gaining the impression that they are little more than terse lists of theological words, dull catalogues of ideas which conspicuously fail to capture our imaginations or excite our minds. Yet when rightly understood, their words serve as triggers for the recollection of what is traditionally described as the 'deposit of faith' – a repository of insight and wisdom which is only partially capable of being expressed in ordinary human language. It is almost as if we need to invent a new language to cope with the realities of the life of faith.

The creeds are not definitive and exhaustive accounts of the contents of the Christian faith, but are rather summary descriptions of the vast expanses of the landscape of faith, intended to invite us to explore further this distinctive landscape. The creeds set out an itinerary of exploration and discovery, aiming to ensure that we attain a comprehensive grasp of the contents of the Christian faith by identifying the points at which we must pause and reflect, ensuring we have omitted nothing of importance.

What has been entrusted to the Christian Church down the ages, so briefly summarized in the creeds, is a way of seeing and thinking about the world and living within it which focuses on the life, death and resurrection of Jesus Christ. The New Testament speaks of the 'mind of Christ' (1 Corinthians 2.16), an acquired habit of understanding and imagining ourselves and our world which allows us to see things as they really are, stripping away illusions and misunderstandings. It is both expressed in and safeguarded by the Christian Bible and creeds, and nourished by the preaching and worship of the Church. The short statements of the creeds are verbal cues to recall and reflect on much deeper truths, issuing invitations to believers to recollect and savour the power of the core memories and beliefs of the Christian community down the ages.

Throughout this work, I shall highlight the importance of (theological vision)— of cultivating the habit of seeing through appearances, and discerning what lies beyond and beneath them. Just looking at the world is not good enough; we can only see the world properly by being trained to see it – by acquiring the art of discernment that arises through initiation into the Christian tradition, both rationally and imaginatively. The New Testament often uses the analogy of an athlete preparing for a race, in which natural gifts are honed and developed by training (1 Corinthians 9.24–26). We are likewise called upon to develop our ability to see, partly through a grace-wrought transformation, and partly through developing habits of attentive observation.

This process involves the creative interplay between divine grace and human wisdom. It is by grace that our eyes are healed and we are able to see; yet we are called upon to develop a discipline of vision, so that we may see more clearly. The Christian way of seeing reality is neither naturally acquired nor naturally endorsed. It comes about through the Christian revelation, which brings about a transformation of our perception of things. As we shall see later, this process of developing our capacity to see is an aspect of our growth in faith which is nourished and sustained by the Church, which serves as a community of learning and discernment.

So how can we visualize the role of the creeds in helping us to see properly? In what follows, we shall consider four analogies that are helpful in illuminating both the distinct nature of

Christianity in general, and the purpose and place of creeds in the life of faith in particular.

The creed as a map

The philosopher Mary Midgley argued that our world is so complex that we need 'multiple maps' if we are to make any sense of it.[2] No single angle of approach or way of looking at things is good enough to do justice to the many layers and aspects of human existence – they can only be adequately accommodated by using a plurality of overlapping models. A failure to do this merely leads to an improper reductionism, in which our failure to use proper mapping tools leads to an impoverished and truncated understanding of a complex reality. In addition to maps of the physical world, we need some way of representing deeper truths about human existence, and relating these to our everyday experiences. One map helps us to understand the shape of our world, and how it works; another helps us to understand our true nature and destiny, and why we are here. We need both maps to inhabit this world meaningfully, and explore it.

Again, one map might allow us to grasp the physical features and structures of our world, helping us to locate mountains, oceans and cities; another map might help us grasp the existential shape of life, allowing us to find meaning, value and purpose. These two maps need to be superimposed on one other, allowing us both to journey through our physical world and to discover our true meaning and purpose. The maps work at different levels, yet both are essential to human wellbeing and flourishing.

In fact, most of us are familiar with this idea of 'multiple maps', working at different levels, to understand complex aspects of our world. Think of Julius Caesar crossing the River Rubicon, just south of the Italian city of Ravenna, in 49 BC. The Roman historian Suetonius is one of several writers to tell of how Caesar led an army southwards over the Rubicon from Cisalpine Gaul to Rome. This action can easily be mapped on to the physical terrain of Italy, so that we can follow the course of Caesar's march southwards towards Rome.

Yet the reason why Caesar's crossing of the Rubicon is of such historical importance can only be appreciated by overlaying another map on this event. The Rubicon marked a political frontier between the territories of the Roman provinces and the area controlled directly by the Roman republic itself. This political map shows us that in crossing this river, Caesar was declaring war against the Roman republic, thus precipitating a civil war. If we are to appreciate the full significance of this event, the physical and political maps need to be overlaid. We need a stereoscopic vision of this event. Physically, Caesar crossed a river; politically, he crossed a regional boundary illegally, and so caused a crisis in Rome.

The same principle applies to theological maps of meaning. The New Testament sees the death of Jesus Christ on a cross as being of decisive importance. The creeds declare that Jesus was 'crucified under Pontius Pilate', making clear that this execution can be dated *historically* to the period during which Pontius Pilate was prefect of the Roman province of Judaea (AD 26–36). This event can also be located *geographically*, in that it took place somewhere immediately outside the ancient city walls of Jerusalem, and *legally*, in that Christ did not simply die, but was executed as a criminal under Roman law.

Yet this historical, geographical and legal mapping of the crucifixion of Jesus Christ is simply not good enough to disclose its full significance. An extra layer of interpretation is needed. Paul, repeating the compact summary of the Christian faith that was passed on to him after his conversion, locates the deeper meaning of Christ's death using a *theological* map. It was a prophetically predicted event which had the potential to transform the human situation. 'I handed on to you as of first importance what I in turn had received: that Christ died for our sins in accordance with the scriptures' (1 Corinthians 15.3). Jesus Christ thus did not simply die; he died *for our sins*. This theological interpretation of the crucifixion is reiterated by the creeds: Christ 'was crucified also for us under Pontius Pilate'.

The Christian creeds thus provide us with a framework for integrating multiple perspectives on the significance of Jesus Christ, insisting that this was a real historical figure with a transhistorical significance. The full meaning of Christ is not bound to any one time and place, but is porous to historical, geographical and cultural boundaries.

The creed as a light

As I set out to explore the complex world of the Christian faith, I began to read writers who would become my travelling companions as I tried to grasp and assimilate its core beliefs. Like many before me, I discovered the works of C. S. Lewis, and began to grasp the imaginative – and not merely the rational – appeal of Christianity. One sentence from one of his lectures to the Oxford Socratic Club captured my imagination, and has shaped my thinking ever since about the role of creeds in helping us to make sense of the world. 'I believe in Christianity as I believe that the Sun has risen, not only because I see it, but because by it I see everything else.'[3]

Lewis's analogy of a rising sun illuminating a landscape is both imaginatively winsome and theologically informative. As Lewis intended, it is best explored by turning it over in our imagination, and working its many angles. His image invites us to see ourselves as standing on a mountain ridge just before dawn, and look down on a dark and misty landscape, tinged with the rays of the rising sun. As we stand in solemn stillness, the valleys below us begin to glow. Slowly, the landscape is bathed in light, and the enfolding mist disperses. We can see what was already there but was previously obscured by the misty darkness.

Lewis's finely crafted analogy helps us grasp that Christianity's capacity to clarify the complex landscape of our world is an indication of its truthfulness. We are a people who once walked in darkness, travelling through a half-glimpsed world. Now, however, we have been enabled to see, through a divinely enriched human act of beholding which does not invent a world of our own creation, but discerns a real world that we previously could not see.

Yet Lewis's analogy of the sun conveys more than the intellectual capaciousness of the Christian faith, which illuminates our world so that we can make sense of it. It also highlights the human inability to achieve such insight unaided. Many Christian writers understand the human condition in terms of impairment of theological vision. Left to our own devices, we do not see properly, and so fall into the trap of defining reality simply in terms of what our impaired vision allows us to see. We are like Plato's prisoners, trapped in their dark underground cave, who think that what they see determines what there is to be seen.

The New Testament regularly uses the image of the restoration of a diminished human vision as an analogy for the transformative and regenerative power of the gospel. The healing ministry of Christ involved the restoration of vision (Mark 8.22–26). Paul's conversion is described in terms of the falling of scales from his eyes (Acts 9.10–19), leading him to suggest that the gospel removes a veil so that we can see the things of God for what they really are (2 Corinthians 4.3–4).

Yet *we still do not see with total clarity*. Lewis's emphasis upon the sense-making capacity of faith can perhaps too easily be misunderstood to mean that the Christian sun illuminates every aspect of the landscape so that no shadows remain. The German theologian Martin Luther offers a helpful corrective to this overstatement. Luther reminds us that some aspects of that landscape remain shrouded in darkness and shadow, and that we are often obliged to journey across and through those shadowlands, walking by faith rather than by sight (2 Corinthians 5.7). We are still walking in the dark, rather than in the full light of God's glory. Our grasp of reality is thus only partial and deeply ambivalent, which sometimes leads us to doubt and despair. Faith is about entering darkness, trusting that God sees and upholds us, even if we do not always see God.

For Luther, the cross of Christ offers us the most secure and reliable standpoint from which to view and cope with these deep ambiguities within the natural order, human culture and our own experience. We live in a dark and tormented world, yet can take comfort from knowing that Christ inhabited this world of apparent meaninglessness. We stand with him and alongside him as we journey through life in the midst of suffering, bewilderment and death.

Lewis is right: our faith gives us a lens through which we can interpret the world, making sense of its ordering and its enigmas. Yet Luther is also right: our faith enables us to journey through darkness and despair, even when there are times when its lens seems to yield a picture that is not fully in focus. With this point in mind, let us move on to consider that image of the creed as a lens in more detail.

The creed as a lens

The imagery of seeing ourselves and our world through glass has long been recognized to be theologically illuminating. In his poem 'The Elixir', George Herbert uses the analogy of looking through a glass window to illustrate the transformative potential of the gospel. This acts as the basis of a coherent account of the transformation of vision and action that Herbert clearly considered to be integral to the Christian faith. The poem affirms and illuminates the capacity of the Christian faith to transform our perceptions of the world, and hence our behaviour within it. Yet this ability to 'see' God in all things is not a natural human capacity, but is a habit or skill that is acquired from God. We can only see the world rightly if we are trained to look at things in a certain way that is not itself given in the natural order of things. Yet we can look at things in different ways. Herbert uses the analogy of a glass window to make this point:[4]

> A man that looks on glass,
> On it may stay his eye;
> Or if he pleaseth, through it pass,
> And then the heav'n espy.

Herbert here contrasts two quite different possible modes of engagement with a piece of glass – a 'looking on' and a 'passing through'. I might look at a window, seeing it as an object of interest in itself, perhaps focusing on the quality of its glass. Yet there is a deeper way of interacting with this window. We can *look through* it rather than *look at it*, thus using this window as a means of gaining access to what lies beyond it. The window now functions as a *gateway to vision,* rather than being itself the *object of vision.* It becomes a means of gaining access to a greater reality, rather than being the object of study itself.

Herbert's point is that the gospel makes possible a new way of seeing things, throwing open the shutters on a world that cannot be fully or properly known, experienced or encountered through human wisdom and strength alone. Christian doctrine offers us a subject worthy of study in its own right; yet its supreme importance lies in its capacity to allow us to pass through its imaginative gateway, and behold our world in a new way. For Herbert, Christian doctrine aims to make us into faithful disciples, in that it helps us to understand our faith and grow in wisdom by developing habits of thought and action that faithfully reflect and communicate the Christian gospel.

Yet the image of glass can be developed in another way. A lens is a piece of glass which enhances the capacity of human vision – as in a telescope or microscope. Galileo famously discovered that a telescope enabled him to look at the night sky and behold sights that none had seen before him – such as the craters and seas of the moon, and the myriad of stars within the Milky Way. The Christian faith, as set out in the creeds, is like a telescope, which enhances the reach of our natural vision so that we can glimpse something of God – a topic to which we shall return later in this work.

The image of a telescope is helpful in another way. I might be walking along a sandy beach on a beautiful day, surveying the deep blue ocean stretching far into the distance. I might notice something moving on the horizon, and use a telescope to see what it is. To begin with, I see only a shapeless and fuzzy blur. Yet as I bring the image into focus, the shapeless blur is transformed into a crisp and vibrant image of a yacht in full sail. We can think of the Christian faith as a lens that brings the meaning of life into focus. Secularism offers a rather different lens, which lets us see less – and thus persuades some that there is less to be seen.

Some might see human life as 'a tale told by an idiot, full of sound and fury, signifying nothing'. We might think of the young Joy Davidman, who summarized her early loss of faith in a neat aphorism: 'In 1929 I believed in nothing but American prosperity; in 1930 I believed in nothing.'[5] Yet using the wrong lens means that the world *seems* out of focus and distorted. We need a new lens if we are to see things more clearly. What some see as something random, meaningless and chaotic, without any underlying order or significance, is brought into focus and given meaning and value by the imaginative theological framework of the Christian faith.

As the philosopher Ludwig Wittgenstein pointed out, faith in God brings life into focus, and conveys meaning through helping us realize that we are thinking and living in accordance with something deeper and greater than ourselves. 'In order to live happily I must be in agreement with the world. And that is what "being happy" means.'[6] We need to grasp the 'big picture' of the universe, and position ourselves within it, accepting any challenges it may bring to the glib and shallow notions of human goodness and autonomy that have become embedded as unexamined cultural norms.

Yet some people prefer to keep seeing the world through a distorting lens. The philosopher Iris Murdoch pointed out that we often shield ourselves from reality by 'fabricating an anxious, usually self-preoccupied, often falsifying *veil* which partially conceals the world'.[7] The true meaning of things is sometimes too disturbing for our comfort. As T. S. Eliot famously remarked, we do not seem to be able to cope with 'very much reality'.

So why do so many prefer to inhabit an illusory world? The Polish poet and Nobel laureate Czesław Miłosz, who lived under a particularly unpleasant form of totalitarianism in Communist Poland, argued that the roots of this oppressive ideology ultimately lay in the rejection of any notion of accountability. People invent a reality that allows them to do what they like without the need to worry about the consequences. Where Karl Marx famously argued that religion was 'the opium of the people', Miłosz argued that the *real* opium of the people is a belief in 'nothingness after death'. We are utterly unaccountable, and can take solace in knowing that we will never be judged for our sins.[8]

Looking at things through a Christian lens, on the other hand, brings our true situation into focus, enabling us to realize that we cannot go on as we are. To use a medical analogy: the Christian framework of meaning acts as a diagnostic tool, showing us that something is wrong with us, and telling us the treatment that is required if we are to be cured. We are liberated from the delusion that all is well, and shown what needs to be done if things are to be put right.

The creed as threads of a tapestry

A final image which I have found helpful in thinking about the place of Christian doctrines – such as those set out in the creeds – is that of threads woven together to produce a tapestry. The creeds can be thought of as the integration of the multiple themes of the Bible, in which each of these themes is connected and correlated with others, yielding a vision of reality which transcends the sum of its individual parts.

Christian beliefs are not like a set of individual, unrelated ideas. We cannot think of Christianity as a series of isolated boxes containing individual ideas – such as creation, the Incarnation, salvation and the Trinity. These ideas are interconnected, like a web, held together by the compelling and persuasive vision of reality that is made possible by the Christian gospel. The image of a web points to a series of interconnected strands of belief that is stronger and more robust than any of its individual parts.

Or, to go back to our original image, the individual threads of Christian belief are woven together to create a fabric which discloses a pattern – a pattern that could not be seen by considering any single thread in isolation. We cannot speak of the Christian understanding of the identity of Jesus Christ without reflecting on the nature of God, the nature of salvation, the role of the Holy Spirit, or our understanding of human nature – to mention just the more obvious themes, to which others can easily be added.

To study any single doctrinal theme is actually to study the whole web of faith, the 'grand narrative of the gospel', as it intersects at this node, or as it focuses on this theme. Christian doctrines are connected together, supporting and informing each other. They lead on to and into each other, so that the explorer can set out from any landmark in the landscape of faith, and find that the paths taken will lead to all the others.

Think again of a map of an island landscape, showing towns that are connected by roads. The map helps us to realize that we can visit every town on the island through this network of roads radiating outward from each of these hubs towards its neighbours. We cannot study individual Christian beliefs in isolation, but need to appreciate the coherence of Christian doctrine. Each element is woven into the fabric of faith. As Christians reflect on the significance of Jesus Christ, they find themselves linking up with related ideas, such as the doctrine of God, the idea of salvation and understanding of human nature.

We must avoid thinking of individual doctrines as self-contained, watertight compartments, each of which may be grasped without reference to anything else. This compartmentalizing attitude is encouraged by theology textbooks – and my own are sadly no exception – which break the rich landscape of Christian theology down into manageable segments. While this is a good educational strategy, it fails to bring out how these individual doctrines combine together to yield a greater vision of reality.

Yet we need to make sure that we never think of Christianity as simply assent to a set of ideas. There is something deeper. Some, such as C. S. Lewis, would find this in the Christian 'meta-narrative' – the story of God, which in turn gives rise to doctrines about God. Doctrines help us to avoid the failure that the poet T. S. Eliot warned about – namely, being unable to grasp the true significance of our experiences. We need a framework of interpretation which helps us to understand what a story or experience really means. Otherwise, to draw on the well-known line from Shakespeare's *Macbeth*, life simply becomes a tale that is 'full of sound and fury, signifying nothing'.

Yet for Lewis, doctrines are always secondary to the story. Others would locate this deeper reality in a relationship with God, or an encounter with God, perhaps through reading the Bible. Doctrine is necessary and important, but it is not what *really* matters. We know and trust God; we accept doctrines as an enrichment of, not a substitute for, this experience and relationship.

Let's go back to the image of a tapestry of faith, in which the individual threads are woven together to disclose a pattern.

The creeds take some trouble to identify the core threads of faith, aiming to ensure that we leave nothing important out as we begin the process of weaving them into our personal tapestries of faith. The New Testament speaks of all things 'holding together' or being 'knit together' in Christ (cf. Colossians 1.17). Christianity thus reassures us of the *coherence of reality*. However fragmented our world of experience may sometimes seem, there is an underlying 'big picture' which holds things together, its threads connecting together in a web of meaning what might otherwise seem incoherent and pointless.

This brings us to one of the core implications of this 'weaving' model of Christian beliefs. It points to individual believers as active interpreters, not passive recipients, of the core ideas of the creeds. Each individual Christian may take the same basic threads and weave them into a tapestry with a different pattern. Does this mean that Christianity has been distorted, or reduced to the subjective whim of the individual weaver? No. It merely recognizes one of the most important points about theology: namely that individual believers develop their own personal understandings of their faith, which address their own situations, reflect their own histories and are expressed in their own language. Each believer develops a personal articulation of faith which partially represents what they have found in the rich Christian depository of faith, how they make sense of it and how they enact it in their lives.

Should this disturb us? No. It is the inevitable result of the way in which human beings 'know' reality. We acknowledge the reality of what is known, as something that exists beyond the knower, while at the same time recognizing that this process of knowing something involves interacting with it and assessing how it relates to us. It involves a mental dialogue or conversation between the knower and what is known, in which the structures of the Christian faith are connected up with the situations we face and issues that concern us.

Problems begin to arise, however, when someone begins to think that their private or personal vision of faith ought to be normative for everyone. That's why creeds are so important. They politely and firmly remind us that Christianity has a public vision and public statement of its core beliefs. We are free to apply and assimilate these as we see best; we are not, however, free to change them. 'Though Christianity is unquestionably a *personal* experience, it is equally unquestionably not a *private* experience' (William Barclay).

The creeds set out a public vision of the Christian faith which emerged and found acceptance within the community of faith over time, and this filters out subjectivity of judgement. A creed is not a personal statement of faith, drawn up by an individual (however important); it is a public statement of the faith which gradually emerged within Christian communities as they reflected on their rich heritage and tried to express this as succinctly as possible.

Moving on

Throughout this work, I have emphasized that Christianity offers a 'big picture' of reality, and that it is this vision as a whole – rather than any of its individual details – which proves so persuasive and compelling. C. S. Lewis was drawn to Christianity for much the same reason as he loved some of the classics of medieval literature: an ability to 'embrace the greatest diversity of subordinated detail'.

That's why we need to appreciate the coherence of faith, and realize how each Christian belief or doctrine offers its own distinct 'little picture' which turns out to be an integral part of the 'big picture'. Imagine you are standing on an alpine peak, looking down at a breathtaking sunlit landscape. After a few moments, during which you are held captive by its beauty and scale, you decide to try to capture the scene. You start taking photographs – a few panoramic shots, followed by more detailed studies of the woods, mountains, streams and towns you can see. Yet each of these snapshots fits into the panorama, which allows you to see how each belongs in its own place within the bigger picture. The big picture positions and contextualizes the snapshots, confirming the coherence and unity of the landscape as a whole.

To make sense of individual snapshots of an alpine vista, we need to first take in the greater panorama, which positions and contextualizes each of these smaller pictures, allowing us to see them as part of a greater coherent whole. Similarly, to understand individual Christian beliefs, we must first catch sight of the greater vision, of which they are part. Now there is nothing wrong with snapshots – they often provide welcome detail of complex landscapes. Yet there is clearly a danger that certain approaches to theology just offer us those snapshots, and fail to show us the panorama.

The creeds thus identify the constituent threads of Christian belief, and leave it to us to weave them together into a coherent 'big picture'. It is this vision as a whole – rather than any of its individual details – which proves so persuasive and compelling, appealing to the imagination, not merely the reason. The big picture comes first; the details come later. The Christian faith allows us to see patterns in the apparent chaos of our world; to perceive a melody, when others only hear a noise. Instead of being overwhelmed with *information*, we are enabled to discern *meaning*.

This naturally leads us to reflect on how those creeds emerged, and why they are so helpful to Christians as they reflect on their own personal faith. In the next chapter, we shall look briefly at the origins and functions of creeds.

3

A cloud of witnesses: why we need creeds

Ambrose of Milan once wrote that the creed is 'a spiritual seal, our heart's meditation and an ever-present guardian; it is, unquestionably, the treasure of our soul'.[1] The creeds are hedges, enfolding and protecting the rich pastureland of faith; they are fences, safeguarding the wells of living water that sustain the life of faith. They are closed caskets of treasure which we are invited to open and explore. It was too easy for me, in my first months of faith, to confuse the fences and the wells, failing to appreciate the distinct *genre* of the creeds, and hence missing their point.

The creeds are primarily communal Christian confessions of faith, setting out the vision of reality that has given – and still gives – life, purpose and direction to individual believers and to the Christian community down the ages. When I recite the creeds, I think of myself as doing three things. First, I am calling to mind the 'big picture' which underlies the Christian faith, which helps me make sense of my world and life. Second, I am affirming that I am part of a believing community which sees this document as mapping out the beliefs that make it distinctive. I thus see myself as an inhabitant of the landscape of faith, not as a tourist or an outside observer. And third, I am recognizing that, in embracing Christianity, I am declaring my willingness to discover and explore what I have not yet encountered, refusing to be limited by my present understanding of my faith.

The creeds are thus aspirational and invitational, giving us a framework for both exploring its individual themes and discovering the greater reality of which they are part. To borrow an image from Teresa of Ávila, the Christian faith is like a mansion

with many rooms to explore. Most of us, however, fail to progress beyond the entrance hall. The creeds map out this mansion
of faith, encouraging us to become familiar with its many rooms,
and learn to live in them.

One of the most important functions of the creeds is to challenge individualist versions of the Christian faith. 'This is the
way I see it – so this is the way things are.' All of us have our own
personal creeds, adapted to our needs yet limited by our perspectives and concerns. Yet the creeds transcend these limits
placed on the capacity of any one individual fully to take in the
vast landscape of the Christian faith. C. S. Lewis realized that his
own grasp of faith was enriched by entering into the visual frame
of other people. His limited personal vision was thus extended,
expanded and enriched. 'My own eyes are not enough for me,
I will see through those of others . . . Like the night sky in the
Greek poem, I see with a myriad eyes, but it is still I who see.'[2]

The creeds are thus communal documents which bear witness
to what Christians down the ages have found to be trustworthy
and authentic readings of the Christian faith. They are there to
help us by questioning our own personal grasp of our faith, and
to enrich us by showing us what more there is to discover
and appreciate. They do not suppress our individuality, but enable us to grasp something that our individual limits prevent us
from seeing fully. They thus help a Church which has become
preoccupied with 'relevance' to relearn a forgotten way of doing
things and recapture lost attitudes, arousing the echoes of a rich
past to enrich the present.

Some, however, are concerned that the creeds seem cumber-
some and bureaucratic, presenting the Christian faith as if it
merely consisted of a catalogue of beliefs, devoid of imaginative
power and existential engagement. Surely we could do better than
this? Or perhaps even do without them altogether? After all, no
other major world religion uses creeds – not even other mono-
theistic faiths, such as Judaism or Islam. And they seem curiously
incomplete. They make no reference to the Bible, nor do they offer
any profound insights into the meaning of life. They seem like
institutional policy documents, which fail to capture the intensity
or depth of the Christian believer's relationship with Jesus Christ.

Do we really need creeds?

So can we do without creeds? What exactly would we lose if we were to cease using them? Surely all that we need to do is love God, and do our best to live out an authentic Christian life in the world? It's easy to understand why some long for what they call an 'undogmatic Christianity' – a faith which expresses itself in the deep personal qualities and activities of love, commitment and authenticity, rather than the somewhat impersonal and dull language of theology.

Yet Christian discipleship engages and makes demands of all our faculties. 'You shall love the Lord your God with all your heart, and with all your soul, and with all your mind, and with all your strength' (Mark 12.30). It demands that we *think* about our faith. Theology arises because we are rational creatures, and feel impelled, both morally and intellectually, to give the best account of reality that we can. Calling for an 'undogmatic Christianity' amounts to little more than issuing a crude embargo on using our minds to think about matters of faith.

The Christian creeds are the natural outcome of a personal encounter and sustained engagement with the person of Jesus Christ. We are drawn to the gospel accounts of Christ, finding he appeals to something deep within us. Yet we need to try to put into words precisely what it is that *we* have found, and ask how what *others* have found could further enrich our own experience and understanding. The creeds are a witness to what Christians have found to be intellectually satisfying summaries of their faith down the ages, and are there to guide and enrich us in our own journeys of faith.

To make this point, let us consider an episode in the Gospels which might at first sight seem to indicate that there is no need for creeds. The gospel accounts of the calling of the fishermen Peter and Andrew, whom Jesus Christ encountered on the shores of the Sea of Galilee (Mark 1.16–20), makes no reference to creeds or any formal statement of faith. Jesus Christ speaks these simple words to them: 'Come, follow me.' And having found Christ to be an utterly compelling figure, the first disciples leave behind their nets – on which their living depended completely – and follow this strange figure. They choose to entrust themselves totally to him, discerning that he is someone truly special, yet not quite understanding who he is. Yet the first disciples were not required to recite a creed before they were allowed to follow Christ. So if the heart of faith is about entrusting ourselves to Jesus Christ, why make this so much more complicated?

This is a perfectly fair question. Yet the point to appreciate is this: although Peter and Andrew's journey of faith began on the shores of the Sea of Galilee, it did not end there. As we read the Gospels, we observe how the disciples' faith deepens and solidifies as they gradually come to understand more about the identity and significance of Christ. In the beginning, they trust him; as time passes, this personal trust is supplemented with – but never displaced by – beliefs about him. How did Jesus Christ fit into the story of Israel? What was so special about him? What were the implications of following him? How did he fit into their own personal stories? And answering those questions led to the gradual emergence of an understanding of the full significance of Christ. Personal trust was thus both *consolidated and enriched* – not *displaced* – by a framework of beliefs.

Whenever the disciples had to explain who Jesus Christ was, or why he was so important, they found themselves having to use *words* to express their *beliefs* about him. The creeds are the carefully chosen words that the early Church agreed on to try to capture what lay at the heart of the Christian faith. They describe the Christian faith, as a sketch map describes a landscape. It is true that the New Testament does not set out a formal creed. Yet it is equally true that it contains many creedal statements. Some of these early Christian statements of faith were very short – such as the simple confession 'Jesus is Lord!' (Romans 10.9; 1 Corinthians 12.3). Yet the New Testament also contains a number of slightly longer creedal statements, such as the following:

> There is one God, the Father, from whom are all things and for whom we exist, and one Lord, Jesus Christ, through whom are all things and through whom we exist.   (1 Corinthians 8.6)

I handed on to you as of first importance what I in turn had received: that Christ died for our sins in accordance with the scriptures, and that he was buried, and that he was raised on the third day in accordance with the scriptures.

(1 Corinthians 15.3–4)

Cyril of Jerusalem argued that the creeds were to be seen as a 'synthesis of faith', which was intended to set out the 'teaching of the faith in its totality', by gathering together the core themes of the Bible – such as those just noted – and weaving them into a coherent whole.

Yet many remain suspicious of creeds, finding them un-attractive in their language, and alienating in their concepts. Surely Christianity needs a more welcoming and affirming inter-face with the wider world than these? Christianity managed per-fectly well without creeds during its first few centuries, when it was in the process of expanding. So why do we need them now?

There's a perfectly fair point being made here. Historically, Christians did indeed manage to get along without any for-mal creeds for the first three centuries of the Church. Yet this was not because they had no interest in what they believed, but because the political situation of the era made it impossible for Christians to meet to agree on universal public norms of faith throughout the Christian world. Christianity spread across the Roman Empire with astonishing speed, yet remained an illegal religion, prohibited from meeting in public. With the conversion of the Roman emperor Constantine in 313, everything changed. Christian leaders from throughout the empire were finally able to gather together at Nicaea in 325, and agree the contours of a common creed.

Yet even before the Council of Nicaea, Christian individ-uals and congregations had formulated some basic summaries of Christian faith. By around 190, we can begin to see collec-tions of texts very similar to the modern New Testament tak-ing shape, along with 'confessions of faith' very similar to the modern Apostles' Creed. These collections of texts and 'confes-sions of faith' were used by individual congregations, and seem to have been spread mainly through the movement of Christians across imperial frontiers. The leaders of Christian communities in the great metropolitan cities of the Roman Empire – such as Alexandria, Antioch and Rome – developed their own distinct ways of teaching the faith, giving rise to prototypes of the creeds. Those used in Rome were especially significant, on account of its status as the 'eternal city', the capital of the empire.

The Apostles' Creed had its origins in the early Church as a profession or confession of faith made by converts at their baptism. The early Church placed great emphasis upon the importance of the baptism of converts. During the period of Lent (the period from Ash Wednesday to Easter), those who had recently come to faith were given instruction in the Christian faith. Finally, when they had mastered the basics of faith, they would recite the Apostles' Creed together, as a collective public witness to the faith in which they believed, and which they now understood. Faith had now been reinforced with understanding.

These converts would then be baptized with great ceremony and joy on Easter Day itself, as the Church celebrated the resurrection of its Lord and Saviour. In this way, the significance of the baptism of the believer could be fully appreciated: he or she had passed from death to life (Romans 6.3–10). Baptism was a public demonstration of the believer's death to the world, and being born to new life in Jesus Christ.

At their baptism, which marked formal admission to the Christian community, believers were asked to confirm their faith individually, by responding to three questions or 'articles':

1 Do you believe in God the Father Almighty?
2 Do you believe in Jesus Christ, the Son of God?
3 Do you believe in the Holy Spirit?

Though these questions were sometimes asked in more extended and elaborate forms, this basic threefold pattern was widely used in both the Western and Eastern churches. In part, it reflects the 'Great Commission' of the risen Christ to his disciples: 'Go therefore and make disciples of all nations, baptizing them in the name of the Father and of the Son and of the Holy Spirit' (Matthew 28.19). The answers given to these three questions were not seen as representing full accounts of the Christian faith, but simply as summaries of its most important themes.

By answering 'I believe', those who were about to be baptized affirmed their commitment to the Christian way of thinking – to its overall 'big picture', not simply to its three leading articles.

The emergence of the creeds

From the end of the second century, documents which are clearly recognizable as creeds began to be used by prominent churches and Christian leaders as convenient summaries of faith. These statements gradually became known as *regulae fidei* (a Latin phrase meaning 'rules of faith'). Justin Martyr, an influential Christian theologian based in Rome, was arrested in 165. At his trial before the Roman prefect, he refused to worship or sacrifice to the traditional Roman gods, and instead declared his faith in the Christian God, using these words:[3]

> We worship the God of the Christians, whom we believe to be one from the beginning, the maker and fashioner of the whole creation, visible and invisible; and the Lord Jesus Christ, the Son of God, whose coming to be present with the human race as the herald of salvation and teacher of good disciples had been proclaimed beforehand by the prophets.

Reciting the creeds thus aligns us today with a community of faithful believers stretching back into the days of the Roman Empire. It reminds us that we are surrounded by a 'great cloud of witnesses' (Hebrews 12.1) as we ourselves journey along the Road, running the race of faith in the amphitheatre of the world. The creeds are a reminder of the importance of the inter-generational transmission of faith, in which one generation hands down to the next the words, ideas, practices and images that it has found helpful in expressing and nourishing its faith.

One of the most important of these 'rules of faith' is now known as the 'Apostles' Creed', or the 'Creed of the Apostles'. There is no doubt that the material included in this creed is authentically apostolic, in that it is deeply rooted in the New Testament. The Apostles' Creed served three important functions. First, it was a shared statement of faith, easily memorized through constant repetition in public worship, through which new Christians could confess and summarize their faith in Jesus Christ. Second, it served as a highly useful preaching and teaching tool, giving an outline of the basic themes of faith for further discussion and exploration, especially in sermons. And third, it provided a convenient synopsis of faith, helping Christians to explain the main points of their faith to outsiders and inquirers.

Yet Christians have always been clear that they do not believe *in* these creeds; they rather regard them as convenient summaries or outline sketches of a faith which is far deeper and richer than any words could express. The creeds are outward verbal expressions and summaries of a living faith, expressed and embodied in a larger quest for holiness, prayer and worship. They are sketch maps of a landscape, taking a radically different form to what they attempt to represent.

Although the creeds present an *adequate* summary of faith, they do not provide an *exhaustive* or *comprehensive* account of faith. There are omissions, which some might find surprising. For example, the creeds make no reference to the relation of the Christian Church and Israel, nor to Jesus Christ representing the fulfilment of Old Testament prophecy – a major theme in Matthew's Gospel and some of Paul's letters. There is no discussion of Christian understandings of human nature, or of grace. The Apostles' Creed also omits any *explicit* reference to the divinity of Jesus Christ, a deficiency which is corrected by the Nicene Creed. Nor is there any mention of the sources and norms of Christian belief, such as the Bible.

In the previous chapter (pages 18–31), I set out four ways of thinking about the function of creeds which may be helpful as we read the Bible and try to make sense of the world around us and within us: as a map, a light, a lens and a tapestry. Each offers an imaginative framework of interpretation, through which we can interrogate our experiences and try to work out what they really mean. Christianity offers us a new way of seeing, understanding and experiencing our world which often means recalibrating the way in which we naturally perceive things and evaluate their meaning. But where do we see things *from*? In thinking about the role of the creeds in the Christian faith, we need to reflect further on how believers relate to the landscape of faith. Do they stand above it, or are they themselves part of that landscape?

The camera and the narrative

Once more, let us imagine an exotic tropical island, shimmering in a sunlit ocean. We are approaching it by air, with high resolution cameras slung beneath the aircraft, ready to photograph its landscape and features with complete accuracy and objectivity. In successive sweeps, the aircraft photographs the island's beaches, rivers, mountains and towns. All are precisely located. The camera is an impersonal and uninvolved observer of the landscape, which records its physical features indifferently from a distance. Later, the photographs can be converted into maps, showing the precise location of the island's many features and points of interest. The photographs might even feature in a traveller's guide to the island.

Yet these photographs do not tell us what it is like to live on that island; they merely identify the physical features of its landscape. They illuminate the context of life on the island, but they do not tell us whether the island's inhabitants are happy and healthy. They show up centres of population, but tell us nothing about the moral dilemmas that face the people of the island, or their deepest existential concerns and fears. People appear merely as objects on the landscape, not living beings who have to make choices, cope with difficulties and try to become better people.

This way of understanding the creeds as objective, indifferent statements of Christian belief is the perspective of a scholar, an outsider, even a nominal Christian – someone who is not concerned or involved in these beliefs, who may have an academic interest in ascertaining what Christians believe, but is not caught up in their web of meaning.

There is, however, a second way of approaching that island landscape. This is the perspective of an inhabitant of the island – someone who is embedded in its physical and social landscape. The aircraft and its cameras offer a privileged perspective, in which impersonal and disinterested observers might look down

on the island, and map its features. The view from the aero-
plane's cameras is totally objective and utterly impersonal. It is
devoid of any of the personal qualities – such as compassion and
love – which make human life meaningful.

The inhabitants of that island, however, are affected by its
landscapes. This is where they act out real ethical dramas that
are invisible to the aircraft's cameras. Floods, earthquakes and
famines are not interesting phenomena to be observed indifferently from a safe distance; they are life-changing events which
shape the existence of human beings and other life forms on the
island. In trying to make sense of their experience of life, people
tell stories. These narratives help us to organize our experience
into a connected whole and allow us to remember people and
events that are important to us.

The airborne camera may give a completely objective view of
the island, yet in terms of what is happening on that island, it is
seriously inadequate, reporting only on what can be seen from
the surface. These two maps – physical and existential – need to
be brought into dialogue. Photographs and stories need to be
brought together in a creative interplay.

Earlier, we noted George Herbert's important distinction between looking *at* Christian belief and looking *through*
Christian belief (pages 24–5). The camera in the aircraft is a
detached observer which looks at the landscape below, offering a physical depiction of what is seen. The inhabitant of the
island is a participant, an actor in the process of living who offers
an existential account of what is experienced, and attempts to
cope with what cannot be understood or changed, and transform what is malleable and ductile. In this sense, the inhabitant
is creating the landscape of faith, not simply observing it. The
camera in the aircraft may photograph the paths along which
these wayfarers travel, yet it cannot tell that the wayfarers have
created these paths by the process of travelling itself.

These two perspectives are significantly different. Both, however, are possible ways of reading the creeds. Those creeds are
objective public statements of faith, yet they need to be assimilated and appropriated by individuals, who interpret and apply
them to their experience of living in the world. There is clearly

room for productive and positive interaction between these two aspects of the creeds, valuing their respective strengths, yet being alert to their weaknesses.

Perhaps the best analogy to help us explore these two ways of thinking about life was developed by John Alexander Mackay, a Scottish theologian who became president of Princeton Theological Seminary. In what follows, we shall consider his famous analogy of the Balcony and the Road.

The Balcony and the Road

Mackay spent some time living in Spain during the 1910s. While observing Spaniards relaxing after dinner in Madrid, Mackay watched some people walking along the streets of the city and others seated on the balconies of houses, high above the streets, looking down on the bustling scenes below. Mackay noted how the elevated vantage point of those on the balcony allowed them to overhear the conversations of the people walking along as they went about their business. The people on the balcony were spectators of, not participants in, the stream of life that was passing below them on the street.[4]

Mackay came to see the Balcony and the Road – I shall capitalize these from now on – as two different perspectives or ways of thinking about the Christian faith. The Balcony represented 'the perfect spectator, for whom life and the universe are permanent objects of study and contemplation'. Life on the street below is best observed in a detached way from a safe distance. We observe what is going on, but it doesn't affect us. The Balcony gives an 'objective view of things', from which all subjective relevance is eliminated.

Yet Mackay believed that the real place of faith was on the Road, where 'choices are made and decisions are carried out'. Here, faith is about a way of *living* – about taking decisions on what to do, where to turn and how to live. Those on the Balcony are *onlookers*; those on the Road are *wayfarers*. The people on the Balcony might watch people moving about below, and speculate idly on where these people are going, what they are worried about or where the road leads to. But when you are on the Road, these are not idle speculative questions. Life on the Road involves a 'first-hand experience of reality'. Truth is something to be *done*, not merely to be *thought*.

This framework of the Balcony and Road helps us in many ways, not least because it alerts us to two quite different ways of reading the creeds. Some read the creeds from the perspective of the Balcony. From this viewpoint, they are objective and detached summaries of Christian belief, from which any personal involvement or engagement is eliminated as a matter of principle. They are impersonal statements of belief – ideas that distinguish Christians and mark them off from other communities of faith. They could be read by outsiders in much the same way as early Western anthropologists approached native cultures – as objects of curiosity, not to be taken seriously, except to help make sense of how these strange people lived.

Yet from the Road, the creeds are seen very differently. They are statements of core beliefs that are to be trusted. They are precious, hard-wrought guides to a journey, distilling the wisdom of those who have already travelled along the Road, passing down both encouragement and insight to those who follow them. The creeds give a framework to the wayfarers on the Road to enable them to make sense of that journey, organizing and interpreting their personal experiences, and reassuring them that this Road actually leads somewhere.

The difference between these two perspectives can be seen from considering the problem of suffering, to which we shall return later (pages 154–69). From the Balcony, making sense of suffering is like a logical puzzle. How can a good God allow suffering? On the Road, however, the issue is how we cope with suffering. How can we keep going in the face of suffering? How can we live with loss, bereavement and the thought of our own death? How can we support others in the same situation, while also finding comfort and compassion? The approaches to suffering developed by people on the Balcony simply do not connect with the needs and concerns of those on the Road.

One of the most interesting illustrations of this point comes from the long career of C. S. Lewis. *The Problem of Pain* (1940), Lewis's first work of apologetics, was widely read, and remains greatly appreciated. Yet it takes a view from the Balcony, leading to an over-intellectualized and detached approach to suffering. When Lewis experienced traumatic grief himself on the Road, following the death of his wife from cancer in 1960, he found his own earlier ideas to be of little use in coping with his emotional pain. Lewis subsequently wrote *A Grief Observed* (1961), which took a very different approach from that set out earlier in *The Problem of Pain*. Lewis now offered a view from the Road, which engaged fully and honestly with the emotional turmoil of those experiencing loss as they travelled through life.

This helps explain why so many people find Christian biographies more helpful and interesting than works of theology. Biographies tell the story of a lived life; of someone who has worked out how to cope with living out faith in the world, and can pass on a legacy of advice, wisdom and encouragement. 'Here's a problem I encountered. And here's what I found helpful. Maybe it will help you as well.' Theological books can – though it must be said that many do not – enable their readers to make more sense of things. But that's for the Balcony. On the Road, we need travelling companions – people who have walked through the landscape of faith before us, and can pass on to us the wisdom that they picked up along the way.

In this opening section of this work, we have reflected on the origins and purpose of creeds. We are now ready to begin with the substance of those creeds, as they set out the basics of faith. In the remainder of this book, we shall use the outlines of the creeds to explore the core elements of the Christian faith.

Part 2

THE FIRST ARTICLE:
THE LIVING GOD

4

What can be trusted? The nature of faith

———◆◆———

'I believe'. In uttering these simple words, Christians declare that they have discovered a place of refuge, a safe anchorage for the soul, a way of seeing the world that makes sense, and a firm place on which they may stand. The first declaration of the creeds is thus not so much an item of belief, but an assertion of the need for faith to lead a meaningful life in the first place. For the Christian, faith is both trusting that there is a 'big picture' of life, and a decision and commitment to step inside this way of seeing ourselves and our world, and live it out. It enfolds a way of understanding our world, and a commitment to live and think on its basis, as we find ourselves transformed in and through our faith.

Yet it is not simply Christians who believe. Any moral, political, religious or anti-religious world view demands faith, in that its core beliefs cannot be demonstrated to be true. As the Greek philosopher Xenophanes argued, life involves a 'woven web of guesses'. To hold to any belief or moral value is to *judge* that these are true and trustworthy, while knowing that they cannot be proved. I mentioned earlier my sense of dismay when I realized that my youthful atheism, which I had fondly believed to be self-evidently true, was actually a judgement – an interpretation of the world – rather than an evidentially compelling factual statement about it.

There are no knock-down arguments that compel us either to believe in God or to believe that there is no God. If a decision has to be made, it takes the form of a judgement about what is the most trustworthy belief. Everyone has a creed that begins – whether implicitly or explicitly – with the words 'I believe'.

Christians simply make their faith commitment open and transparent, where others prefer to conceal or downplay it. Some might respond to this analysis by arguing that it makes *every* belief legitimate. It does not. Faith is about motivated judgement, which requires that there be good reasons for coming to such a conclusion, even though this conclusion itself cannot be demonstrably proved.

A feigned absence of faith was one of the more puzzling features of the New Atheist movement. Christopher Hitchens rather pompously declared that his faith was 'no faith'. Yet even a casual reading of his atheist manifesto *God is Not Great* (2007) showed it to be littered with unproven (and usually unprovable) value judgements and beliefs. This form of atheism is simply an intellectual bubble, a closed belief system, impervious to argument and evidence.

Yet not even the natural sciences can deliver secure answers to the deepest questions we would rightly ask ourselves about our meaning, value and purpose. Science makes judgements about which is the best theoretical representation of some aspect of our world. These judgements are clearly rationally motivated, and grounded in the evidence. Yet they remain provisional reasonable beliefs, not proven facts. Now this does not reduce us to despair; it simply highlights the importance of faith in making judgements that cannot be proved to be true yet rightly command our intellectual loyalty as trustworthy.

Yes, we live in an age of doubt and uncertainty. Yet this is not a recent development. In fact, we have *always* lived in such a world, but managed to deny it until the force of evidence was such that we had to come to terms again with this unsettling yet suppressed truth. The bygone 'Age of Reason' tried to ignore or conceal our situation, in much the same way as medieval supporters of Ptolemy's geocentric model of the solar system tried to overlook the evidence indicating it was fatally flawed.

Now we can see that the slick and shallow rationalism of the past was a distraction from the real question: how we can live without certainty, yet without being at the same time overwhelmed by doubt and despair. No human world view – religious, political or atheist – can prove its deliverances, and we must learn to live within them with uncertainty and the possibility of error. The hard rationalism of the 'Age of Reason', by proposing and then trying to enforce arbitrary criteria for proof, merely created anxiety and distress as it became clear that reason simply could not meet these inflated demands.

This point was set out clearly by the English philosopher Thomas Hobbes, who derided those who proposed 'right reason' as a universal and objective criterion for political, social, moral or religious ideas. Unfortunately, this was not some notion that was hardwired into the structures of the universe. Far from being an objective and universal judgement, it was simply a subjective perception on the part of powerful individuals whose influence was sufficient to create the impression of a cultural consensus. 'Commonly they that call for right reason to decide any controversy, do mean their own.'[1]

Meaning is not something that can be proved to be true or false. It hovers within the penumbra of rationality, unverifiable yet somehow essential to human wellbeing and flourishing. As the philosopher Ludwig Wittgenstein suggested, we seem to need more – much more – than what logic, mathematics and science can provide if we are to lead meaningful lives. 'We feel that even if *all possible* scientific questions could be answered, the problems of life have still not been touched at all.'[2]

In the end, we all have to make decisions about what beliefs and values command our assent and loyalty. The supreme goal of the truth-seeking mind is to find what is truly worth loving and truly capable of being trusted. G. K. Chesterton once quipped that 'the object of opening the mind, as of opening the mouth, is to shut it again on something solid'.[3] We all want to find something secure and trustworthy on which we can build our lives. We may trust people; we may trust beliefs. Yet in both cases, we have to make a judgement about their reliability and trustworthiness. Martin Luther pointed out that everyone needs to base their lives on something or someone. 'Your god is whatever you have set your heart upon, whoever it is that you trust.'[4] Religious faith is fundamentally about what we really value, find meaningful and yearn to possess. Each of these three aspects, though in different ways, is engaged and fulfilled by the Christian vision of God.

The opening words of the creed are thus as much an invitation to trust God as they are an affirmation of the trustworthiness of belief in God. They invite us to share the faith of Abraham, who trusted God's promises and set out into the unknown (Genesis 12.1–4), and all those who came after him who trusted in this same joy-giving, life-changing God. Yes, Christianity is about certain ideas, which we believe, but it is more fundamentally about a God whom we discover to be trustworthy, and invite to become the foundation and lodestar of our lives. Faith acknowledges and trusts a God who journeys with us, even when we pass through dark times and places.

What is faith?

It is natural for us to read the opening words of the creeds – 'I believe' – and interpret them in the light of their use in contemporary culture. Yet, as Ludwig Wittgenstein pointed out, we need to listen to how a community uses language, in that the same words may have special or developed meanings in one context which are not present in another. Christianity uses three critically important terms – faith, hope and love – in a distinct manner, which can only be understood through attentiveness to Christian preaching and worship, and especially the language of the Bible. To gloss 'I believe in God' as 'I think (but can't prove) there is a God' misses the point of what the creeds are saying. The subtlety of the Christian understanding of faith eludes categorization purely in terms of rational assent.

The Swiss theologian Emil Brunner dismissed rational conceptions of faith as *Fürwahrhalten* – in other words, simply taking something as being true. It fails to appreciate that faith is prompted in part by an *affective* response to its object. For some, God may indeed be the endpoint of a logical argument; yet for others, we are captivated by the glory of God, or held spellbound by the beauty of God. Some find themselves to be emotionally compelled to faith by the beauty of – for example – the Christian doctrine of the Incarnation, which then shapes their attitudes and goals in life. Yet this emotional response is a gateway to intellectual reflection, in which we seek to understand what we love.

Anselm of Canterbury famously spoke of the discipleship of the mind using the Latin slogan *fides quarens intellectum* ('faith seeking understanding'). We come to understand what we have learned to love, beginning to grasp the inner logic of the vision of God that we have found to be beautiful, radiant and compelling.

We need to recall that the creeds date from as early as the fourth century, and we have to ask what the words would have meant *at that time*, rather than assuming that they have the same meaning as today. The Apostles' Creed, for example, opens with the Latin word *credo*, which is almost always translated as 'I believe'. Yet the proper meaning of *credo* at the time when the creeds were written was 'to trust or confide in a person or thing; to have confidence in; to trust'.[5] While we now tend to think of faith in terms of a theoretical judgement, the creeds see it as a personal commitment.

Faustus of Riez, writing in the fifth century, explains that to believe (*credere*) in God means to 'respond to God in worship and adoration, by giving ourselves and our affections completely over to God'.[6] Part of that devotion is what I have called the 'discipleship of the mind', which aims to help us develop habits of thought that are rooted in the realities of the Christian faith, rather than passively echoing the dominant ideas of our culture.

The historian Pierre Hadot has pointed out that the word 'philosophy' was mainly used in the Classical world to mean *an intellectual expression of a way of life*. Philosophy was about giving intellectual substance to a way of life, and developing a code of conduct reflecting its core values.[7] Beliefs and lifestyle were seen as two sides of the same coin. This helps us to understand why the early Christians often spoke of their faith as a 'philosophy', a way of life leading to wisdom and goodness, and regularly depicted Christ as wearing a *pallium* – a philosopher's cloak.

The creeds think of faith in terms of commitment and entrustment, in which believers place their trust and hope in a trustworthy God. There is, of course, a sense in which the creeds affirm the truthfulness of the Christian faith. Yet historically, Christianity did not see itself as a 'religion' (as we would now use that word) with a set of beliefs to which we must assent, but as a trustworthy and reliable way of thinking and living which we

51

are invited to enter. The creeds sketch the outlines of this new pattern of thought and life, listing the key themes of Christian ways of thinking and living. We, as interpreters of the creeds, are invited to give depth and colour to these terse statements.

So how should we then think of faith? How can we retrieve this more authentic way of thinking about what it means to 'believe in God'? Perhaps the simplest approach is to think of faith as having three main aspects or elements, each of which is part of a greater whole, but none of which in itself adequately describes that whole.

To begin with, faith involves *assent*. Faith believes that certain things are true. 'I believe in God' includes the idea 'I believe that there is a God'. There is, of course, much more to faith than this. Yet before we can begin to say anything about what God is like, we need to assume that there is a God in the first place. When I was an atheist, I assumed that Christian faith was nothing more than intellectual assent to God's existence (something which I regarded as highly implausible). Yet as I explored Christianity, I realized that my earlier understanding of faith was totally inadequate. It was an outsider's view, inattentive to the actual ways in which Christians lived, spoke and thought.

Second, and perhaps more importantly, Christian faith is also to be seen as *trust*. When I declare that 'I believe in God', I am not just saying that I believe God exists. I am also affirming my trust in this God. Faith is not purely intellectual, enlightening the mind while leaving the heart untouched. Faith is the response of our whole person to the person of God. It is a joyful reaction on our part to the overwhelming divine love we see revealed in Jesus Christ. 'Faith is not only the assent of our minds to doctrinal propositions: it is the commitment of our whole selves into the hands of a faithful Creator and merciful Redeemer' (William Temple). Through faith, we accept and embrace God and the transformed existence that this relationship of trust makes possible.

Christians don't just believe; they believe *in someone*. A true friend is not merely a friend who actually exists, but someone I can trust to behave as a friend in situations of need or loss. Faith is not just believing that God exists; it is about anchoring ourselves to that God, and resting securely in doing so. Whatever storms life may bring, the anchor of faith will hold us firm to God.

And finally, in the third place Christian faith involves a *commitment* to God, our decision to allow the 'God and Father of our Lord Jesus Christ' to be present with us, to guide us, support us and transform us. It is a joyful and willing self-surrender to God. It is a throwing open of the doors of our lives, and inviting God to enter, not merely as our guest, but as our Lord. It is about stepping into the Christian 'big picture', and allowing the contours of our lives and actions to be shaped by its vision of the good.

God's commitment to us demands a commitment from us in return. Faith thus leads to obedience – a willingness to trust and obey the God whom we love. Faith is a personal relationship with God, in which we find ourselves being transformed and renewed in and through this relationship.

We noted earlier the close links between the creed and baptism in the early Church. At that time, to admit to being a Christian in the Roman Empire of the second and third centuries was to open yourself to ridicule, discrimination, victimization and possibly much worse. To come out as a Christian was a matter of real courage. When Christian converts declared that they believed in God, in Jesus Christ and in the Holy Spirit, they were not just telling the world *what* they believed about Jesus Christ, they were telling the world *that* they believed in Jesus Christ.

Thinking more about faith

The creeds aim to set out the richness of faith in God. Faith is about seeing the 'landscape of vision', in which we catch a glimpse of a greater and more beautiful vision of reality than anything the world can offer. We come to trust this vision of reality, which becomes our guide to thinking and living in the world, committing ourselves to living as if this magnificent vision of reality is true. We believe it is true. Yet, like every other 'big picture' of life, we know that we cannot prove it comprehensively and completely – but we still believe it may be trusted and entered, and that we can inhabit this world authentically, joyfully and hopefully.

Christian writers down the ages have distinguished two senses of the word 'faith'. First, it refers to 'a faith by which we believe' – that is to say, the act of trust and assent which says 'yes' to God, and reaches out to grasp and hold fast to God as the secure ground of our life and thought. Second, it refers to 'a faith which we believe' – that is to say, a set of beliefs, such as those laid out in the creeds. In this sense of the word, faith refers to the *content* of what we believe, rather than the *act* of believing and trusting. Creeds relate mainly to faith in the second sense of the word – but they nevertheless presuppose faith in the first sense of the word.

Some like to think of Christianity as a fixed set of beliefs which we are simply called to learn by heart. Yet we are all called out to wrestle with the Bible and the Christian tradition, trying to connect our ideas together in a way that we find meaningful and framing them in language that we understand, while at the same time listening to the rich witness of the Christian past, which offers us wisdom and insight as we reflect.

The Swiss theologian Emil Brunner brought out the need for constant attentiveness towards the gospel and our world of thought, so that the Christian faith could continually be brought into connection and dialogue with a changing world. 'The gospel remains the same, but our understanding of the gospel must ever be won anew.'[8] The discipleship of the mind is about this process of exploration and synthesis, which invites us to allow the Christian faith to illuminate the anxieties of our age, and speak meaningfully and faithfully to those concerns.

Some Christians take refuge in the simplistic faith of their childhood, or the certainties of the Church of the past. Yet we are called to grow in our faith, as we begin to appreciate its hidden depths through a process of reflection, interrogation and exploration. We cannot freeze faith in one of its past forms – whether it is our own childhood or defining moments in Christian history. We can always find nourishment from the Christian past; yet we can too easily become trapped in a nostalgic bygone world when we ought instead to rise to the challenges of the present moment. If we find that we live in an age of anxiety and uncertainty, we must find out how the rich deposit of faith can speak into this present situation.

If certainty is unattainable outside the highly restricted and unrepresentative areas of logic and mathematics, this does not mean that we are reduced to bewilderment and forced to take refuge in arbitrary theories that we find pleasing or consoling. Christian faith is not certainty in any mathematical or logical sense. It is something deeper than that – what Martin Luther called *fiducia*, a confidence that is neither blind trust nor mathematical certainty, but a principled trust in what has been found to be worthy of that trust.

Having faith in God is about trusting God. Beliefs represent an attempt to put the substance of that faith into words. While creeds are secondary to our trust and commitment, that does not mean they are unimportant or that we can do without them. The relationship between the believer and God, expressed in prayer and worship, needs to be explored in words and ideas. The medieval theologian Anselm of Canterbury made this point in his slogan 'faith seeking understanding'. We are called upon to love God with our minds, as well as our hearts and souls (Matthew 22.37). Part of the life of faith is a desire to understand more about whom and what we trust.

Faith and the quest for meaning

Human beings are meaning-seeking creatures who weave webs of meaning to guide and govern our lives. We live in a strange and baffling world of space and time, trying to work out answers to our deepest questions. What is the point of life? Why are we here? Do we really matter? Yet there is a problem – a problem which is airbrushed out of the picture by an overconfident breezy rationalism, but which is recognized and confronted by faith. *We cannot prove that any of the answers we give to the great* *questions of life are right*. All of them go beyond what reason and science can prove. Proof is only possible in the very limited realms of logic and mathematics. But how well do these relate to what Karl Popper called 'ultimate questions' – the really big questions about the meaning and value of life? Both logic and mathematics possess an elegant and austere beauty, yet they exist in an eternal and changeless world of their own, which seems to bear little relation to the changing world in which we live.

I admire the certainty and elegance of mathematics and formal logic, the only two areas of human thought in which any degree of certainty is possible. Yet each of these two worlds is the creation of the human mind, bearing little relation to the everyday world of human life and experience. Logic is really an analysis of the processes of human thought, rather than a study of any reality outside the human mind. Its perfection is grounded in its abstraction. It tells us a lot about the rules of thinking, but nothing about the world in which we live.

The fact that mathematics seems capable of expressing the deep structures of the universe is quite remarkable and calls out for an explanation that goes beyond the mere assertion of good fortune. Happily, as we shall see (pages 83–91), the Christian doctrine of creation offers one such explanation.

Our quest for trustworthy answers to life's ultimate questions ends up by exposing the frailty and provisionality of human thought. The English philosopher John Locke took great pleasure in the pursuit of truth. 'I know there is truth opposite to falsehood, that it may be found if people will, and is worth the seeking, and is not only the most valuable, but the pleasantest thing in the world.'[9] Those words could easily serve as the motto for the intellectual aspirations of the natural sciences, philosophy and Christian theology.

However, Locke was also acutely aware of the limited capacity of human reason to penetrate and comprehend the strange world in which we live. After surveying the significant problems we confront in trying to make sense of this world, Locke remarked: 'From all which it is easy to perceive what a darkness we are involved in, how little it is of Being, and the things that are, that we are capable to know.'[10]

Locke has a point. We struggle to grasp and represent our universe. After all, scientists now tell us that we can only see about 4 per cent of our universe; the remainder is made up of dark matter or dark energy that we cannot see, detect or even comprehend. Its existence is inferred from its gravitational influence on the very limited parts of the universe which can be seen, but dark matter and energy themselves continue to elude all detection.

That's just the way things are. Alexander Pope pointed out this disconcerting truth about our capacity to understand our world in his *Essay on Man*. We are 'born but to die, and reasoning but to err', trapped in an unsettling shadowy world suspended tantalizingly between scepticism and certainty.[11] We live in a twilight realm between scepticism and certainty, and have to work within this framework. For Pope, the category of faith thus extends beyond the limited realm of religion to embrace human knowledge as a whole. Shallow truths can be proved; deep truths have to be trusted.

Everyone needs faith – even atheists. Richard Dawkins, one of England's best-known atheists, demands that religious people should prove their beliefs. Yet he seems to be unable, even unwilling, to apply this criterion of truth to his own beliefs. Dawkins seems to be haunted by the realization that his own belief system failed the critical test that he himself had set it. This intellectual unease was seen in Dawkins's remarkable admission that he was actually an agnostic at an Oxford debate with the Archbishop of Canterbury in February 2012. While the audience was astonished at the candour of this admission, its logic is unassailable: Dawkins believes something he cannot prove.

It is helpful to set these issues against a broader backdrop. The philosopher and intellectual historian Isaiah Berlin pointed out that there are three basic categories of human convictions:

1 those arising from empirical observation;
2 those that can be established by logical deduction;
3 those that cannot be confirmed in either of these ways.

The first two of these categories embrace what is held to be known reliably through the natural sciences on the one hand, and what can be proved through logic and mathematics on the other. The third category concerns the values and ideas that have shaped human culture and given human existence direction and purpose down the ages – but which cannot be proved by reason or science.

Isaiah Berlin's point was elegantly simple. The beliefs that give human life meaning and purpose – such as social or ethical values, political beliefs, and religious or anti-religious ways of thinking – cannot be proved to be true, yet cannot be deemed to be irrational for that reason. Christianity, which is one set of such convictions, offers a coherent and rationally motivated view of the way the world is. And, like other 'big pictures', it cannot be demonstrated to be correct.

We live in a world characterized by a spectrum of rational possibilities, from 'demonstrably false' on the one hand to 'demonstrably correct' on the other. For Berlin, the convictions that we find meaningful and plausible lie towards the middle of that spectrum, occupying a position of faith rather than certainty. This is not a problem, save for those who demand that all beliefs (except their own) can be proved. 'We hold many beliefs that have no unimpeachably rational justification, but are nonetheless reasonable to entertain' (Terry Eagleton).

Reason, as the great Italian poet Dante once noted, has 'short wings'. What thinkers of the 'Age of Reason' had hoped to be an eagle that could soar high above the earth, carrying them aloft on its wings, turned out to be a turkey, capable only of short bursts of flight. Sadly, some of those who boast of being 'free-thinkers' are simply imprisoned within a defunct and discredited eighteenth-century rationalism.

For Christian thinkers, religious faith is not a surly and sour rebellion against reason, but a principled revolt against the imprisonment of humanity within the cold walls of a rationalist dogmatism. Human logic may be rationally adequate, but it is also existentially deficient. Faith declares that there is more to life than this. It doesn't contradict reason but transcends it. It elicits and invites rational consent, but does not compel it.

The great 'Age of Reason' held that human reason could sort out all the great questions of life without the need to appeal to a higher authority – or, indeed, to any other authority beyond itself. But by the outbreak of the First World War, it was obvious that the Enlightenment quest for truth was in deep trouble. The 'Age of Reason' was seen to deliver spurious certainties, being both inattentive to the complexity of reality and unrealistic about the capacities of human reason.

One major concern was that the Enlightenment's appeal to reason as the ultimate reliable source of authority could not itself be verified. How could it possibly be checked to make sure it was reliable? Rationalism argued that reason itself could demonstrate its own authority. Yet this was simply to use reason to prove reason, so that human reason served as both judge and jury in its own defence. The rationalist argument for the authority of reason turns out to be circular, presupposing its own conclusions.

The recent rise of postmodernity is really not a symptom of irrationalism (as irritated rationalists tend to suggest), but is actually a protest against the intellectual overstatements and the existential inadequacy of rationalism, as well as the authoritarianism it has encouraged. People came to realize the obvious problems with an approach to life that is *determined* – as opposed to merely being *informed* – by reason, and protested against those who tried to shoehorn them into such a dreary rationalist cage.

Only shallow truths can be proved. The deep truths that bring meaning and purpose to life lie tantalizingly beyond the realm of logical or scientific proof, and we have to learn to live with this. That's what Bertrand Russell was getting at when he remarked that philosophy teaches us 'how to live without certainty, and yet without being paralyzed by hesitation' (page 7).

We live in an age of uncertainty, and there is no going back to the cosy and easy certainties of the past. We have rightly become suspicious of those who offer slick and easy answers to what we know are complex questions. Yet this does not mean that we are entering a phase of irrationalism or a lazy complacency that holds that all beliefs are equally valid. It remains important to offer reasons for our beliefs, and to reflect critically on why we believe them to be right. But we now know that *no* conviction that is worth holding can be proved, and we have become willing to grasp the nettle of living with uncertainty.

The limits of reason

Reason is a useful critical tool, but it is an unreliable foundation for truth. It is too shallow to meet our existential needs, or to cope with the profundity and complexity of our universe. It is not surprising that old-fashioned rationalism, which limits reality to what can be proved by logic and mathematics, has been given such a hard time in recent years. Eighteenth-century writers who developed such a confidence in the autonomy and competence of reason knew nothing of the empirical psychological research of recent decades, which has highlighted the flaws – such as the phenomenon of cognitive bias – in natural human reasoning processes. We now know that we need to treat unaided human reason with a healthy degree of suspicion, celebrating it when it works well, but being alert to how easily it can go wrong – for example, by confusing contemporary cultural norms with the secure conclusions of pure reason.

Most people are now willing to draw a much-needed distinction between 'thin' and 'thick' approaches to reason. The 'thin' approach limits knowledge to the proven abstract ideas of logic and mathematics, while the 'thick' approach recognizes the many beliefs that human beings may reasonably hold without being able to prove them by the highly restrictive methods of logic. Here, reason embraces desire, imagination and meaning, and opens up a richer vision of life.

Faith is a principled conviction that a certain way of thinking is trustworthy, reliable and relevant. It's a way of seeing things that can't be proved to be right, yet proves to be reliable. Yet it is more than this. It is about entering into this way of thinking, and allowing it to become a way of living. It is about embracing a 'big picture' of reality which is capable of catching our imagination, illuminating our reason and creating an ethical vision for how we should live in the world. While science takes things apart so that we can see how they work, faith puts them back together again, so we can see what they mean.

Christianity is about transcending limits and rebelling against rationalist taboos. It's about expanding our vision of life as we appreciate the depths of reality, rather than limiting our vision to the very restricted realm of what we can prove. It is one of the most assured results of philosophy that reason has its limits, as do logic and science. All three can be useful in helping us avoid making mistakes. But knowing what is wrong does not tell you what is right. The elimination of what is false is a necessary step to truth, but it is not a sufficient step. Knowing that you cannot draw a circle with six sides does not help us find, let alone grasp, the truth, beauty and goodness that lie at the heart of a meaningful human life.

Life sometimes seems chaotic and purposeless to us because we are situated within the flow of things, and cannot extricate ourselves from it to catch a full glimpse of reality. We cannot stand above life and see it from a God's-eye perspective. To use an image that we considered earlier (pages 42–4), we long to stand on a Balcony looking down on the Road of life, which alone might be able to disclose that we have a meaningful place in a coherent universe. Yet our place is on the Road, not the Balcony. There is no privileged standpoint from which we can observe our world. We cannot stand above the flow of life and history, and have to make sense of it from within.

The Balcony is a place of privilege, in which we look at the Road below us and can see with a clarity and comprehensiveness denied to those who are on the Road. The Balcony offers a God's-eye view of things, whereas the wayfarer's vision is limited to what can be seen from the Road. The wayfarers on the Road cannot rise above it, but must try to make sense of it from within the process of journeying.

The 'Age of Reason' thought that human beings could climb up to a rationalist Balcony, and see everything clearly and comprehensively. Now this seems to be little more than a charming dream or a heartbreaking delusion. Our vision is limited to what can be seen from the Road. We cannot escape from its limiting perspectives, and have to learn to work with them. The philosopher Thomas Nagel has emphasized that we cannot escape the condition of seeing the world from our particular insertion in it, so that every viewpoint on the world or life is actually a 'view from somewhere',[12] not the God's-eye view to which the 'Age of Reason' aspired.

Everywhere around us, there are hints and clues of a world beyond the frontiers of reason, which we are invited to explore and inhabit. We may hear snatches of its music in the quiet moments of life. Or scent its fragrance wafted towards us by a gentle breeze on a cool evening. Or hear stories of others who have discovered this land and are ready to share their adventures. All these 'signals of transcendence' encourage us to believe that there is more to existence than our everyday experience. As G. K. Chesterton pointed out, the human imagination reaches beyond the limits of reason. All true artists, he argued, sense that they are 'touching transcendental truths' and that their images are 'shadows of things seen through the veil'.[13]

In the end, faith is about more than the intellectual acceptance of ideas. It is about holding fast to certain things that we believe can be trusted. Early Christian writers compared faith to an anchor. We are like boats, who find safety in a harbour, secured to something and someone safe, reliable and trustworthy. Faith is indeed about trusting God. But it is also about entrusting ourselves to God, realizing that God will always be our place of refuge and peace, our harbour in the midst of life's stormy seas.

Becoming part of God's story

Finally, let us return to think about a phrase I used earlier in this work, when I spoke of the 'grand narrative of the gospel'. Christianity affirms that there is a bigger story of which we are part. At the core of the Christian 'big story' or 'grand narrative' are the themes of creation, fall, redemption and final consummation. A good and beautiful creation is spoiled and ruined by a fall, in which the creator's power is denied and usurped. The creator then enters into the creation to break the power of the usurper, and restore things through a redemptive sacrifice. Yet even after the coming of the redeemer, the struggle against sin and evil continues, and will not be ended until the final restoration and transformation of all things.

It is often said that we live within a world that is shaped by stories – by narratives which tell us who we are and what really matters. But which of these stories can we trust? One of the dominant narratives of Western culture tells us that we are here by accident, meaningless products of a random process. We can only invent meaning and purpose in life, and do our best to stay alive – even though there is no point to life.

There is, however, another story, which takes a very different approach. The Christian story – outlined above – tells us that we are precious creatures of a loving God, redeemed through Christ and called by God to do something good and useful in this world while we travel through it on our way to the new Jerusalem.

These two stories are totally incompatible. They can't both be right. So which do we trust? And which do we choose to *enter*? The creeds help us to see that we are called into God's story. This means that we are not merely people who look at this story from outside. We realize that we have been invited to be part of it. We have been written into the story, and have roles to play and things to do which help advance that story.

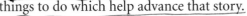

One way of thinking about faith is to see it as a willingness to become part of God's story. It is about realizing that there is a 'grand narrative', and that we are invited to step into this and move it on. Our own story is thus given significance, meaning and purpose because it becomes part of this greater story.

We are now ready to move on to deal with the first major article of the Christian faith, as set out in the creeds: believing in God the Father, creator of heaven and earth.

5

A rock: God as the ground of our existence

———◦◦———

The creeds are often criticized for being too brief and terse, failing to engage both our reason and imagination. There is doubtless some truth in this; however, we must remember that they are *creeds*, not sermons. The power of the creeds lies at least as much in what they *suggest* as in what they actually state. They are to be judged by their capacity to guide and open up informed reflection and engagement, rather than by the brevity of their formulations.

Their brief statements are intended to open up an expansive vision of the Christian landscape, to act as triggers to our memories and imaginations as we correlate their brief statements with the rich deposit of faith. They help us identify what lies within the treasure chest of the Christian faith, and create a sense of expectancy as we prepare to explore them. They are like a concert programme, listing the works to be performed. They are like the menus that proud hosts provide for their guests as they gather for dinner, letting them anticipate the delicacies they will later be enjoying. The words are not the anticipated reality; they merely map out what to expect, and heighten our attentiveness in order to enhance the quality of our engagement with it.

An explorer's guide to the landscape of the Christian faith could begin from just about any point. A good case, for example, could be made for beginning with the fascinating figure of Jesus Christ, and exploring the multiple paths that radiate outwards from him. The creeds, however, are quite clear about where the exploration of the landscape of faith should begin – with the Christian vision of God. 'I believe in God, the Father Almighty, creator of heaven and earth.'

These phrases are the creeds' sketch map of the Christian belief in God and mark our starting point for our journey of exploration. Where some guides might begin with the coastline and end up with the capital city, the creeds take us straight to what they regard as the chief article of the Christian faith – the living and loving God. *This* God is the one we can trust, and who is worthy of this trust.

But do the creeds do justice to this chief article? Many people who have had a profound experience of the living God find that the creeds' statements about this God seem somehow terribly banal, even unreal. Take a woman who has felt herself overwhelmed by the closeness of God at the birth of her first child. Or a student who experiences an awesome sense of God's forgiveness as she prays. Or someone who, like the present writer, has been out alone in an Arabian desert in the depths of the night, and caught a sense of the immensity of God amidst the solemn and still splendour of the starry heavens.

All these people have felt the presence of God. And when they turn from this deeply moving experience to consider the somewhat flat statements of the Christian creeds, they often feel a sense of deflation and disappointment. These seem stale, cold and impersonal in comparison with what they know of God. They just don't seem to measure up to the real thing.

But the creeds are not meant to evoke a sense of wonder and awe at the presence of God. That's what worship is all about. Instead, they provide an outline sketch of the Christian faith, proving a framework capable of respecting and accommodating our experiences, so that we can appreciate their meaning.

The creeds are like maps telling us where to find food and water on an island. They point to the realities of Christian experience and the joy of knowing God – but, like every sign, they must never be confused with what they signify. They are skeletons supporting the living organs of faith, conduits for the springs of living water that will refresh the soul, and keys to the gates of the new Jerusalem. They do not deliver grace or joy, but help us to find them.

One reason why Christians enjoy reading spiritual autobiographies – such as Augustine's *Confessions* or C. S. Lewis's

Surprised by Joy – is that these flesh out the structures of the creed in the shape of transformed lives. Christianity is manifested in one way in the doctrines of the creeds and in another in the lives of believers. Augustine and Lewis both help us to see how the basic structures of the Christian faith came to life for them, and took on a deeper significance, engaging both their hearts and minds. Both these writers – alongside many others – allow us to see how the terse statements of the creeds are expanded, enriched and embodied in their lives. As with G. K. Chesterton, their faith in God thus becomes 'less of a theory and more of a love affair'.

So just who is this God? And what difference does faith in this God make?

Which God are we talking about?

Which God are the creeds talking about when they speak of God? The 'abstract philosophical idea' so beloved of armchair philosophers? Or Homer's grudge-bearing Greek Olympian deities, who were out to settle scores after being snubbed by upstart mortals or outwitted and outmanoeuvred by other gods? No. The creeds bear witness to the God who is made known in and through Jesus Christ, and invite us to linger, ponder and savour all we know about this God.

Some of the finest and most poetic passages in the Old Testament speak of God's graciousness, majesty and love. God is like a shepherd, who journeys with us, guiding and protecting us. God is like rain in a parched desert, bringing refreshment and new life to our souls. This is not a God whose existence we acknowledge in our minds, but a God who captures our imagination, enters into a relationship with us, and is the one whom we learn to trust and adore.

Yet the word 'God' seems inadequate. It is a generic idea designating a category of beings rather than one specific god. In fact, the word 'god' would not really have conveyed much information in the world of the ancient Near East. The Egyptians, Babylonians, Canaanites and Assyrians all worshipped multiple gods. To speak of 'god' did not convey enough information to identify any of them. Which one do you mean? Which god are you talking about?

Israel increasingly came to describe its own special divinity as the God who called Abraham, Isaac and Jacob, and the God who led Israel out of captivity in Egypt into the promised land. The New Testament develops this further, seeing the life, death and resurrection of Jesus Christ as opening new windows through which God may be seen and known. Christ both *tells* us and ✳ *shows* us what God is like. He is the 'image of the invisible God' (Colossians 1.15), who makes God visible and tangible. 'The Word became flesh and lived among us, and we have seen his glory' (John 1.14). In his words, Jesus Christ teaches us about what God is like, and how we ought to behave as a result. Yet in his person and actions, Christ *shows* what God is like.

The Christian tradition developed the special term 'Incarnation' to express the idea that Jesus Christ *embodies* God. God is with us – not merely in the sense of being on our side (though that's a rather wonderful idea), but also in the sense of standing alongside us, sharing our story and journeying with us. God's commitment to us is expressed in action, not simply in words. God does not speak to us from a distance, but comes to where we are in order to meet us. We shall return to this theme later.

The God who is proclaimed by the creeds is thus not some abstract impersonal entity, but a living reality who engages, calls and loves us, and whom we are invited to know and trust. Some people think of God as a remote and inaccessible being, some kind of a 'life force' rather than a person who loves us. As C. S. Lewis pointed out, God is not just some impersonal 'force' behind the universe. Though God may well be *more* than personal, God is certainly not less than this. This is the God who stands at the heart of the biblical narrative and the Christian faith – the God of Abraham, Isaac and Jacob, and the God of Jesus Christ.

My own journey of faith took me from atheism to Christianity. To begin with, I tended to see belief in God as superstitious nonsense, lacking any warrant in reason or experience. Probably because I enjoyed reading Homer, I tended to think of God along the lines of Classical Greek mythology: the gods were just bigger versions of human beings, doing the kind of things that we do (only on a larger scale). I could see no good reason – in fact, I struggled to find *any* reason – to believe that any god existed.

I agreed with Bertrand Russell, who suggested that belief in God was like believing that there was a china teapot revolving in an elliptical orbit between Earth and Mars. In other words, God was an item within the universe, capable of being disclosed and discovered by science. So if science couldn't discover God, there was no God to be discovered. And that, as far as I was concerned, was the end of the matter.

So I thought of God as something or someone within the universe, raising impossible questions about the *location* of God and – perhaps more importantly – the *origins* of God. If everything has a cause, what caused God? Suppose we can track the origins of everything in the universe to something we call 'God'. Why should the buck stop there? Why should we not ask what brought *God* into being? It seemed to be an unanswerable question. And for that reason, I assumed it was a fatal intellectual blow against the existence of God. I was wrong – but in a helpful way.

Christians have always insisted that God is the ground of our being, not something (or even someone) within our universe. Where some philosophers struggle to accommodate the idea of our universe somehow bootstrapping itself into existence, Christianity speaks of a God who is not a constituent element of our universe bringing that universe into being. God creates the universe *with* time, but not *in* time.

God is not part of the furniture of the universe – whether a cosmic teapot or something even more exotic – but is rather to be seen as some fundamental agency which is not conditioned or caused by anything outside itself. God is the source of the universe, not one of its many components.

The word 'god' does not designate something that can be observed within our world, like a dog, cabbage or pencil. If some friends from a strange world in which there were no cabbages were to ask me what they looked like, I could invite them to come and inspect some cabbages in my garden. However, the question of God simply cannot be answered in this way, since God is not something observable in our world. Nor can we solve the problem by the intellectually vacuous procedure of quoting dictionary definitions of God as they amount to little more than summaries of what people think the word means or designates. If there *is* a god, we need that god to tell us – or, better, *show* us – what a god is like. *You* tell us your name. *You* tell us what you are like.

For Christians, God is the foundation and the central theme of the 'big picture' of Christianity – both the canvas on which this picture is painted and a major element of the picture itself. It makes sense for the creeds to begin here, precisely because this is where the story of our universe begins and where it will end. The Christian doctrine of creation gives us a powerful answer ✷ to the question of why there is something rather than nothing.

The appeal to the imagination: biblical images of God

The nineteenth-century poet Lord Tennyson once said that most English people picture God as an enormous clergyman with a long beard. I very much doubt that this is a helpful way of thinking about God. However, it does draw attention to the fact that we need to visualize God in some sort of way. How often have we been reminded that a picture is worth a thousand words?

Images engage our imagination, opening up our capacity to grasp a complex reality by *seeing* it, not just by thinking about it. The great early Church theologian Augustine of Hippo, for example, did not see the Bible as a set of theological propositions to be assembled by rational synthesis, but as calling for an intuitive, imaginative, symbolic, image-making apprehension of biblical truth, perhaps paralleling the approach of a poet rather than a logician. The Bible provides a series of highly effective pictures of God (such as 'God as father', 'God as shepherd' and so on), drawn from everyday life. Although none of these images is adequate in itself to disclose the full picture of God, they can be brought together to give a more comprehensive cumulative vision of the nature and character of God.

One of the most familiar and well-loved biblical images of God is found in Psalm 23: 'The LORD is my shepherd'

(Psalm 23.1). So what does this image tell us about God? Many things, including the loving care of the shepherd for his sheep. This theme is developed further in the New Testament, especially in the parable of the lost sheep (Luke 15.3–7). Here the shepherd actively seeks out any lost sheep in order to bring them home. Jesus Christ is spoken of as the 'good shepherd', who would go so far as to lay down his life for the safety of his sheep (John 10.11–16).

Yet there is another aspect of this image, which speaks to us especially in times of uncertainty or periods of doubt. Some feel that they are eternal nomads, doomed to sail vast and stormy seas for ever and never enter harbour. There is nowhere that they can call their true home; they are always in transit between temporary destinations. Others may believe that God is specifically located in a particular place; its destruction or loss thus shatters our heart's desire, and the basis of our identity. Yet Christians hold that God journeys with us as we cross the landscape of faith. Wherever we go, our God goes with us.

> If I take the wings of the morning
> and settle at the farthest limits of the sea,
> even there your hand shall lead me,
> and your right hand shall hold me fast. (Psalm 139.9–10)

A second image of importance is that of God as a rock (e.g., Psalms 18.2; 28.1; 42.9; 78.35; 89.26; Isaiah 17.10). This image is not intended to suggest that God is inanimate and static; rather, it conveys powerfully and vividly the idea of a God who brings both security and stability. Life's storms and floods may beat around us; yet God is a rock who will not let us down or let us fall (Psalm 42.7–9). Like a rock, God is our place of refuge, our hiding place, the firm foundation upon which we may base our lives and our faith.

This idea is vividly developed in the Sermon on the Mount, in which Christ speaks of building a house on a rock rather than on sand (Matthew 7.24–27). Any human construction – whether a house or an attitude to life – must rest upon a secure foundation if it is to survive. It cannot be built upon shifting sands, but needs to be grounded upon something permanent and enduring. In thinking of God as a rock, we are invited to reflect upon the fact that it is God, and God alone, who is unchanging and permanent, despite all the changes we see going on around us. It is on the rock of God alone that we should build our house of faith, knowing that only in this way can we weather the storms and floods of life.

To appreciate the importance of images such as these, we shall return to Plato's famous analogy of a group of people who have lived their entire lives trapped within a dark underground cave, illuminated only by the flickering flames of a fire. They know nothing of a world beyond its grimy walls: their vision of reality is limited to this dark, shadowy place, illuminated only by the firelight.

Now suppose someone were to find her way into this cave from outside – from the vibrant real world of fresh air, bright sunlight, trees, mountains and brilliant blue skies. How could she explain to those in the cave what this other world is like, when nobody in the cave has any experience of this bright and brilliant alternative reality? In the end, she would have to use things within the world of the cave as analogies for the greater reality that lies beyond it.

Wanting to tell her captive audience about trees, she might pick up some pieces of dead wood lying in the cave, which would be used as fuel for the fire. She could explain that trees were like these pieces of wood, but were alive, bigger and covered with bright green leaves. Trees are *like* bits of wood – but they are *more than that.* Or a puddle of stagnant water in the corner of the cave might become an analogy, however inadequate, for the rivers and lakes of the outside world. A lake is like that puddle – except it is deeper, wider and more beautiful. The known and familiar is thus used to open windows of vision to another domain.

To say that God is our shepherd is to affirm that God is in some ways (but not all) *like* a shepherd. This image helps us visualize God's care, guidance and protection. It assures us that God journeys with us. Yet there is more to God than this. The image is only a starting point for our journey of exploration of the landscape of faith, and needs supplementation by others.

Now, images can be misunderstood. Every analogy breaks down if it is pressed too far. Some might think that the image of 'God as a rock' means that God is lifeless. Yet other images of God in the Bible affirm God's vitality and power. God cannot be defined exclusively in terms of one image. One of the most important tasks of Christian theology is to ensure that such biblical images and analogies are woven together to give us the fullest possible picture of God. They are the threads that need to be brought together to help us see the 'big picture'.

The creeds use one such image of God in mapping the landscape of faith – God as father. So what is meant by this image? In the next chapter, we shall explore this point in more detail.

6

The God and Father of our Lord Jesus Christ

———◆◈◆———

'I believe in God'. But *which* God? The world of ancient Israel was populated by a rich array of gods which were often seen as local or regional divinities. At the time of Christ, the civilized world recognized many gods, most notably the civic deities of the Roman Empire (such as Jupiter and Venus), or those of Classical Greece (such as Zeus and Diana). As Christianity gained traction in the Roman Empire, Christians needed to make it clear which of these gods stood at the heart of their faith.

One way of identifying this God was through naming individuals who had known and trusted this God in the past, and shaped their lives accordingly. In the Old Testament, this God could be designated as the God of Abraham, Isaac and Jacob. In the New Testament, this designation was expanded: Christians knew and trusted the 'God and Father of our Lord Jesus Christ' (Ephesians 1.3; 1 Peter 1.3).

At first sight, this New Testament way of speaking about God might be seen as little more than indicating that Abraham, Isaac, Jacob and Jesus Christ all believed in the same God. While this is true, it is inadequate. For the New Testament, Christ is 'the image of the invisible God' (Colossians 1.15). Christ is not simply an exemplar of faith in God; he is the means by which this God may be known more reliably and fully. God the Father is seen in and through the life and teaching of God the Son. To develop this point, we need to say more about this important image of God as father.

God as father

'I believe in God, the Father Almighty.' These familiar opening words of the creeds invite us to explore what it means to speak of God as 'father'. Earlier, we noted how the Bible uses rich and imaginatively compelling images to help us to think about God. The image of a human parent is used extensively in both the Old and New Testaments to help us visualize God.

Although the strongly patriarchal structure of society at the time inevitably meant that emphasis was placed upon God as father (e.g., Jeremiah 3.19; Matthew 6.9), other passages encourage us to think of God as our mother (e.g., Deuteronomy 32.18). Just as a mother can never forget her child, so God will not forget the people of Jerusalem, who were then exiled in Jerusalem (Isaiah 49.15).

One reason why the creeds speak about faith in God as 'father' is because this way of speaking *about* God and speaking *to* God was used by Jesus Christ. The Lord's Prayer – widely regarded as a 'model prayer' for Christians – opens with the phrase 'our Father'. So in using this language, the creeds are simply following the example of Jesus. Christians believe and trust in the same God who was known, obeyed and revealed by him.

Yet speaking of God as 'father' does not mean that God is *male*. God *creates* male and female, but God *is* neither male nor female. Gender is an aspect of the created order, not a characteristic of God, who stands above these sexual identities. Since God transcends the human distinction between the sexes, human language struggles to express God's distinct characteristics using words that are intended to relate to human contexts. The social roles that are sometimes specifically linked with one or other gender throughout human history are not divinely ordained, but are cultural contingencies, which change over time.

The long tradition of Christian reflection on the Bible has tried to do justice to the use of both maternal and paternal images of God. Although the default position has often been to refer to God using male models, there are many examples of the use of female analogies to communicate the love and care of God or Christ. For example, in the eleventh century Anselm of Canterbury used maternal images to open up some aspects of the ministry of Jesus Christ, asking us to think of Christ as a mother who gathers her chickens under her wings, like a hen.

So what points does thinking of God as a father or mother help us to grasp? Perhaps there are two that stand out as being particularly important.

First, this image helps us grasp that God has called us into being. We owe our existence to God. Just as our human parents brought us into being, so God must be recognized as the author and source of our existence. Thus at one point in their history, the people of Israel are chided because they have failed to remain close to God, who brought them into being in the first place. 'You forgot the God who gave you birth' (Deuteronomy 32.18).

The second point made by the image of God as mother or father is the natural love of God for us. The basis of God's love for individuals is not our achievements, but because of God's parental relationship to us. 'It was not because you were more numerous than any other people that the LORD set his heart on you and chose you – for you were the fewest of all peoples. It was because the LORD loved you' (Deuteronomy 7.7–8).

This rich imagery thus helps to lodge a series of themes in our imagination: that we owe our origins to God; that God, like our parents, brought us into being; that God cares and provides for us. This is a good starting point for reflecting further on one of the most important insights of the creed: that God is not an abstract principle or power but a personal reality. We shall consider this in the next section.

A personal God

At the heart of the Christian faith lies a personal God. We need to be clear from the outset that not all conceptions of God are like this. The Classical philosopher Aristotle thought of God in highly impersonal terms as a 'prime mover'. Aristotle did not (and indeed could not) speak of a love of God for us in any sense. For the rationalist philosopher Baruch Spinoza (1632–1677), it was (just) possible to allow that human beings could love God;

yet this love could not in any way be reciprocated by Spinoza's abstract and impersonal God.

Christians talk about God using words which have strongly personal associations. God is someone whom they love – and who loves them. God is someone who may be trusted. The Christian practice of prayer expresses a gracious relationship which 'is simply trust in a person whose whole dealing with us proves him worthy of trust' (John Oman).

A 'personal God' is thus a God with whom we can exist in a relationship that is analogous to that which we might have with a parent, friend, spouse or lover. Our identity is expressed within a network of relationships in which we both *belong* and *matter*, whether as a member of a family, as a friend, or as a colleague – or as a child of the living God. And by existing within this nexus of relationships, we find ourselves changing and growing as we gradually assimilate our faith.

The Christian Bible does not use the specific language of a 'personal God'. Yet the fundamental themes of this idea are unquestionably present in the Bible, and are expressed in a number of ways. To begin with, God is not understood or spoken of as an abstract principle or source of energy, but as someone who has a *name*. For many biblical writers, a name conveyed someone's personal identity and characteristics. Calling 'on the name of the Lord' in times of trouble (Joel 2.32) is about appealing to the faithfulness and constancy of God. The 'Lord God of Israel' is the God who could be trusted in the past – as, for example, in the exodus from Egypt, and the entry into the promised land – and can still be trusted today.

One of the great themes which dominate the Old Testament in particular is that of the covenant between God and Israel, by which they mutually bind themselves to one other. 'I will be their God, and they shall be my people' (Jeremiah 31.33). The basic idea underlying this is that of a personal commitment of God to Israel, and of Israel to God. The notion of a personal God also underlies the biblical metaphor of the 'face of God'. To be allowed to see the face of God was seen as a mark of divine favour, intimacy and acceptance. One of the most engaging ideas of the New Testament is that the face of God is disclosed in Jesus Christ (2 Corinthians 4.6).

One of Paul's leading images for the transformation of humanity as a result of the death and resurrection of Christ is reconciliation – an idea that is clearly based on the restoration of human personal relationships. Paul uses exactly the same Greek word to refer to the restoration of the relationship between God and humanity that he uses in connection with the restoration of the relationship between a man and his wife who have fallen out with each other. The transformation through faith of the relationship between God and sinful human beings is held to be like the reconciliation of two persons, such as an alienated husband and wife (1 Corinthians 7.11; 2 Corinthians 5.18).

This strongly personal notion of God is also reflected in the Christian vision of heaven. Some religious people argue that the ultimate goal of humanity is to lose our distinct identity, so that we become like nameless drops of water in a vast ocean. Christianity takes the view that we matter to God as individuals. The courts of the new Jerusalem are not occupied by disembodied spirits, purged of their history and memories, but by individual believers, renewed and restored, yet continuous with our earthly selves. The relationship with God that we knew on earth will be continued and consummated in heaven, even if our imaginations struggle to grasp what this might look like.

For Christians, God is the guarantor of our personal identity. A relationship with God is what makes us special, and gives us a distinct identity and value. God treats each of us as a person, not as an object. God calls and knows each of us by name. 'Do not fear, for I have redeemed you; I have called you by name, you are mine' (Isaiah 43.1).

As we shall see (pages 95–100), the belief that human beings bear the image of God is perhaps the best intellectual defence against dehumanization. Underneath our tattered external appearance, our lowly status in the eyes of the powerful and self-important, lies the iridescent splendour of God, marked indelibly on our nature. Realizing that we bear this divine image reminds us that there is something worth saving, even in the worst of us, from which a renewed and restored creation can emerge by grace.

It is helpful here to consider what overtones the phrase 'an impersonal God' would convey. This phrase suggests a God who is distant or aloof, who deals with humanity (if God deals with us at all) in general terms which take no account of human individuality. The idea of a personal relationship, such as love, suggests a reciprocal character to God's dealings with us. This idea is incorporated into the notion of a personal God, but not into impersonal conceptions of the nature of God. There are strongly negative overtones to the idea of 'impersonal', which have passed into Christian thinking about the nature of God.

God as a person: some implications

Appreciating that God is personal is central to a right understanding of the creeds. Let's look at some insights that will help us grasp this more fully. First, in speaking of God as a person, we are making it clear that we can *know* God, not merely know things *about* God – for example, that God is gracious, righteous and faithful. 'This is eternal life, that they may know you, the only true God, and Jesus Christ whom you have sent' (John 17.3). To 'know' God in this sense is about experiencing, loving and desiring God, not simply possessing information about God.

This way of thinking about God also helps us to make sense of the process of growing in our faith. What do we mean when we speak of deepening our faith? When I was beginning to explore Christianity, I tended to think of 'growing in faith' as acquiring additional factual information about Christianity – such as knowing details of the geography of the Holy Land or the dates of various kings of ancient Israel. Happily, I came to realize that it was about coming to know God better, not merely knowing more about God. It is about the quality of our relationship with God, not the quantity of information we have acquired about Christian history. The image of a personal God helps us to see spiritual growth in terms of a deepening relationship with God, shaped by prayer and worship as much as by reading theology textbooks.

Being remembered by God

In 2008, I began the research for a new biography of C. S. Lewis. This involved reading everything he had written in chronological order, as well as the large amount of literature about him. While exploring collections of documents in archives in Oxford and elsewhere, I came across many early photographs of Lewis and his friends dating from the 1910s and 1920s. Some showed him with small groups of people, others as part of larger gatherings. It was easy to identify Lewis himself and some of those who played an important role in his life – such as his father, his brother and his childhood friend Arthur Greeves.

But there were some other people in those photographs whom neither I nor any of those I consulted could identify. All too often, I had to pencil the word 'unknown' beside their images, even though they were clearly important members of Lewis's circle of family and friends. Once, they mattered: now they were forgotten; their memory and identity had simply faded out of history, like the ink on a piece of writing paper that was being washed away by a spilled glass of water.

The great fear of Old Testament writers was that they too would be forgotten by others, and maybe even by God. When the people of Jerusalem were in exile in Babylon, far from their homeland, they wondered if God had remembered them. The image of a personal God who loves, remembers and values people came into its own in that situation. 'Israel, you will not be forgotten by me' (Isaiah 44.21). This important theme of being remembered is brought home in the powerful image of the intimate relationship between a mother and her infant child. A mother might conceivably forget her nursing child; yet God could never forget Israel. Yet the rich analogy of God as a mother who could never forget her child is supplemented by other images reinforcing this point. 'See, I have inscribed you on the palms of my hands' (Isaiah 49.14–16). We are, so to speak, permanently etched into God's very being. God remembers us, even when we fail to remember God.

God almighty?

The creeds go on to speak of believing in an 'almighty' God. Those with unhappy experiences of political or institutional authoritarianism will naturally react with deep suspicion to any idea that God is 'almighty'. All too often, this idea of power is linked with the suppression of freedom, or the whimsical rule of tyrannical monarchs or national leaders. Yet to be almighty is not merely to be able to do anything you want; it is to be utterly unaccountable to anyone for your actions. So what does it mean to speak of God being 'almighty'?

Once more, we have a translation issue that needs to be noted. The creeds here pick up on a Greek word that the early Christians used to refer to God – *pantokrator*. This is used at several points in the New Testament (e.g., Revelation 4.8), and is often translated as if it were an adjective: 'almighty'. However, the Greek word is actually a noun, and is best translated as 'ruler of all', or perhaps 'sovereign'. The point being made is simple and important: no earthly ruler can compare or compete with God. There is no source of true authority outside or beyond God. To be a Christian is to recognize the supreme lordship or sovereignty of God, who stands over (and sometimes against) civic authority.

This helps us to understand why the early Christians refused to worship the Roman emperor, and faced martyrdom as a result. The so-called 'imperial cult' developed in various forms in the regions and municipalities of the eastern Roman Empire around the year 100. Most of these regarded the emperor as a divine figure, to whom temples, altars and priesthoods were to be dedicated.

Worship of the emperor became seen as a sign of loyalty to the empire, with refusal to conform to the imperial cult being interpreted as treason or sedition. Christians felt that they had no option but to refuse these demands to worship the emperor, even though many Romans regarded it as little more than a civic formality. Christians, however, saw this as denying the sovereignty of their God, or that Jesus Christ was the Lord of their lives.

The creeds are really affirming the idea that God alone is Lord of our world, rather than the notion that God is omnipotent. No earthly ruler or authority should be allowed to usurp the place of God. 'You shall have no other gods before me' (Exodus 20.3). Yet although this places the emphasis upon God being 'sovereign' rather than 'almighty', we cannot avoid thinking about what it means to think of God as 'omnipotent' or 'all-powerful'.

Many people think that affirming their faith in an 'almighty' God means believing in a God who can do anything and everything. I have no doubt that some Christians also think like this – but they really ought not to. We have allowed ourselves to become enslaved to words, captivated by the lure of the word 'almighty' – which, as we have seen, is not even a good translation of the vocabulary of the creeds. There are many things that God cannot do, such as create a square circle, or draw a triangle with four sides. These are simply things that cannot be done – by God or by anyone else. Triangles have three sides; to draw a shape with four sides is to draw something else. Four-sided triangles do not and cannot exist. The fact that God cannot draw a triangle with four sides is not a problem. It just forces us to restate our simple statement in a slightly more complicated way. 'To say that God is almighty means that God can do anything that does not involve logical contradiction.'

Yet it soon becomes clear that there are real difficulties even with this modified definition. Let's ask another question to help us identify the problem. Can God break promises? Since there is no logical contradiction involved in breaking promises, it would seem that, if God can do anything that does not involve logical contradiction, God can certainly break a promise. The logic seems obvious.

Yet I hope that my readers will be deeply uneasy with this line of thought. The idea of God breaking promises doesn't seem right. It seems to reduce God to our level. It suggests that God is like fallen and fallible human beings.

Let's ask another question. Can God tell lies? Once more, there is no logical problem here. Yet many will feel a deep sense of ethical unease. Why? Because God – or, at least, the *Christian* God – is not like that.

These two probing questions help us to see that the question is not really about *omnipotence*, but about *character*. Christians believe in a trustworthy God, who does not break promises or tell lies. It is true that no *logical* principles would be infringed if God behaved in such a way, but something much deeper would be violated – our understanding of the character of God.

There is a world of difference between a whimsical god – like some of Homer's unpleasantly self-centred Olympian deities, who constantly needed to be cajoled and humoured – and a faithful

God, who may be relied upon and trusted. The creeds make it clear which God they are talking about. And it's not one of Homer's.

For Christians, God is trustworthy and faithful – and trustworthy and faithful people just don't do these kinds of things. The biblical witness to the nature and character of God protests against a God who would betray, deceive or lie. Indeed, the Hebrew word that most biblical translations render as 'truth' really means 'something that you can rely on'. God makes promises – and having made those promises, stands by them.

At the human level, power is seen as something that corrupts us. We might hope that power will enable us to express a good character; too often, it seems to destroy that character. 'If you want to test a man's character, give him power' (Abraham Lincoln).

The British politician and historian Lord Acton (1834–1902) was probably right when he rather cynically observed that 'power tends to corrupt, and absolute power corrupts absolutely'. As a result, 'great men are almost always bad men'. Human nature is morally fragile and is placed under such severe stress by the temptations and privileges of power that it often proves incapable of resisting them. This issue lies at the heart of one of the greatest works of twentieth-century literature – J. R. R. Tolkien's *The Lord of the Rings*. The master ring seemed to offer power to its possessors – but in reality, it enslaved them. Tolkien shrewdly realized that the possibility of possessing absolute power revealed what people were really like.

This theme is explored powerfully in the gospel temptation narratives. Before Jesus Christ began his public ministry in Galilee, he was tempted in the wilderness. It is important to realize that these temptations were fundamentally about the abuse of power (Matthew 4.1–11). Why not turn stones into bread? Christ, however, reserved his power for the healing and salvation of the world, not his own personal gain. His temptation confirmed his character.

In this chapter, we have explored something of what it means to speak of God in personal terms, and how this illuminates aspects of the Christian life. Yet the creeds have another insight about God that they invite us to incorporate into our vision of the landscape of faith – namely, the idea of God as creator. We shall turn to consider this theme in the following chapter.

7

In the beginning: God as creator

Once more, imagine that you find yourself cast ashore on a mysterious island following a plane crash in the middle of the Pacific Ocean. As you look around you, you find yourself bombarded with questions. Where are you? How can you get home? Are there any others who can help you? Yet one question that is bound to occur to you, sooner or later, is this: whose island is this? Might you have landed on forbidden or hostile territory?

One of the most familiar, and probably one of the best, explorations of this question is found in C. S. Lewis's *The Lion, the Witch and the Wardrobe*. Four children find themselves entering a mysterious wintry world through a gateway concealed in a wardrobe. As they explore this land, they hear different stories about Narnia. Some say that Narnia is the realm of the White Witch; others, that it is really the realm of the noble lion Aslan, who brought it into being in the first place. In his absence, he has been usurped by the White Witch. But one day, Aslan will return, and restore Narnia to what it was really meant to be. The children realize that a physical map of Narnia is not enough. It needs to be supplemented with a different kind of map, which deals with questions of origins and destiny – a narrative that is partly provided in *The Lion, the Witch and the Wardrobe*, but which is amplified in the prequel, *The Magician's Nephew*.

Christianity affirms that God brought the universe into existence, and in so doing established an order within nature which reflected God's character. Some peoples in the ancient Near East believed in national gods, whose sphere of influence was limited to a geographical region – such as Egypt or Babylon. For ancient Israel, recognizing God as creator meant that the 'Lord God of hosts' was the Lord of *all* the world. This idea became particularly important during the period of exile, when most of the population of Jerusalem was deported to Babylon, far from their own native land. God's presence and activity was not limited to a specific geographical region, but was universal.

The Christian idea of creation

So what is the Christian doctrine of creation? What are its core themes? It seems to me that there are three key insights. In the first place, the Christian understanding of creation is about *origination*. The world has not always existed. It came into being – not by accident, but by an act of will. This leads into the second core theme – that of *intentionality*. The universe did not simply happen; it was *made* to happen, and it was *meant* to happen.

The third aspect of the language of creation is that of *signification*. The universe is like a signpost to its creator, pointing beyond itself to its ultimate source and origin. It echoes or expresses the character of God in a scaled-down yet recognizable manner. 'God was a creator, as an artist is a creator' (G. K. Chesterton). The universe bears the imprint of God, revealing something of the divine splendour and wisdom. 'The heavens are telling the glory of God; and the firmament proclaims his handiwork' (Psalm 19.1).

Each of these aspects of the doctrine of creation deserves further exploration, beginning with the theme of origination. The Christian view that the universe came into being was widely criticized during the period of the early Church by secular writers, most of whom followed the Greek philosopher Aristotle in holding that the world had existed eternally. Christians found themselves facing ridicule. How could anyone in the sophisticated Greek cultural world take the Christian faith seriously when it contradicted one of the core teachings of Aristotle?

Similar ideas were deeply embedded in the scientific community in the not so distant past. By the first decade of the twentieth century, most scientists had come to the view that the universe had always existed. Any religious language of 'creation' was meaningless. The scientific wisdom of that age was that it was absurd to suggest that the universe had a beginning. Or that it would have an end.

Yet science has now changed its mind about this. From around 1920, growing evidence began to suggest that the world originated in what we now call the 'Big Bang' – a cosmic fireball which expanded to form our present universe. The scientific community slowly came round to this way of thinking. One of the reasons for their reluctance to accept the 'Big Bang' was that this seemed to be an embarrassingly 'religious' way of thinking. Atheist astronomers such as Fred Hoyle were alarmed that this new scientific understanding of the origins of the universe seemed uncomfortably close to a Christian idea of creation.

However, agreement that the universe had an origin does not necessarily mean that there is a God, or that the Christian doctrine of creation is right. It certainly *suggests* these things; it is *consistent* with them; but it does not *prove* them. Some atheist scientists would argue that the universe just happened. Maybe it came into being by a process that we don't understand. Maybe it even caused its own creation. Not unreasonably, Christians point out that these seem rather clumsy and forced ways of trying to avoid the obvious fact that what we now know about the origins of the universe fits neatly into the Christian 'big picture'.

The second aspect of the doctrine of creation, intentionality, affirms that God meant to create the world – and us. This world is not an accident and nor are we. We can speak of life having a purpose and the universe having a meaning. However, these are not ideas that can be read off the world, like colour, temperature or height: they are more profound notions, lying beneath the surface of things. The Christian 'big picture' gives us an intellectual framework that allows us to discern purpose and meaning in the world around us, as well as in our own lives. It invites us to stop thinking of the natural world as a *given*, and instead to appreciate it as a *gift*.

The third aspect of the doctrine of creation, signification, helps us to see that God's character, like that of any artist, is expressed in the creation. When understood correctly, the world around us echoes and reflects something of God. Once more, the Christian 'big picture' – of which the doctrine of creation is an important element – gives us a lens for looking at the worlds around and within us. When I was young, I often lay awake at night, tracing the patterns of the stars through my school dormitory window. I found this a deeply melancholy experience at that stage in my life, as I had rejected any belief in God. When I looked at the stars through an atheist lens, it seemed that I was alone in a vast, meaningless universe which was completely indifferent to my presence. Those silent pinpoints of light in the night sky became symbols of the brevity of my own existence and the futility of life.

After discovering Christianity, I looked again at those same stars but now through a different lens. What I had once seen as symbols of transience and pointlessness took on a new meaning. The God who had created those had also created me. Even though I was insignificant in relation to the grand scale of the cosmos, I was known, loved and valued by God (Psalm 8.3–5).

The beauty of the creation thus echoes the greater beauty of God. This world may only be a scaled-down version of something greater, but we sometimes catch fragments of the melodies of the new Jerusalem floating by, as on a passing breeze. Perhaps nothing can fully prepare us for heaven when we finally enter it, except the thought that it will be like the very best of this world, only better. We can appreciate the beauty of the island, while realizing this beauty is a sign of something still more wonderful that awaits us.

One more point needs to be made. There was some divergence between Christian writers of the first three centuries as to whether creation involved God imposing order and structure on some existing material, or bringing material into existence from nothing (Latin: *ex nihilo*). The philosopher Plato thought of creation in the former way, suggesting that God created the world by imposing form on some shapeless mass. Some Old Testament passages can be interpreted in this way, leading some early Christian writers to take a similar view.

However, by the end of the third century, the consensus had shifted, with most Christians holding to the idea of creation from nothing. This seemed to be clearly stated in the prologue to John's Gospel: 'All things came into being through him, and without him not one thing came into being' (John 1.3). It seemed to make more sense to read Old Testament texts dealing with the theme of creation through this lens. An increasingly sophisticated reading of the Old Testament creation narratives led major Christian writers of the second and third centuries – such as Irenaeus of Lyons – to argue that *everything* had to be created by God from scratch.

The creeds themselves make no *explicit* statements on this matter. However, the Nicene Creed's statement that 'all things were made' through Christ seems to reflect these ideas in John's Gospel, suggesting that it ought to be seen to *implicitly* endorse the notion of creation from nothing.

Ways of thinking about creation

So how is the idea of creation to be visualized? What images help us to grasp its significance? As I look at the long Christian tradition of wrestling with this issue, three ways of representing the idea of creation seem to be of especial importance.

The first of these rose to prominence during the period of the early Church, and has philosophical roots in the Platonic tradition. Creation is here seen as being analogous to light or heat being radiated from the sun, or from a human source such as a fire. This image of creation (hinted at in the Nicene Creed's phrase 'Light of Light') suggests that the creation of the world can be regarded as an overflowing of the creative energy of God. Just as light derives from the sun and reflects its nature, so the created order derives from God and expresses the divine nature. This way of thinking is often referred to as 'emanation'. There is, on the basis of this model, a *natural* or *organic* connection between God and the creation.

However, the image of a sun radiating light, or a fire radiating heat, seems to imply some kind of automatic or mechanical emission of heat or light. Yet Christianity has consistently emphasized the intentional decision on the part of God to create, which this model does not express particularly well. Furthermore, this way of thinking about creation is very impersonal, contrasting with the notion of a personal God whose divine personality is expressed in both the act of creation and the subsequent form of that creation.

A second image is that of God as a master builder, who intentionally constructs the world according to a specific design (for example, Psalm 127.1). This powerful image conveys the ideas of purpose, planning and a deliberate intention to create. This way of envisaging creation highlights both the skill of the creator and the beauty and ordering of the resulting creation.

I was an undergraduate at Wadham College, Oxford. Its dining hall was decorated with portraits of leading former members of the college, including Sir Christopher Wren, who went on to become an architect after leaving the college. In 1666, the Great Fire of London badly damaged the original St Paul's Cathedral, and a decision was taken to commission a new building. Wren's fame ensured he was selected as the designer, and the current St Paul's, completed in 1710, remains one of London's most famous landmarks.

For several years, I worked at King's College London, and had an office in central London. I often visited the cathedral, enjoying its elegance and beauty. I would occasionally hear visitors asking cathedral staff where they could find a memorial to Christopher Wren within the cathedral. Yet the cathedral itself is a memorial to Wren. On a circle of black marble on the main floor beneath the centre of the great dome, there is a Latin inscription which includes the words: 'Reader, if you are looking for a memorial, look around you.' Wren's wisdom and skill are best appreciated not through any kind of verbal eulogy, but by admiring the masterpiece he created. The creator's genius is seen in the creation itself.

Thinking of creation as an act of design and construction appeals to the human imagination. However, the image has a potential weakness, in that it portrays the act of creation as giving shape and form to something which is already there – an idea which does not fit easily with the doctrine of creation *ex nihilo*. Nevertheless, the model helps us to see that God creates an ordered and rational world which is open to investigation by the natural sciences.

A third approach is to think of God not so much as a builder, but as an artist or novelist. Many Christian writers, from various periods in the history of the Church, have spoken of creation as the 'handiwork of God', comparing it to a work of art which is not only beautiful in itself but expresses the personality of its creator. We often speak of an artist 'putting something of himself' into a painting, or a novelist telling a story that is profoundly shaped by his or her own experience and concerns. Both the painting and the novel are works of art in themselves which nevertheless convey something of the character and wisdom of their creators. (It is not surprising that book festivals have become so important in recent years, given that they allow people who admire particular novels to encounter and express their appreciation to those who created them in the first place.)

Living within the creation

So what difference does the idea that God created our world make to the way we think about how we inhabit the landscape of faith? The belief that God created our world is a lens which brings our world into a new focus, allowing us to see aspects of the landscape that we might otherwise have missed, and helping us to appreciate its deeper significance.

One important question we are forced to confront is our own status within this landscape. Are we lords of all we survey? Is this world our possession, so that we may do with it as we please? The Christian doctrine of creation provides us with a framework for understanding our relationship with the natural world. Where some ideologies allow us to exploit the world for our amusement and profit, a Christian perspective insists that the natural world is God's precious creation, which we do not possess or own. Rather, it has been entrusted to us. We are given the privilege of accountability, in that we are called to be stewards of God's creation. The outlines of a rich environmental ethic are laid down by the Christian 'big picture', inviting us to consider how we might implement these.

Yet there is another issue of importance, which is linked with the Christian idea of the intentionality of creation – both of the world and of ourselves as human beings. Some believe that we have found our way into this strange and puzzling landscape by accident. The French biologist Jacques Monod argued that we are an accidental and meaningless presence in an equally accidental and meaningless universe. We have to face up to the fact that we are like gypsies who live on the fringes of an alien world which is deaf to our music and indifferent to our hopes.

We are not *meant* to be here. We find ourselves in a world which is neither of our making nor of our choosing. In fact, we are not meant to be *anywhere*. Nature is simply a prison in which we find ourselves trapped, the landscape through which we are passing on a journey that goes nowhere. The universe doesn't know we exist – and it doesn't care.

We cannot help but wonder about the world in which we find ourselves, and our place within it. Is this universe our home – even if only for an astonishingly short time, in terms of the vast expanse of cosmic history? Or is it our prison, which prevents us from achieving our true potential? Or are we like sojourners, passing through it on our way to somewhere else? Do we really belong here?

The Christian 'big picture' allows us to see our world in a new way. No longer is it a meaningless and faceless void; it bears the imprint of God. Psalm 8 offers perhaps one of the most eloquent reflections on this theme. We may feel overwhelmed by the immensity of this universe, with its vast starry skies. Yet God has placed us within this world, where we are meant to be. It is stamped and studded with signs of God's presence and glory; and we, who bear God's image, can discern those signs, and, illuminated and empowered by grace, may reach out and embrace the God who created us and our world. Yet we need to see this world rightly – as it really is – rather than be trapped within materialist ways of thinking that impoverish its significance.

Perhaps most importantly of all, this world allows us to anticipate another world, which is our true ultimate goal. A Christian framework of meaning allows us to see that this is an interim location, a place through which we are passing, rather than our ultimate destination. So does this mean that we disengage from this world? That we disregard its beauty or its challenges? Certainly not. There is work to be done to make this world a better place. We can be committed to its wellbeing without becoming absorbed or overwhelmed by it.

Few have now heard of the poet and religious writer Frederick Langbridge. Yet he penned two lines that are helpful in illuminating the human situation from a Christian perspective.

> Two men look out through the same bars:
> One sees the mud, and one the stars.

The point Langbridge was trying to make is that we need to see the stars to live in the mud. It is by sustaining the hope of heaven that we are enabled to live authentically in this world. His language mirrors that of the New Testament:

> Since, then, you have been raised with Christ, set your hearts on things above, where Christ is seated at the right hand of God. Set your minds on things above, not on earthly things.
>
> (Colossians 3.1–2, NIV)

In this chapter, we have explored some basic aspects of Christian thinking about God as the creator of the world. Yet what about human beings, who are such a significant presence within that world? For Christianity, human beings are also part of God's creation, while standing out from the remainder of the created order in a number of respects. In the next chapter, we shall consider the enigma of human nature.

8

The enigma of humanity: the climax of God's creation

————

One of my favourite stories from the Classical age tells how the Greek philosopher Aristippus of Cyrene was shipwrecked on an Aegean island during a storm. As it happened, Aristippus had landed on the island of Rhodes. However, he had no idea of the identity of this strange place. Was it inhabited? Would he be able to find anyone to help him? As he walked along the shoreline, he spotted some geometric patterns traced in the sand. Like Robinson Crusoe discovering a footprint on the beach of his deserted island, Aristippus had noticed something that made him realize he was not on his own. Only a human being could have traced those patterns.

Since the beginning of recorded history, people have looked at the patterns we see in the world around us and wondered about their deeper meaning. We see rivers and pastures, stunning mountain ranges in the distance and starry skies above. What are they all about? Where did they come from? Do they point to a bigger story? Is this our true homeland or do we really belong somewhere else? Are there tracings in the fabric of the world which tell us we are not alone, or help us ascertain our true origin and destiny?

Who are we? Why are we here? Do we really matter? These questions bring us to the Christian understanding of human nature. The creeds make no explicit reference to what Christians believe about human nature. Yet at one point, they draw aside a curtain so that we can glimpse something of this distinctive way of thinking about the mystery of human nature and destiny. In exploring the significance of Jesus Christ, the Nicene Creed declares that the great drama of Christ's life, death and resurrection took place 'for our salvation'. We shall think about the meaning of this rich term 'salvation' in due course. But for the moment, we need to note an important point: for Christianity, human beings need to be saved in the first place. There is some flaw, some fault or defect in human nature that needs to be healed and put right.

In our explorations of the landscape of faith thus far, we have looked at several aspects of the Christian 'big picture', and the way of looking at our world that it makes possible. We have used this powerful vision of reality as a lens, bringing aspects of our world and our experience into sharper focus. Yet now we are going to use this lens to look at ourselves, as if it were a magnifying mirror, showing us up as we really are rather than as we would like to think we are.

The enigma of human nature

So what do we find reflected in this mirror of disclosure and unveiling? Christianity holds a profoundly realistic view of human nature, recognizing that we are capable of great good on the one hand and profound evil on the other. Christianity 'is a hard, tough, exacting and complex doctrine, steeped in drastic and uncompromising realism' (Dorothy L. Sayers). As individuals and as a society, human beings display qualities of both greatness and wretchedness.

Where a shallow secular humanism uncritically proclaims the moral and rational excellence of humanity, Christianity tempers this with the awkward truths of human selfishness and a tendency towards self-deception. It creates space for us to speak of human evil, and challenges the great delusion of our age – that humanity is intrinsically good.

For Augustine of Hippo, we suffer from an illness whose symptoms include a stubborn and persistent refusal to accept that we are ill in the first place. This judgement is difficult to ignore or sidestep in the light of the history of the twentieth century, as extermination camps and technologically enhanced warfare allowed human beings to inflict more destruction and suffering on their fellows than at any point in the past. It is hard to speak of human progress when this leads to murder on an industrial scale.

The historian R. G. Collingwood offered a blunt challenge to inflated notions of human perfectibility and excellence: 'The chief business of twentieth-century philosophy is to reckon with twentieth-century history.' If human beings are so wonderful, why have they created such chaos and unleashed such destruction? New technologies have given us an unprecedented capacity to heal on the one hand, and to maim and destroy on the other. It is as if we now possess God-like powers resulting from technology, set alongside a disturbing trend to an animal irrationality which many believed (and hoped) had been left behind in our evolutionary history.

This suggestion of the fragility of human goodness on the one hand, and a propensity towards selfishness on the other, has provoked predictable howls of outrage from those with vested interests in defending the glory of human reason and judgement. Algernon Swinburne, one of Victorian England's more colourful atheists, is perhaps best remembered for his delusional assertion of the moral and intellectual glories of humanity, delightfully innocent of the horrors of the twentieth century that would fatally undermine his core belief:

Glory to Man in the highest! For Man is the master of things.

Swinburne and his followers dismissed any idea of humanity as having flaws or defects as pessimistic, insulting and judgemental. Yet pessimism is simply an optimist's dismissive term for realism. There is nothing insulting or judgemental about asking that humanity faces up to its flaws and tries to work out what to do about them. The problem lies with those who deny there is a problem, rather than those trying to work out its solution.

The New Testament's judgement of the human situation is more of a diagnosis than a condemnation. It recognizes that the process of healing and restoration requires an evaluation of the nature of our problem. My physician would not be insulting me nor behaving judgementally if he were to tell me that I had pneumonia – something which I, lacking medical training, could not do, and might not want to do, given its unsettling implications. In making that diagnosis, my physician would not be criticizing or patronizing me, but simply telling me the truth about myself as the first stage in healing me. The motivation behind that diagnosis would be a desire to heal, not to belittle.

Blaise Pascal provided what many regard as one of the finest accounts of the enigma of human nature, which he framed in terms of the awkward and unresolved interplay between human grandeur and misery. We are raised up by noble thoughts which inspire and uplift us; yet we are pulled down by base thoughts and motivations which threaten to damage or even destroy us. The more enlightened we become, the more we become aware of both our greatness and our vileness.

Pascal suggests that many humanist philosophies exalt human greatness while overlooking our darker side, or emphasize our shadow side while sidelining our capacity for greatness.

So how do we account for what seem to be these fatal inconsistencies within us? For Pascal, the Christian 'big picture' offered a coherent account of what at first sight seems to be an enigma – the incoherence and self-contradictions within ourselves. We bear God's image, which raises us upwards; yet we are sinful, which draws us downwards.

In the next two sections, we shall explore these two elements of a Christian understanding of human nature, and how they illuminate the profound ambiguities and apparent self-contradictions of human nature.

Being drawn upwards: the image of God in humanity

'What are human beings that you are mindful of them?' (Psalm 8.4). From the beginning of history, human beings have wondered about their place in the greater scheme of things. Why are we here? What is our destiny? What is the meaning of human existence? Is there a grander vision of reality within which we have a special place? The Christian doctrine of creation offers the beginnings of an answer. It helps us to deepen our understanding and appreciation of the world in which we find ourselves placed.

We are part of God's creation, and must learn and accept our place within that created order. This insight is deeply counter-cultural, and often provokes a ferocious reaction. Some argue that the world would be a better place if we got rid of God altogether, and put human beings in his place. Many of the more idealistic writers of the nineteenth century insisted that the only way to eliminate the ills of the world was to enthrone humanity as Lord of the earth. Yet paradoxically, this exalted view of humanity spawned the dehumanizing ideologies of Nazism and Stalinism. A more sober estimation of humanity's moral capacities has slowly crept back into favour, which recognizes our tendency towards self-deception and delusion.

Yet although Christians believe that humanity is part of the created order, this does not mean that we are *indistinguishable* from the remainder of creation. We stand out within the landscape of faith, having been set a little lower than the angels and been 'crowned with glory and honour' (Psalm 8.5). Men and women are created 'in the image of God' (Genesis 1.27). This brief yet deeply significant phrase opens the way to a right understanding of human nature and our overall place within the created order. Although humanity is not divine, it possesses a relationship with God which is different from that of other creatures. *Humanity bears the image of God.* For some, this is a statement of the privileged position of humanity within creation. Yet for most Christian theologians, it is above all an affirmation of *responsibility* and *accountability* towards the world in which we live.

So how are we to understand this special relationship to God? How can we visualize this 'image of God'? A number of ways of making sense of this idea have been developed within Christian theology, of which we will consider four. These are not to be seen as mutually inconsistent, so that we have to choose one as right and dismiss the remainder as wrong. They are better seen as offering different but potentially complementary insights into the notion, capable of being woven together into a richer account of what it means to bear God's image.

The first of these ways of understanding the 'image of God' interprets it as an affirmation of the authority of God over humanity. Within the cultural context of the ancient Near East known to the biblical writers, the authority of a monarch was often asserted through the display of images throughout their domain (think, for example, of the golden statue of Nebuchadnezzar, described in Daniel 3.1–7). To be created in the 'image of God' might thus mean that we are accountable to God, or living within the sphere of the sovereignty of God.

The Genesis creation account locates the origins of sin as lying partly in a refusal to accept such limits on human autonomy. One of the leading themes of the 'Golden Age of Atheism' following the French Revolution of 1789 was that human beings were their own masters, and could do as they pleased. They were accountable to nobody save themselves. There was no higher authority to which they were answerable. Although some saw this as a liberating doctrine, others feared it opened the doors to oppression by removing any transcendent obstacle to totalitarianism, or ruthless exploitation of other human beings or the earth's resources.

A second approach to the 'image of God' emphasizes the harmony between human reason and the rationality of God as our creator. This theme was explored by many writers in the early Church, and can be seen especially clearly in Athanasius of Alexandria's famous treatise *On the Incarnation*. Recently, this approach has been developed further by the physicist turned theologian John Polkinghorne, who argues that there seems to be some kind of 'resonance' or 'harmony' between the ordering of the world and the capacity of the human mind to discern and represent it. A Christian explanation of the deep-rooted resonance between the rationality present within our minds and the rationality observed within the world lies in the rationality of the creator of both the natural order and the human mind.

This way of interpreting the 'image of God' suggests that humanity possesses some inbuilt tendency to find its way towards God – a tendency which is challenged and occasionally subverted by our innate tendency to want to remain autonomous and independent. We possess a kind of rational or imaginative template which draws us towards God, partly because it offers a coherent and plausible way of making sense of our world and experiences.

There are some interesting parallels here with the modern discipline of the cognitive science of religion, which strongly suggests belief in transcendent beings arises through normal human processes of thought, not in opposition to them. Religious beliefs and commitments are a natural aspect of being human, arising naturally from human cognitive processes that are not dependent on culture.

If correct, this means that secular humanist aspirations for a totally secular human world are unrealistic, in that religion will naturally re-emerge, even where it has been suppressed by the state – as, for example, in the remarkable resurgence of religion following the collapse of the Soviet Union. It also suggests that people who do not think of themselves as religious possess natural capacities and tendencies which have either not yet been activated by any triggers in their environment or experience, or been suppressed by social or cultural pressures. We do not understand why we are hardwired in this way, although there is clearly some overlap with the idea of the 'image of God' as a rational template leading to a heightened attentiveness towards God within the world.

Perhaps most importantly, it challenges the lazy assumption of Western culture that 'humanism' unambiguously designates an anti-religious attitude. If it is natural for human beings to have religious inclinations, how can 'humanism' defend suppressing these? The answer, of course, is that what Western culture refers to simply as 'humanism' is really a *specific form* of humanism – secular humanism. Every 'humanism' is dependent on a prior understanding of human nature. Secular humanism regards religion as detrimental to human flourishing; Christian humanism sees God as the key to human flourishing and well-being. Perhaps we need to ask some hard questions about those who naïvely presume that the meaning of 'humanism' is as self-evident as it is secular.

A third approach to the 'image of God' envisages it as making a statement about the innate human tendency and capacity to relate to God. To be created in the 'image of God' is to possess the potential to enter into a relationship with God, so that we are incomplete and unfulfilled until and unless we relate to God. This theme has played a major role in Christian spirituality. It is found, for example, in a famous prayer of Augustine of Hippo: 'You have made us for yourself, and our heart is restless until it finds its rest in you.' Human beings only achieve their true identity, goal and meaning when they relate to God.

In recent years, the word 'humanism' has been monopolized by those promoting what is actually a 'secular humanism' based on an anti-religious or atheist world view. The real meaning of the term 'humanism' is, however, very different: it is about enabling human beings to achieve their full potential. *Christian humanism* – the phrase is not a self-contradiction – is a philosophy of life which holds that to be truly human we need to relate to God.

This form of humanism is found in leading Renaissance thinkers such as Erasmus of Rotterdam or Thomas More, who believed that knowing and loving God endowed – and was intended to endow – human life with dignity and meaning. Any form of humanism is ultimately dependent on a 'big picture' which sets out a vision of human nature and destiny. There is no 'neutral' humanism, in that each form of humanism reflects and rests upon foundational assumptions about the true nature and goal of humanity.

A fourth approach is especially associated with literary authors, such as J. R. R. Tolkien, who see the 'image of God' as an imaginative narrative template. On this approach, human beings tell stories which are subtly governed or shaped by a Christian 'grand story', so that echoes of Christian ideas and values are to be found in pagan myths. For Tolkien, human beings create such stories under the influence of God: 'We make still by the law in which we're made.'

It is possible to regard Tolkien as offering a Christian version of the 'archetypes' set out by the Swiss psychoanalyst Carl Jung. For Jung, these were universal, archaic patterns and images that were embedded in the human unconsciousness and shaped our thinking without our realizing it. Tolkien's point is similar, in that he argues that, since we bear God's image, we unconsciously create stories which echo our origins in God. We are actually 'co-creators', in that our creative imaginations are already shaped and influenced by God.

Being drawn downwards: the concept of sin

The 'Age of Reason' argued that reason and science enabled fundamentally good people to progress towards enlightenment and moral perfection. Reason and science would put an end to conflict and social tension, enabling humanity to progress towards an ideal society. When I was a morally earnest teenager, I gladly accepted this belief in the constant improvement of the human condition through science and technology. Yet I have reluctantly abandoned this belief, because the evidence simply does not support it. One of secular humanism's greatest failings is its inability to concede that there is something *wrong* with human nature, and face the consequences of this admission.

Our forebears of the eighteenth and nineteenth centuries might have dreamed of a bright new world of social justice and world peace, but the massively destructive Great War of 1914–18 put an end to this dream, exposing it as a sad and unsustainable delusion. The Enlightenment told us that war was caused by religion, and by giving up on religion the world would become a safer place. Yet historians are agreed that religion played virtually no role in causing the Great War.

Nationalism, pride, greed and utter stupidity were all major contributing causes to this devastating war. But how did human beings manage to get themselves into this mess? How did they trigger such a frenzy of destruction, with incalculably negative implications for the wellbeing of human society? Why did rational creatures do something so irrational?

And what about the Second World War? The significance of the Nazi extermination camps for any account of human nature can hardly be overlooked. They prompted the philosopher George Steiner's famous observation that someone could read great poetry or play great music in the evening, and then take part in mass murder on an industrial scale the next day. How could such dehumanization have come about?

It is hard not to avoid reflecting on the dark and disturbing ✳
question of whether there is something in human nature that
inclines us to do evil, even when we pay lip service to the good.
That steers us to do things we know we shouldn't do, or fail to do
the things we know we should. That enables us to turn a blind
eye to the blatant irrationality of certain courses of action, even
persuading ourselves that these are actually quite rational.

Much secular thinking about ethics is based on the assumption that we naturally want to do the right thing. But what if
there is some fatal flaw, some irrational or delusional tendency,
within human nature that inclines us to doing what suits our
own agendas, when we know perfectly well that we ought to be
doing something else? Or to invent alternative truths, when real
truths are too disturbing for us to bear?

In Christian theology, this flaw within human nature is
called sin. This notion, prematurely dismissed by many modern
self-congratulatory visions of humanism, tries to articulate what
is *wrong* with us, and what can be done about it. We cannot see
things as they really are. Our eyes are dimmed and unfocused,
requiring both divine healing and training if they are to see our
world and ourselves properly. And even if we could achieve such
a proper vision, we are trapped within our own self-referential
schemes of thought that dispose us not to want to accept, still
less act upon, such a true knowledge of ourselves. The problem
involves both intellect and will.

Humans resist being reduced to purely good or purely evil.
Rather, we are forced to confront the enigma of human complexity and ambiguity, even in the face of our own instinct to deny
or suppress ideas that we find threatening or disturbing. Sadly,
the simplistic narratives of fundamental human goodness and
inevitable progress – such as those thin and superficial philosophies which dominated the bygone 'Age of Reason' – have to
be rejected as myths. They represent a blind faith in a utopian
human nature which bears little obvious relation to what we see
in history and culture, especially in the darker moments of the
history of Europe in the twentieth century.

We need a better narrative if we are to do justice to reality
and face up to its implications. That means we have to look for

a richer, if more disturbing, view of reality to help us here in facing up to selfishness and evil – such as Carl Jung's concept of the 'shadow', Richard Dawkins's notion of the 'selfish gene', or the Christian concept of 'original sin' – which boldly faces up to this disquieting aspect of human nature that the 'Age of Reason' understandably but wrongly preferred to gloss over.

Unpacking the idea of sin

Christianity uses the broad term 'sin' to designate the problem with human nature. Although it is tempting to try to offer a simple definition of sin, this inevitably ends in reducing a rich and deep concept to something shallow and superficial. Sin is something that demands to be described in all its fullness, not truncated for the purposes of allowing a neat little definition. In what follows, I shall map out three aspects of the Christian understanding of sin – each of which is a thread that needs to be woven together with the others to disclose a fuller picture of sin, rather than determining that picture by itself. These three aspects of sin are illustrative, not exhaustive. There is more that needs to be said, and these examples are intended to help flesh out a description of sin, not provide a comprehensive account of it.

The first theme of the Christian understanding of sin is an impairment of theological vision. We are unable to see ourselves, our world and God properly. There are limits on what we can see of the landscape of faith, or of God. If we try to use reason to find our way to God, we end up with an attenuated impersonal notion of God – what Pascal called the 'god of the philosophers' rather than the personal 'God of Abraham, Isaac and Jacob'. Human reason may find itself drawn towards God, yet it proves incapable of rendering God faithfully and fully.

We need help if we are to know God, otherwise we are limited to a realm of hints, suggestions and partial insights which conceal as much as reveal the truth about God. The Christian notion of revelation – which is really an aspect of the Christian understanding of God – sets out the idea that God *tells* us and *shows* us what we could otherwise not grasp or see.

Second, we can think of sin in terms of moral guilt. We have either done things that fail to live up to the standards that might be expected of us, or we have deliberately subverted our notions of God. This can be interpreted in terms of human failure to do what is good as much as deliberately choosing to do what is wrong. As the Roman poet Ovid pointed out two thousand years ago, we recognize and approve what is good – but we seem to end up doing something much worse. *Video meliora, proboque, deteriora sequor.* One of the more troublesome aspects of much human ethical thought in the eighteenth and nineteenth centuries is the reluctance on the part of so many of the philosophers of that age to accept that human beings might deliberately choose to do something which is wrong.

A third way of describing sin is to think of it as an illness. This sets out the idea that there is something wrong with us – that this is not the way we are meant to be. We have become infected with a virus which has reduced our capacity to live normally. We may want to be restored to the way we were before, but we are unable to achieve this unaided. We need to be healed by a competent physician, who understands our situation, and is able to begin the therapeutic process.

If we are afflicted by an illness, there is little point in trying to deal purely with its symptoms. While we can try to reduce their impact through medication, the real solution lies in curing the condition which caused them in the first place. It is the underlying medical condition which needs healing, not its symptoms. Well-meaning moralists might declare that all would be well with the world if everyone ceased being selfish and became good instead. Yet that's like asking people to stop coughing when they are suffering from a respiratory tract infection. The solution is to cure the infection, not issue endless (and pointless) demands that the unfortunate victim suppress one of its most obvious symptoms.

For Augustine of Hippo, the Christian gospel promised the cure (though not an *immediate* healing) of this sinful disposition, allowing us to break free from natural inclinations towards sin and evil. Augustine suggested that the Church was like a hospital, in which those who were damaged or wounded by sin could find healing and restoration under the care of a competent physician.

This way of thinking about sin helps us to see that sin is not something that is banished from the human life by grace. It is like an infection that is removed slowly over time by the healing process. There is no instantaneous transformation of the human situation. It is like someone receiving medical care who is recovering from an illness, yet who is not yet fully healed. They are on their way to recovery, but have yet to arrive. We are thus caught up in a conflict between sin and grace, still unable to do the good that we would like to, and finding ourselves dragged down into patterns of thought and behaviour that we know to be wrong or less good than what we are called to achieve.

Christian theology holds that sin is not something which begins to enter our lives at some age of majority. The phrase 'original sin' is used to refer to an innate human tendency towards sin. It is not something that we pick up from our environment or discover as we grow up. There is an inclination or predisposition to sin within us from our birth, as part of our natural endowment. Individual sinful actions or attitudes are to be seen as the result of some inbuilt flaw within human nature which inclined them towards sin.

In affirming the reality of sin, Christianity is not lapsing into despair about humanity. The creeds invite us to steer a middle course between a naïve optimism and a cynical pessimism. By telling us the truth about ourselves, Christianity diagnoses both our situation and our options for the future. Yes, we are weak – but we can walk in God's strength. Yes, we want to do our best – but somehow we seem to mess things up. Yes, our lives can go horribly wrong – but we can start again.

The two fundamental outcomes of the Christian understanding of humanity can be set out simply like this: we need to be realistic about ourselves, and realize that God longs to heal our wounds, illuminate our minds and support us as we walk through life. A sobering realism about ourselves must always be tempered by a knowledge of the graciousness of God. As Augustine of Hippo once put it: 'Christ is your salvation, so fix your mind on Christ. Accept his cup of salvation, for he heals all your diseases . . . Your life has been redeemed from corruption; there is no need to be afraid ever again.'[1]

Augustine's emphasis on the importance of Christ in disclosing the truth about the human situation and making possible its transformation leads us to think about his identity and significance in more detail. We now turn to deal with one of the most distinctive and fundamental aspects of the Christian faith – the person and work of Jesus Christ.

Part 3

THE SECOND ARTICLE: JESUS CHRIST, LORD AND SAVIOUR

9

The two maps: exploring the identity of Jesus Christ

'I believe in Jesus Christ'. The creeds introduce Christ as a real historical figure who lived in a specific place and age, yet who transcends the limits of geography and history. Christians do not simply share Christ's belief in God, thus seeing their faith essentially as an act of solidarity with him. They recognize that, in some way, Christ offers us a lens through which we may see God, a nexus of interconnection between God and the world, and an insertion of divine presence and activity within the world that has the potential to transform us.

To believe in Jesus Christ is certainly to affirm his existence as an historical figure. Yet we need to go much further than this. There is a need for theological attentiveness towards Christ as the centre and focus of our faith – a loving and committed concern to go as far and as deep as we reasonably can, in order to bring out the full meaning of Christ's identity and agency.

The creeds sketch the history of Jesus Christ, without adding detail, colour or mood. We learn that Christ was born of Mary, and that he was crucified under Pontius Pilate. Yet there is a total silence about the period between his birth and death – nothing which even hints at the richly textured picture of the life and ministry of Christ that we find in the four Gospels. Many find themselves disappointed at the creeds' flat statements, which seem inadequate and pale in comparison with the vibrant picture of Christ we find in the Gospels.

Yet the creeds are not meant to be substitutes for the Gospels. Maurice Halbwachs – a pioneer in the field of 'collective memory' – once defined history as 'an intellectualized reordering of the past to fit it into a coherent framework'. The creeds offer an 'intellectualized reordering' of the gospel narratives, allowing us to see their patterns and grasp their significance. We stand back from the events of the Gospels, and try to discern the 'coherent framework' they disclose. This 'big picture' mingles historical narrative with intellectual reflection and interpretation.

We need to use two maps to make sense of Christ – one of which is historical and the other theological. The creeds rehearse history while supplementing this with a theological commentary: born, suffered and crucified; Son of God, Incarnation and salvation. Yet they also rehearse theology, and supplement this with an historical commentary. The point being made is that Christianity is rooted in history, yet not limited to history.

The first Christians used images to convey their understanding of Christ, and there is much we can learn by reflecting on those images. Unable to meet in public due to the hostility of the imperial Roman authorities, the early Christians dug into the soft basaltic rock around the city of Rome and constructed the long underground tunnels we now know as the Catacombs. Here they would gather for prayer and worship, and bury their dead in large stone coffins known as sarcophagi. These early Christians inscribed symbols of their faith on the walls of these tunnels and the surfaces of the sarcophagi. Two of these are especially important in helping us understand how ordinary Christians then thought of Christ as their companion on the Road, offering them comfort and guidance.

First, Christ was portrayed as a philosopher, holding the trademark philosopher's travelling staff in one hand and a gospel book in the other. In Classical culture, a philosopher was a teacher of wisdom, whose instruction enabled people to live and die well. With his staff, Christ conquered death; with his gospel, he brought the truth that philosophers had long searched for, but was now fulfilled in his coming, enabling people to see things as they really were.

Second, he was depicted as the good shepherd (John 10.14), carrying lambs on his shoulders (Luke 15.4–5). The good shepherd cared for his sheep, seeking those who were lost, and carrying them home when they were exhausted or wounded. They had heard his voice call them by name, and they would follow nobody else.

It is easy to understand the imaginative power which these symbols of divine compassion, care and commitment had for believers within a Roman imperial environment that was often intensely hostile to the Christian faith. They engage us at the existential level, telling us whom we may trust in situations of uncertainty, doubt and distress. They can still speak deeply to Christians today, especially when they feel under threat from an intolerant culture. Faith is about making a principled decision to entrust ourselves to Christ as our trailblazer, companion and guide as we journey along the Road.

But what does it mean to speak of Christ in these terms? For example, how do we understand a 'trailblazer'? As someone who leads us along familiar paths, or rather as one who establishes, at great personal cost, a path that did not previously exist, and then leads us along it to safety? To ask these questions is to move into the areas of Christian theology traditionally described as 'the person of Christ' (or sometimes 'Christology') and 'the work of Christ' (or sometimes 'atonement' or 'soteriology'). These involve focused attention on the identity and function of Jesus Christ as part of the discipleship of the mind. They supplement and undergird our trust in Christ, expanding our vision of his identity and significance so that we understand more clearly who Christ is and the difference that he makes to our lives.

To open our discussion of how we can begin to develop these more sophisticated approaches to our understanding of Christ, we may think a little about how we use maps to make sense of our world.

The two maps: historical and theological

The creeds do not present Jesus Christ as a theological dogma or a philosophical riddle, but as a real historical figure who transcends the limits of any and all historical contexts. E. C. Bentley's *Biography for Beginners* (1905) opens with a startling observation that helps us in our reflections at this point:

> The art of Biography
> Is different from Geography.
> Geography is about maps,
> But Biography is about chaps.

Jesus Christ is indeed a person, not an abstraction or a disembodied idea. Yet to appreciate the importance of this person, we need to use maps of meaning to help us grasp his full significance. No single map is adequate to the task of disclosing what the New Testament calls the 'boundless riches of Christ' (Ephesians 3.8). We need multiple maps to bring out the full significance of Christ – not some one-dimensional pastiche which results from limiting ourselves to a single angle of approach.

We might use an historical map, which discloses Christ as a Galilean artisan who lived and was executed by the Roman authorities on the basis of what was probably a fabricated charge of religious sedition. Yet although this might be part of the 'big picture' of Christ, it is totally inadequate in itself, failing to explain or unfold what Christians found – and find – in Christ that elicits worship and adoration. It is a 'story-book faith' (William Tyndale), which reduces Christ to the level of other historical figures, such as Pontius Pilate or Julius Caesar.

This approach became popular during the 'Age of Reason', which found the traditional Christian account of the identity and significance of Christ to be rationally challenging. The 'quest for the historical Jesus' set out to locate Jesus on a purely historical map, based on the deeply flawed assumption that this could be done objectively and empirically. Yet such historical reconstructions of Jesus lead to him becoming a distant figure, lost in the mists of history, and so entangled in the cultural specifics of first-century Judaea that he loses any relevance to us today.

Now, we need to be quite clear that both the New Testament and the Christian creeds are emphatic that Jesus Christ was a human being, an historical figure who lived and died in a specific part of the world at a specific time. The Gospel of Luke in particular locates Christ historically and geographically as precisely as was possible by the standards of the day. Yet this is only part of the 'big picture' of Christ. If we treat this as the whole truth, we fail to grasp why Christ is of such luminous significance. 'Though we once knew Christ from a human point of view, we know him no longer in that way' (2 Corinthians 5.16).

Christ really was a human being who wept, became tired, who cared for others, was angered by religious hypocrisy, and who suffered and died. Yet he was more than this, without ever becoming less than this. The question concerns the precise nature of this 'more'. We need to use every tool at our disposal to help us grasp why Christ stands at the heart of the Christian faith, and his implications for the life of faith. That's why we need a theological map, and not simply an historical map, if we are to grasp the full significance of Christ.

It is often said that the four Gospels offer an historical account of Christ, and the other works of the New Testament – such as the epistles – a theological account. There is some truth in this. Although the letters of Paul clearly assume their readers know something of the history of Christ, their primary concern is with preaching about Christ, and developing a lifestyle which embodies his values. Their concern is not with the historical figure of Christ, but with grasping his significance for the life of faith.

Similarly, the Gospels provide a primarily – but not exclusively – historical account of Christ. Yet the Gospels themselves supplement their accounts of what Jesus Christ said and did with deeper reflection on what these mean. The Gospels are not purely factual accounts of the life and teaching of Christ, in that they blend together history and theology, event and interpretation. Fact and interpretation are intermingled. Even in the Gospels, Jesus himself is part of the proclamation.

Furthermore, the process of selection which is such an important feature of the 'period of oral transmission' before the Gospels were written down means that much information concerning Jesus which the early Christians thought insignificant for their purposes is lost. We know nothing about his weight or his height. Yet these details are clearly not considered to be necessary if we are to grasp what is really important about Christ. John's Gospel makes this point succinctly and clearly.

> Now Jesus did many other signs in the presence of his disciples, which are not written in this book. But these are written so that you may come to believe that Jesus is the Messiah, the Son of God, and that through believing you may have life in his name.
> (John 20.30–31)

Realizing that Jesus is the Messiah and Son of God is the gateway to the personal transformation that lies at the heart of the Christian faith.

Christian faith is thus not simply an act of trust; it is an act of *discernment*. We see beyond the empirical historical figure of Jesus Christ, and recognize that we need another map of meaning to make sense of his identity and his significance for us. The creeds provide both these maps, empirical and theological, inviting us to weave them together to disclose the richer vision of Christ which stands at the heart of the Christian faith.

The empirical map on its own is not enough, and at best leads to us discovering an admirable historical personality, too often seen only dimly through a fog of romantic sentiment, from whom we might hope to learn something. Christianity is not like Platonism or Marxism. The ancient Greek philosopher Plato is the originator, not the subject, of Platonism. We know a lot about his ideas, and little about him as a person. But that doesn't matter: Platonism is a way of thinking about the world which is now independent of Plato himself.

In the same way, 'Marxism' refers to the political and economic theories of the nineteenth-century German political philosopher Karl Marx and his colleague Friedrich Engels. Yet Marxism has now become an abstract system of thought which is detached from its founder. Marx himself is not part of the Marxist world view, but is seen as the philosopher who introduced these ideas into the flow of history. The ideas are now judged in terms of their own intellectual merits, not on the basis of the moral character of their originator.

The relationship between Jesus Christ and Christianity is, however, strikingly different. Christians do not see Christ simply as a religious teacher, nor do they understand Christianity as just the set of religious and moral teachings originating from him. Jesus Christ is himself part of the Christian proclamation. Christ does not merely show us how to live, teach us what is true, or point us towards where life may be found. He himself is what he brings – the 'way, and the truth, and the life' (John 14.6). On a theological map, Christ is the point of intersection of time and eternity, the crossroads at which God and humanity meet.

Yet a theological map is also inadequate, if taken in isolation. It reduces the living historical figure of Christ to intellectual abstractions which are disconnected from history. We cannot love or relate to ideas, or feel that these ideas have any interest in us. Yet when taken together and laid over the person of Jesus Christ, these two maps enable us to discern a real historical figure of flesh and blood, who lived, suffered and died – and yet who transcends the restrictions of any time and place, disclosing the face of God and enabling us to grasp the hope of eternal life.

In exploring all the intellectual options at their disposal, some early Christians were drawn to the use of a purely theological map to construct a coherent understanding of the identity and significance of Christ. The outcome of this process was a view known as 'Docetism' (from the Greek verb *dokein*, 'to appear'). Christ may have possessed the outward appearance of being human; in reality, he was a theological phantasm, a purely divine figure with an accidental and inconsequential presence in history.

This view was disowned by mainstream Christianity, which regarded it as an inadequate interpretation of the New Testament that failed to capture one of the most precious insights of the doctrine of the Incarnation – that God entered into history, and in doing so became vulnerable. We shall reflect on such matters further in the next chapter. But at this stage, we may merely note that the doctrine of the Incarnation has emerged as *the* defining Christian map of meaning for Christ. This map continues to be used because it represents a trustworthy rendering of the landscape of faith, having been tried and tested down the centuries by generations of believers anxious to ensure the best possible way of framing their faith and safeguarding its insights.

When the old maps failed

A close reading of the first three Gospels (often known collectively as the 'synoptic Gospels') reveals a process taking place that helps us think about how we frame our understandings of

Christ. To begin with, Christ's disciples tended to think of him using their inherited Jewish maps of meaning. Yet as they journeyed with Christ, they began to realize that these maps were not good enough to accommodate what they saw and heard. The old wineskins simply could not contain the new wine of Christ – it caused them to burst under the strain (Mark 2.22).

Our starting point is the familiar story of the calling of Simon and his brother Andrew on the shoreline of the Sea of Galilee (Mark 1.16–18). Christ approaches them and, without disclosing anything of his identity or intentions, invites them to follow him. We do not know what thoughts went through their minds, yet there was something compelling about this mysterious figure that commanded their attention and their trust. They left everything and followed him, beginning their journey of discernment and discovery.

Mark, like the other gospel writers, allows us to stand alongside the disciples, hearing what Christ said and watching what he did. As the disciples continued their physical journey around the villages near Galilee, they found another journey taking place in their minds and imaginations – the gradual dawning of insight into the true identity of this strange person. As they listened and observed, they tried to locate Christ on the conceptual maps they had inherited from Judaism. To begin with, this seemed relatively unproblematic. Christ was clearly a religious teacher – and hence could easily be assimilated to the Jewish category of the rabbi. Yet even there, there were tensions with this existing intellectual template. If Jesus was a teacher, he seemed to stand out from others in this category. 'They were astounded at his teaching, for he taught them as one having authority' (Mark 1.22).

The disciples' intellectual discomfort becomes increasingly clear as Christ's ministry unfolded. Not only did Christ teach about the kingdom of God; he healed people as a sign of this coming kingdom. He seemed able to command the forces of nature: 'Who then is this, that even the wind and sea obey him?' (Mark 4.35–41). It was as if the curtain was being lifted on a new era of the history of Israel. Christ did not seem to fit the standard templates.

A conceptual turning point seems to have been reached with the healing of a paralytic in the village of Capernaum (Mark 2.1–12). A large crowd had gathered, and heard Christ declare that the paralytic's sins were forgiven. We too easily lose sight of their significance against the core theological premises of rabbinical Judaism. The 'scribes' – the theological experts of first-century Palestinian Judaism – had no difficulty in identifying the theological implications of these words. 'Who can forgive sins but God alone?' (Mark 2.7).

Those words violated secure theological categories, transgressing borders on the familiar intellectual maps. One conceptual mapping of those words – favoured by the scribes – was that Christ was blaspheming against God, by proposing that he could do something that religious orthodoxy insisted was the unique prerogative of God. But there was another option: the theological maps needed revision.

As Mark's narrative progresses, more pieces are added to the jigsaw. A turning point is reached, geographically and theologically, as Christ and the disciples walk through the villages near Caesarea Philippi, at the base of Mount Hermon, just north of the Golan Heights. Christ asked his disciples to tell him how people were making sense of him (Mark 8.27–31). Who did they think he really was? They told him the main views that they had heard as they travelled: John the Baptist, Elijah or one of the prophets.

The disciples were, in effect, reporting where people were locating Christ on theological maps. Christ, however, pressed his disciples on where *they* would place him on such a map. Their response was unanimous: 'You are the Messiah.' They had come a long way from their first encounters with Christ and now had a fuller grasp of his significance. Yet it was still not enough.

Christ supplemented this theological map in a way that clearly challenged his disciples and caused them genuine theological discomfort. He began to teach them that the Son of Man must undergo great suffering, and be rejected by the elders, the chief priests, and the scribes, and be killed, and after three days rise again' (Mark 8.31). Their theological mapping still had further to go. The popular image of the Messiah in Judaism was that of a triumphant religious hero. Yet Christ was to be a crucified

Messiah – a core element of the New Testament's proclamation of the 'word of the cross'.

The titles of Christ in the creeds

The New Testament provides a rich list of titles for Christ, each of which opens a window of understanding and discernment into his identity and significance. Two of these titles are explicitly mentioned in the creeds: 'Son of God' and 'Lord'. While other titles are important, we shall reflect on these two, given their central place in the creeds.

Christ as the Son of God

The creeds invite us to believe in Jesus Christ as God's 'only Son' and 'our Lord'. So what does it mean to think of Christ as 'Son of God'? Without in any way losing sight of the fact that Jesus was a human being – like us in so many ways, apart from being sinful and thus standing in need of redemption – the creeds highlight the fact that there was something fundamentally different about him. Traditionally, his identity is explored using the 'two natures' framework, which presents Christ as being both truly human and truly divine.

Christians often use the pair of New Testament titles 'Son of Man' and 'Son of God' to designate the human and divine aspects of Jesus. For Paul, Jesus Christ 'was descended from David according to the flesh and was declared to be Son of God with power according to the spirit of holiness by resurrection from the dead' (Romans 1.3–4). The humanity and divinity of Christ are like threads woven together in a seamless fabric; they cannot be separated from each other, because they are both an integral part of the pattern.

The Old Testament occasionally uses the title 'Son of God' to refer to angelic or supernatural persons. However, the title is also often used to refer to the coming Messiah (2 Samuel 7.12–14; Psalms 2.7; 86.26–27). The New Testament develops this idea of Christ as the Son of God in a number of ways. For example, Christ directly addresses God as 'Father', using the Aramaic word 'Abba', which is often thought to express a particularly close relationship (Mark 14.36; see also Matthew 6.9; 11.25–26; 26.42; Luke 23.34, 46).

It is interesting to note how many passages in the Gospel of John make extensive reference to the Father–Son relationship (John 5.16–27; 17.1–26). These passages place a remarkable emphasis upon the identity of will and purpose of the Father and Son, indicating how close the relationship between Jesus and God was understood to be by the first Christians. At every level in the New Testament – in the words of Jesus himself, or in the impression which was created among the first Christians – Jesus is clearly understood to have a unique and intimate relationship to God, which the resurrection demonstrated publicly (Romans 1.3–4).

Of course, recognizing and confessing Christ as the Son of God does more than affirm that *Christ is like God*; it also makes clear that *God is like Christ*. Our God is not one who is hidden from us, as some inscrutable and distant despot. Rather, God's will is made known and God's face is shown in Jesus Christ. The creeds reassure us that Jesus is the gateway through which we have access to God. There is a God; there is a way to this God; and this way has been made known and made open through the life, death and resurrection of Jesus.

Although all people are children of God in some sense of the word, the New Testament holds that Jesus is *the* Son of God. Paul distinguishes between Jesus as the natural Son of God and believers as adopted sons. Their relation to God is quite different from Jesus' relationship to him, even though both may be referred to as 'sons of God'. We shall explore this point later when we consider the idea of 'adoption' as a way of thinking about the benefits Christ obtained for us on the cross.

Christ as Lord

The title 'Lord' is used in relation to Christ in two main senses in the New Testament. It is used as a polite title of respect. Thus when Martha addressed Christ as 'Lord' (John 11.21), she was probably simply treating Jesus with proper deference.

However, there are many passages in the New Testament which refer to Christ as 'Lord' in a different sense. The confession that

'Jesus is Lord' (Romans 10.9; 1 Corinthians 12.3) was clearly regarded by Paul as a statement of the essential feature of the gospel. Christians are sometimes spoken of as those who 'call on the name of the Lord' (Romans 10.13; 1 Corinthians 1.2). But what is implied by this?

The word 'Lord' (Greek: *kyrios*) was regularly used to translate the cypher of four letters referring to God in the Old Testament (often referred to as the 'Tetragrammaton', from the Greek words for 'four' and 'letters'). Old Testament writers were sometimes reluctant to refer to God directly, and tended to use a cypher of four letters, sometimes transliterated as YHWH, to represent the sacred name of God. While other Hebrew words could be used to refer to gods in general, this name was used to refer only to the God of Abraham, Isaac and Jacob. This name refers only to the covenant God of Israel, almost acting as a proper name. It is never used to refer to any other divine or angelic being, unlike other Hebrew words for 'god'.

When the Old Testament was first translated from Hebrew into Greek, the word *kyrios* was generally used to render this sacred name of God. Of the 6,823 times that this name is used in the Hebrew, the Greek word *kyrios* ('Lord') is used to translate it on 6,156 occasions. This Greek word thus came to be an accepted way of referring directly and specifically to the covenant God of Israel, revealed at Sinai, and who had entered into a covenant with his people on that occasion. Jews would not use this term to refer to anyone or anything else, because this would imply that this person or thing was of divine status. The historian Josephus tells us that the Jews refused to call the Roman emperor *kyrios*, because they regarded this name as reserved for God alone.

Yet the writers of the New Testament had no hesitation in using this sacred name to refer to Jesus, with all that this implied. A name which was used exclusively to refer to God by Jewish writers came to be used by the first Christians – most of whom were Jews – to refer to Jesus Christ. This was not some error made by ill-informed writers, ignorant of the Jewish background to the name.

For example, the prophet Joel tells of a coming period in the history of the people of God in which the Spirit of God will be poured out upon all people (Joel 2.28). On that day, 'everyone who calls on the name of the LORD shall be saved' (Joel 2.32). This prophecy is referenced in Peter's great sermon on the day of Pentecost (Acts 2.17–21), which ends with the declaration that 'everyone who calls on the name of the Lord shall be saved' (Acts 2.21). But Peter makes it clear that the 'Lord' in question is none other than Jesus of Nazareth, thus publicly declaring the exalted status and identity of the risen Christ.

Those New Testament writers, such as Paul, who made most use of the term 'Lord' to refer to Jesus were perfectly well aware of its implications. They regarded the evidence concerning Jesus, especially his resurrection from the dead, as compelling them to make this statement concerning his identity. It was a deliberate, considered, informed and justified decision, entirely appropriate in the light of the history of Jesus. He has been raised to glory and majesty, and sits at the right hand of God. He therefore shares the same status as God and is to be addressed accordingly.

When the creeds refer to Christ as 'Lord', they are not simply referring to the idea that Christians see Christ as a normative point of reference, someone whom they recognize as having authority. They are also making a fundamental statement about Christ's relationship to God, which had to be woven into the Christian Church's attempts to develop a coherent theological account of the identity and significance of Jesus Christ – an area of theology which is often referred to as 'Christology'.

Mapping the location of Jesus Christ

We have already explored the importance of mapping in this chapter, noting how we need several intellectual toolkits to do justice to the complexity and richness of the biblical witness to Christ. We have also noted how the imposition of an alien map of meaning – such as that of eighteenth-century rationalism – merely leads to Christ being constrained by the predetermined categories of the map, thus diminishing his status and impoverishing our understanding and appreciation of who he is.

One of the core working assumptions of the natural sciences is that the object under investigation determines both the way in which you investigate it and the extent to which it can be known. A research method that works well in physics thus fails when applied to psychology. We develop maps of meaning that are determined by what it is we are investigating. The same principle applies in theology: we must learn to develop methods of exploring and representing Christ which are adapted for this purpose, not imported from another context, within which they had been created with a quite different objective in mind.

In what follows, I shall look at three ways of mapping Jesus Christ, and reflect on their limits and strengths, while at the same time considering how these help us in the task of constructing a coherent and comprehensive Christology.

Christ as the fulfilment of the hopes and aspirations of Israel

Although the creeds do not make reference to this theme, it is clearly an integral part of the New Testament's understanding of the identity and significance of Christ. Matthew's Gospel emphasizes how events in the life and ministry of Christ can be seen as fulfilling Old Testament prophecy. Christ himself endorsed this point: 'Do not think that I have come to abolish the law or the prophets; I have come not to abolish but to fulfil' (Matthew 5.17). Although the New Testament spoke of a 'suffering Messiah' (a term which would have made little sense to traditional Jewish readers), the fact that Christ is identified with the long-awaited Messiah is an important affirmation of the continuity between the Old and New Testaments.

This framework is also used in the Christian interpretation of the Old Testament. Christians read the Old Testament to understand the history and beliefs of Israel, but also to grasp how Christ represents the fulfilment and transformation of Judaism. The Old Testament thus foreshadows the New Testament, just as the New Testament fulfils the Old Testament. 'The New Testament is concealed in the Old, and the Old Testament is revealed in the New' (Augustine of Hippo).

Early Christian writers developed a form of biblical interpretation known as 'typology', which recognized a correspondence between events, persons or things within the historical frame-work of revelation. Thus the Passover once celebrated in Egypt is seen as prefiguring 'Christ our Passover' (1 Corinthians 5.7, AV), just as the Passover lamb slaughtered in Egypt anticipates the 'Lamb slain from the foundation of the world' (Revelation 13.8, AV). Similarly, the history of Israel in Egypt is to be seen as an anticipation of the history of Jesus Christ in Judaea.

This way of mapping the life, death and resurrection of Jesus Christ anchors him firmly within the history of Israel, showing how a good Jew could embrace Christianity – a theme that is especially important in some of the letters of Paul, who under-went precisely such a process of conversion. Yet this map runs the risk of *limiting* the significance of Christ to those within the sphere of Judaism. We need other maps, if other groups of people are to see how Christ is connected and correlated with their longings, fears and aspirations.

Christ as the fulfilment of Classical wisdom

The New Testament indicates that Christianity soon began to gain a following outside Judaism. So how could the relevance and appeal of Christianity be explained to those who were steeped in the ideas of the Greek philosophical tradition? Writers such as Justin Martyr and Clement of Alexandria developed the idea that Christ was the fulfilment of the age-old human quest for wisdom, and thus represented the culmination of Greek philosophy.

This was often expressed using the Greek notion of *logos* (a Greek term best translated as 'word' or 'reason') – the ra-tional principle underlying the cosmos. There are hints of this idea in the New Testament itself, above all the remarkable dec-laration in the prologue to John's Gospel: 'the Word became flesh' (John 1.14). Plato had argued for the existence of an ideal world lying beyond the world of appearances. So how could this ideal realm be known? Some philosophers of this age spoke of the *logos* as a mediating principle or agent between these two very different, yet interconnected, worlds. But how might this gap be bridged? Who could bring the ideal realm into the everyday world? Clement and Justin both explored how Christ could be understood as the *logos* – the mediator between these two worlds.

Christ as the goal of human longing and desire

A third map of meaning is often used in engaging with the existential unease of Western culture, and its longing for something of true value. Many philosophies seem to offer little more than transient ideas and values that are quick fixes to complex problems. Is there something deeper and more satisfying? This map allows Christ to be correlated with the 'heart's desire' – the quest for existential fulfilment and satisfaction. Writers such as Blaise Pascal and C. S. Lewis have offered impressive attempts to connect these anxieties and aspirations with the fundamental themes of the Christian faith, especially the person of Christ.

Many experience deep feelings of longing or yearning for something as yet unpossessed, a nostalgia for the transcendent, which might somehow transform their lives into something meaningful and valuable. The English poet George Herbert engages such feelings, speaking of Christ as the 'philosopher's stone' who is able to turn the base metal of life into gold. For some, Christ's significance is linked with the interpretative framework of the Incarnation, which affirms that we know and see God in Christ. For others, however, it lies in Christ confronting and experiencing seemingly meaningless suffering, and sustaining those who experience similar traumas and anxieties today. Yet other groups also raise questions about the connectedness of Christ. How, for example, does Jesus Christ relate to the traditional philosophies of China? Or the ancient religious traditions of the Indian subcontinent?

In this chapter, we have explored the need for maps to make sense of Jesus Christ. To use the framework I noted earlier, I have tended to stand on a Balcony and develop maps from that privileged standpoint. But what about the Road? We are now ready to begin a more sustained engagement with three central themes that radiate outwards from him, as these focus on life on the Road – beginning with the remarkable concept of the Incarnation.

10

Incarnation: God with us

As a book-loving teenager, I devoured all kinds of literature, often uncritically and invariably enthusiastically. I developed a particular love for crime fiction, and soon discovered the works of Dorothy L. Sayers, the creator of the aristocratic sleuth Lord Peter Wimsey. Later, as I tried to make sense of my newly acquired Christian faith, I discovered that Sayers had also written extensively in the field of theology. I came across a lecture by Sayers, delivered in May 1940, which helped me grasp the centrality of the Incarnation to the Christian faith:[1]

> The central dogma of the Incarnation is that by which relevance stands or falls. If Christ was only man, then He is entirely irrelevant to any thought about God; if He is only God, then He is entirely irrelevant to any experience of human life.

Sayers helped me to solidify an insight that I had never really managed to formulate properly in words. I had seen something, yet failed to find a way of expressing it verbally. For a few weeks in late 1971, I found myself in a twilight zone as I hovered on the brink between what I had thought to be a solid atheism that I now found to be crumbling beneath me, and a Christian way of thinking that seemed to offer a gateway to a richer and deeper way of living and thinking. I now recall little of this process of transition, save for one question that I found myself turning over in my mind.

By that stage, I could see that assuming the existence of some kind of God made much more intellectual sense than dismissive atheists were prepared to allow. While I was increasingly convinced that it was entirely rational to believe in God, it was still tantalizingly unclear to me whether this belief merely resolved a few intellectual enigmas, or promised something much more satisfying, engaging deeper existential concerns.

I had read Edward Fitzgerald's translation of the *Rubáiyát* of the twelfth-century Persian mathematician Omar Khayyám as a teenager, and regularly found myself pondering one of its stanzas:[2]

> And that inverted Bowl they call the Sky,
> Whereunder crawling coop'd we live and die,
> Lift not your hands to *It* for help – for It
> As impotently moves as you or I.

That seemed to me to summarize the problem with believing in a god as the ground of explanation for our world. Human beings were trapped in history. And God stood beyond this place of our habitation, irrespective of whether we saw this as a paradise or a prison. So how could this God be of any relevance to us?

I was coming to the view that atheism was wrong in its premature dismissal of the utility of the notion of God. The idea was a useful sense-making device for experience and observation. God, however, still seemed to me to be a distant reality standing behind or outside history, a sort of abstract intellectual template who, like the ancient gods of Olympus, was detached from human existential concerns and shielded from the flux of history. Since I was part of history, it seemed to me that God was a stranger to the tragedies and traumas of the historical process within which I existed.

While in this twilight region of intellectual wrestling and occasional bafflement, I stumbled across an answer – or, more accurately, an idea that seemed capable of enormous imaginative and intellectual expansion. It directly addressed my concerns and opened up intellectual possibilities that went far beyond my emerging idea of God as an explanatory agency, and helped move me decisively on from some kind of philosophical theism towards Christianity itself. The idea, of course, was that of Christ as God Incarnate. Perhaps I had come across this idea earlier and failed to appreciate its implications. Yet it now proved pivotal to my growth into the Christian faith.

The concept of the Incarnation can be summed up in the biblical affirmation that the 'Word became flesh and lived among us' (John 1.14). The Greek word translated here as 'lived' more accurately means 'pitched a tent', alluding to the people of Israel's period of journeying in the wilderness of Sinai on their way to Canaan. God shares our journey through the wilderness of this world towards the promised land. The doctrine of the Incarnation thus solidifies one of the great truths of the Christian faith – that God truly cares for us, not as a passive distant observer, but as an active fellow traveller and constant companion. God descends from the Balcony and joins us on the Road.

In this chapter, we shall consider this remarkable idea in more detail, considering both its grounds and its consequences. We begin by setting this idea in its context.

The two natures of Christ: the basis of the Incarnation

'The Word became flesh and lived among us, and we have seen his glory' (John 1.14). These words compress some vivid and powerful theological themes into a few precise words. The Greek term *logos*, here translated as 'Word', possesses a richness and complexity which no English translation can adequately convey. We might rephrase it like this: 'the one who made the world has entered into the world as part of that world, and we have seen his glory'. God, having created the world, now enters into that creation to recreate it and bring it to its intended goal.

So how does God enter into this world? In what form? At what place? When? The classic Christian answer is in that little piece of human history that we call Jesus Christ, who was born under the rule of Herod and crucified under Pontius Pilate. The idea of 'Incarnation' means God taking on human flesh, achieving a double entry into our situation, coming *among us* as *one of us*. The one who was there from the beginning became a human being in order to redeem us. Charles Wesley's famous Christmas carol 'Hark the Herald Angels Sing!' phrases this point memorably:

> Veiled in flesh the Godhead see,
> Hail the incarnate Deity!

Pleased as man with man to dwell,
Jesus our Emmanuel!

There is, of course, the most intimate connection between the idea of the Incarnation and the doctrine of the 'two natures' of Christ – the Christian belief that Jesus Christ is fully God and fully human. There was no doubt in the minds of any of the gospel writers or first Christian witnesses to Jesus Christ that he was a human being. But he was more than that – much more than that. Jesus offered access to God, by both making God known and making God available. As part of their disciple-ship of the mind, Christians had to learn to 'think about Jesus as we do about God' (to quote the second letter of Clement, a late first-century Christian writing which was greatly valued by the early Church). But how was this to be expressed? How could the biblical witness to the identity and impact of Jesus be crystal-lized into verbal formulae? In fact, how could any form of words be good enough to do justice to this remarkable figure?

We can see something of this dilemma in the account of the transfiguration (Luke 9:1–10). When Jesus was transfigured in the sight of the disciples, their initial reaction was to try to pre-serve this moment of glory. Could they not construct 'dwellings' or 'booths', so that this brief and dazzling display of glory might be made permanently accessible? The disciples caught sight of the glory of Christ. But how was this glory to be captured? Karl Barth, widely recognized as one of the most important Christian theologians of the twentieth century, shrewdly pointed out this paradox in one of his earliest writings – his commentary on Paul's Letter to the Romans. God's revelation, he argued, cannot be frozen or pinned down, any more than a bird can be stopped in mid-flight. We can never fully seize the glory of divine revelation.

In one sense, this is what Christian doctrines attempt to do – preserve a mystery, in the full knowledge that human words can never hope to do justice to it. Doctrines were never meant to be a substitute for Christian experience. Rather, they are meant to be a kind of 'hedge', marking out and safeguarding an area of thought about God and Christ which seemed to be faithful to Christian experience on the one hand and to Scripture on the other.

This 'hedging' process was difficult, yet it needed to be done. Jesus needed to be placed on a conceptual map. Initially, it seemed that he had to be calibrated according to the coordinates of humanity and divinity, time and eternity. This raised the most difficult of theological questions, which the Christian Church rightly chose to wrestle with over many years, ensuring that every possible avenue of explanation, every conceivable way of representing this insight, had been evaluated. Many of the models initially evaluated were borrowed from Judaism or Greek philosophy. Might Jesus be some kind of prophet with an especially significant endowment of the Holy Spirit? Might Jesus be a theophany – a temporary revelation of God? Or a philosophical ideal, made known under the limiting conditions of history?

The period of the early Church witnessed exhaustive discussion of many possible ways of conceiving Jesus' identity. One neat solution that some early Christians found attractive was to think of Jesus as God's deputy. God was too busy to do everything – so he delegated the rather troublesome business of saving the world to an underling. It made sense to some at the time, especially as Judaism had already developed the idea that God delegated some of his powers for practical purposes to some kind of archangel or intermediate.

It was neat, but it just wasn't good enough. It didn't really capture the growing sense of excitement about the identity of Christ that we can see in the gospel narratives. Nor did it do intellectual justice to the rich tapestry of witness to the words, deeds and impact of Christ on those around him. Steeped in the knowledge of God's dealings with Israel, they recognized that something *new* had happened – something that just didn't fit the settled patterns of existing ways of thinking.

The new wine: Jesus and God

So what patterns of thought are found in the New Testament that needed to be woven together to disclose a coherent 'big picture' of the identity and significance of Jesus Christ? To illustrate these issues, we shall look at three groups of texts from the New Testament which speak of Christ as performing certain functions or tasks which are specifically and uniquely associated with God. These identify the function of Christ in terms which have clear implications for his identity. Each of them fits easily and naturally into the Christian 'big picture', which recognizes Christ as God Incarnate – one who has inhabited our landscapes.

Jesus is the Saviour of humanity

The Old Testament was quite clear that there was only one saviour of humanity – God. In the full knowledge that only God could save, the first Christians affirmed that Jesus was Saviour. Jesus saves his people from their sins (Matthew 1.21); in his name alone is there salvation (Acts 4.12); he is the 'captain of salvation' (Hebrews 2.10, AV); he is the 'Saviour, who is Christ the Lord' (Luke 2.11, ESV). And in these affirmations, and others, Jesus is understood to function as God, doing something which, properly speaking, only God can do.

As Athanasius of Alexandria emphasized, no creature, no matter how great or holy, can achieve this. If Jesus Christ has brought salvation to humanity, as the creed declares that he has, then he must be God. If Jesus Christ is something other than God – in other words, a creature – then whatever 'salvation' he brings is not the same as that offered by God. Historians note that the early Christians used a fish as a symbol of their faith. Why? Because the five Greek letters which spell out 'fish' in Greek (I-CH-TH-U-S) are the initial letters of the slogan 'Jesus Christ, Son of God, Saviour'.

Jesus is worshipped

Within the Jewish context in which the first Christians lived and thought, it was universally agreed that only God was to be worshipped. Paul warned the Christians at Rome that there was a constant danger that humans would worship creatures, when they ought to be worshipping their creator (Romans 1.23). Yet we know that the early Christian Church worshipped Christ as God. This practice was noted by Pliny the Younger in a famous letter of AD 112 to the emperor Trajan, in which he reports that Christians sang hymns to their Lord 'as God' (*quasi deo*).

Yet the worship of Christ is not a later innovation, but is clearly reflected in the New Testament itself. Thus 1 Corinthians 1.2 speaks of Christians as those who 'call on the name of our Lord Jesus Christ', using language which reflects the Old Testament formulae for worshipping or adoring God (such as Genesis 4.26; 13.4; Psalm 105.1; Jeremiah 10.25; Joel 2.32). Jesus is thus clearly understood to function as God, in that he is an object of worship.

Jesus reveals God

'Anyone who has seen me has seen the Father' (John 14.9, NIV). This remarkable statement highlights the Christian belief that the Father speaks and acts in the Son – in other words, that God is revealed in, by and through Christ, who is the 'image of the invisible God' (Colossians 1.15). To have seen Jesus is to have seen God. Christ is again understood to function as God in this respect.

The New Testament portrays Christ as a human being who wept, suffered, became tired and experienced human emotions. In a sense, the humanity of Christ is a 'given', and cannot be taken away. Yet these three groups of passages clearly point to an understanding of Christ which forces us to think of him as transcending the category of pure humanity. Without in any way denying that Christ was a human being, the New Testament clearly indicates that there is a lot more that needs to be said about his true identity and significance. Christ was indeed a real human being – but he was more than that. The issue was to clarify precisely what this 'more' meant.

In the end, it was clear that the new wine of the person of Jesus Christ simply could not be contained by the old wineskins of existing patterns of religious thought. Not surprisingly, they proved incapable of containing him. New ways of thinking were demanded by this remarkable person. And a new vocabulary had to be developed to cope with this new map of meaning. Nothing that lay to hand proved adequate for the purpose.

By the end of the fourth century, the Church had made up its collective mind and decided that the only acceptable way of describing Jesus Christ was using what has come to be known as the 'two natures' formula – namely, that Jesus Christ was 'truly divine and truly human'. This is sometimes referred to as the 'Chalcedonian definition', set out more fully and formally by the Council of Chalcedon in 451.

If we think of the range of possible interpretations of Christ's identity and significance as being like a field, the Council of Chalcedon marked off and preserved the area of reliable inter-pretations of the identity of Jesus Christ, and invited us to explore them. Other ways of thinking about him were fenced off because they were recognized as being inadequate, impoverished or misleading.

One such way proved especially controversial – the view of Arius, generally known as 'Arianism'.

Arianism: a failed map

During the fourth century, Arius – a theologian based in the great Egyptian city of Alexandria – began to have doubts about whether the Christian idea of the Incarnation should be defended, when it caused offence to some Greek philosophers. Arius argued that Jesus Christ was not divine in any meaningful sense of the term. A rigid boundary had to be drawn between God and the creation. Christ might be supreme within the cre-ation; he was, however, unquestionably part of the created order. And because he was a creature, like us, Christ could not know God fully and properly. His insights into God might have been privileged; they were, however, limited.

Arianism thus emphasized the inscrutability of God. There was an absolute gulf between God and the world of the crea-tures, and it could not be bridged. Christ, himself a creature, did not have direct knowledge of God, and was thus un-able to mediate a direct, reliable and authoritative revelation of God. God's will might be known, although in a very in-direct and roundabout way; God's face, however, remained averted and unknown.

Mainline Christianity offered a theological map which affirmed that Christ was able to reveal God, thus providing a secure link between the revealer and the revealed. Since Christ is God, Christ can disclose both what God is like and what God wants. Christian orthodoxy understood Christ as the mediator between God and humanity, and appreciated that his unique identity as truly divine and truly human was a means of ensuring that this bridge was secure. Only God could disclose the ✳ face and will of God to humanity; only God could save humanity. The Nicene account of the identity of Jesus Christ safeguarded the actuality of both revelation and salvation.

Arianism, however, offered a theological map which failed to establish or permit any meaningful connection between Christ and God – and thus failed to allow humanity either reliable and authentic knowledge of God, or the salvation promised by the gospel. For Arius, Christ had no direct knowledge of God, and thus mediated a second-hand knowledge of God which may have been superior in quality at points to that of other human beings, but was nevertheless equal in kind.

The idea of the Incarnation provides a map which upholds and affirms the core New Testament ideas that Christ makes God known, and transforms our relationship with God. The doctrine of the Incarnation affirms that Christ, as God Incarnate, shows us what God is like. Identity underlies function. This theological framework safeguards the vibrant opening declaration of the First Letter of John: 'We declare to you what was from the beginning, what we have heard, what we have seen with our eyes, what we have looked at and touched with our hands, concerning the word of life' (1 John 1.1).

Yet the main weakness of Arianism is this: God remains on the Balcony, a distant spectator of our struggles. God observes our weaknesses from the safety and security of the Balcony, and sends a deputy to tell us how we ought to behave in this situation. The rich Christian vision of the Incarnation is that of a God who descends from the Balcony on to the Road in order to be with us in the midst of our sorrows and anxiety. Arius's God is like Omar Khayyám's uncaring sky – impersonal, silent and distant. Yet Christianity speaks about – and knows – a God who cares for us and shows that commitment by entering into the flow of human history, becoming vulnerable to human evil and ambition.

C. S. Lewis on the Incarnation

What has someone who lived long, long ago got to do with us today? Or with God? That was the question that troubled C. S. Lewis in 1931. After a period as an atheist, Lewis had recently returned to belief in God. God, he concluded, offered a way of making sense of the world and of human experience which appealed to both his reason and imagination. But how did Jesus Christ fit into this? Why did belief in God have anything to do with him? Lewis wrote to his close friend Arthur Greeves, confessing that he simply could not see 'how the life and death of Someone Else (whoever he was) 2000 years ago could help us here and now'.[3]

Within a year of returning to faith in God, Lewis had found his answer to those questions. Lewis's answer remains important as we think about the landscape of faith. After a long conversation with his colleague J. R. R. Tolkien in September 1931, Lewis began to realize that Christianity was not first and foremost a set of ideas about God and the world. It was about a story – a 'grand narrative' – which captured the imagination and thus opened up new ways of thinking. The creeds arose from reflection on the true and trustworthy story of Jesus Christ.

When rightly understood, the imaginatively compelling story of the birth of Christ was about God entering the world in order to redeem it. The Christmas liturgy and carols set out a powerful vision of a God who enters the world in humility, and is embraced by the imagination as much as it is analysed by reason. For Lewis, the theme of the Incarnation was impoverished if it was reduced to a mere piece of cold and clinical theological logic.

Lewis explored the theme of the Incarnation in an imaginatively engaging way in a remarkable sermon preached in a London church during the Second World War. Lewis had learned how to dive in 1930. Although he initially saw this simply as an enjoyable and exhilarating experience, he began to realize its potential as an analogy for what he had come to see as a core theme of the Christian faith – the Incarnation. In this sermon, Lewis invited his audience to imagine a diver who wants to rescue something precious that has fallen into the mud at the bottom of a deep lake. He asks us to imagine the diver plunging[4]

> down through the green and warm and sunlit water into the pitch black, cold, freezing water, down into the mud and slime, then up again, his lungs almost bursting, back again to the green and warm and sunlit water, and then at last out into the sunshine, holding in his hand the dripping thing he went down to get.

And just what is this 'dripping thing' that led to all this effort and risk on the diver's part? For Lewis, the object of the diver's love and commitment was humanity, who had become lost in the universe. God 'descended into his own universe, and rose again, bringing human nature up with him'.

Lewis's sermon makes a point to which we shall return in the next chapter, as we begin to explore the theme of 'atonement' – namely, that there is an intimate link between the identity and the function of Christ. Who Christ *is* determines what Christ *does*; what Christ *does* illuminates who Christ *is*. For Lewis, the doctrine of the Incarnation helps us grasp that God is an 'eternally perfect' being who also 'in some incomprehensible way, is a purposing, feeling, and finally crucified Man in a particular place and time'.

The significance of the Incarnation

So what insights does the idea of the Incarnation safeguard? The doctrine of the Incarnation tells us that God chose to come and inhabit our world as one of us. In an act of condescension and humility, God entered our history and experienced its violence and degradation. Christ was rejected, flogged, humiliated, and put to death by one of the most painful and degrading means known to the ingenuity of the Romans. There is no need to explain to God what human history is like. In Christ, God descends from the Balcony and stands and journeys with us on the Road – a place of suffering, weariness, pain and uncertainty.

The Incarnation reassures us of God's solidarity with us as we struggle on that Road.

The doctrine of the Incarnation thus undergirds the Christian belief that Jesus Christ is the most trustworthy picture of God we possess. We simply do not have access to any better or more definitive image than this. To trust in the Christian God is to trust the means by which we know this God – supremely, through the words and deeds of Jesus Christ, who is the point of intersection between God and ourselves, the window through which we see God, and the highway by which we come to God. Christ does not simply *tell* us about God; he *shows* us God. Christ does not simply point out the way to God; he takes us to God. The Incarnation is about Christ bringing God to us, so that he might bring us to God. The Incarnation affirms that God is with us – in the sense of both being on our side and being present with us in the midst of the seemingly uncontrollable problems we face. One of its great themes is simply this: we must not be *afraid*, because we are not *alone*.

J. Robert Oppenheimer, one of the twentieth century's most colourful scientists, made a memorable remark after the Second World War, as he realized how important it was to meet and talk to people if you wanted to really understand them. International diplomacy demanded personal engagement. 'The best way to send information is to wrap it up in a person.'[5] This may have some significant shortcomings as a theological strapline, but it highlights a key theme of the Christian faith: in the Incarnation, message and messenger are seamlessly woven together.

Let's look at a classic statement of the doctrine of the Incarnation found in the writings of the theologian Athanasius of Alexandria. In his masterpiece *On the Incarnation*, written around 365, Athanasius set out its basic themes like this:[6]

> So the Son of God became the Son of Man, so that the sons of man, that is, of Adam, might become sons of God. The Word begotten of the Father from on high, inexpressibly, inexplicably, incomprehensibly and eternally, is the one who is born in time here below, of the Virgin Mary, the Mother of God, so that those who are born here in the first place might have a second birth from on high, that is, of God.

The language may at times be dense, but Athanasius's basic idea is clear. God became incarnate – that is, God entered into human history as a real human being – in order to allow those born in time to be reborn eternally. God became incarnate so that we might become the children of God.

The doctrine of the Incarnation thus frames and safeguards one of the most imaginatively dramatic insights of the Christian faith – namely, that the God who created the heavens and the earth chose to come and dwell among us humans beings as one of us. If Athanasius is right, then all we need to know about God is found in Jesus Christ. There may be aspects of God's immense mystery that lie *beyond* Christ, but there is not a God who is *against* Christ, undermining the finality or completeness of our knowledge of God in Christ. The life of Jesus Christ is about God embodied in an historical form in an historical place, making God visible, tangible and available.

The Council of Chalcedon ensures that we think of Jesus Christ in ways that affirm he offers access to God, both making God *known* and making God *available*. As Calvin puts it: 'The Son of God became the Son of Man, and received what is ours in such a way that he transferred to us what is his, making that which is his by nature to become ours through grace.' Calvin argues that Jesus Christ brings together in his person the three great mediatorial offices of the Old Testament – prophet, priest and king. Christ's work may thus be summed up in terms of three offices or ministries. In his *prophetic* office, Jesus is the herald and witness of God's grace. In his *kingly* office, Jesus has inaugurated a kingship which is heavenly, not earthly; spiritual, not physical. Finally, through his *priestly* office, Jesus is able to restore us to divine favour, through offering his death as a satisfaction for our sin.

With these words, we have moved on to think about the Christian understanding of atonement, to be considered in greater detail in the next chapter.

11

Atonement: putting things right

'God left his heavens precisely in order to set the world right' (G. K. Chesterton).[1] With the incisiveness of a theologically informed journalist, Chesterton here pinpointed the golden thread running throughout the Christian narrative. There is something wrong with the world, and with us – something that we cannot put right. Yet God chose to enter our world and restore it to what it ought to have been. The theological term used to refer to this process of 'putting things right' is *atonement*.

The origins of the English word 'atonement' can be traced back to William Tyndale's ground-breaking translation of the New Testament (1526). Tyndale needed to convey the concept of 'reconciliation' to his readers before the now-familiar English word 'reconciliation' had been invented. Tyndale solved the problem by inventing the word 'atonement' to express the state of 'at-one-ment' – that is, reconciliation – between God and humanity as a result of the death of Christ. The term 'atonement' has now come to mean something like 'the benefits that Christ secured by his life, death and resurrection'.

The Lutheran theologian Philip Melanchthon once declared that 'To know Christ is to know his benefits,' not to 'speculate about his natures and the modes of his incarnation'. I first read those words back in 1977, when I was studying theology at Oxford University. To know Christ was – at least in part – to grasp what he had achieved for us. Melanchthon was anxious that we might become trapped in abstract theological speculation, where we ought instead to identify and appreciate the difference that Christ makes to believers. To know the giver is to know the gifts. Christian thinking about the atonement focuses on identifying those benefits, reflecting on how they are linked with the crucifixion and resurrection of Christ, and considering how we might receive them and be transformed by them.

Atonement: discovering the benefits of Christ

As we have seen, Christian theology aims to help us appreciate and understand the 'big picture' of faith in all its fullness. It helps us grasp its comprehensiveness, its richness and its capacity to make sense of things and offer hope and transformation. The creeds tell us about a glorious, loving and righteous God, who creates a world that goes wrong, and then acts graciously and wondrously in order to renew and redirect it, before finally bringing it to its fulfilment.

For this reason, we should not see the doctrine of the atonement in isolation. It is connected with so many other leading themes of the Christian faith, such as the nature of God, the identity of Jesus Christ, and the Christian understanding of human nature. The 'big picture' of faith engages the core questions about who we really are, what is really wrong with us and our world, what God proposes to do about this, and what we must do in response. The doctrine of the atonement is one piece in that jigsaw, joined up to other pieces. There is little point in asking which comes first, or which takes priority. They all converge in the grand vision of the Christian faith.

We can think of the doctrine of the atonement as a node on the spider's web of faith, a point at which multiple strands of theological silk converge and interconnect. One of these strands is the loving purpose of the God who created the world. Another is the realization that human nature is wounded, damaged and broken, and thus needs to be healed, mended and repaired. But we cannot achieve this by ourselves. It lies beyond our natural human capacities, which are in any case impaired by sin.

A central insight of Christian theology is that sinful humanity needs a saviour – someone who is the solution to our problem, not part of it. Only God can save. The doctrine of the Incarnation affirms both that God is with us and that a redeemer has entered the world. If Christ were merely a human being like us, the cross could be understood in terms of a tragic miscarriage of justice, or a magnificent example of someone being executed for their ideals. If Christ were merely God, this would be a remarkable epiphany of divine power, but without any point of contact with the broken human nature that needs to be restored and healed. Yet if Christ is God Incarnate, we have to see the cross in a completely different light – a place where the story of God and the story of humanity intersect in a scene of dereliction and suffering, in which God transforms our situation and gives us hope.

Opening up the idea of 'atonement'

The New Testament affirms that Christ has made possible the transformation of the human situation, and uses a series of rich images which allow us to visualize the form this transformation takes. None of these are normative or exhaustive. They have a cumulative force, like a series of brush strokes which make up a picture. Each of them illuminates one aspect of the Christian understanding of atonement, representing an element of a bigger picture.

One of the fundamental tasks of Christian theology is to unpack the riches of the Christian proclamation. At its best, theology is about holding up the diamond of the Christian 'deposit of faith', and allowing each of its facets to scintillate in the sunlight, disclosing its individual radiance. It is like opening the treasure chest of faith and lifting out its precious contents, slowly and carefully, so that the particular value can be appreciated. Theology aims to set out the full richness of the Christian gospel for public inspection.

An analogy I have long found helpful in explaining the role of theology to university students is that of refracting a beam of white light so that its individual component colours can be seen and studied individually. This process takes place naturally to create rainbows, but was studied scientifically by the great physicist and mathematician Isaac Newton. Newton showed that a beam of white sunlight, entering through a narrow slit in the shutters of his darkened rooms at Cambridge University, could be passed through a glass prism and split into its constituent colours – red, orange, yellow, green, blue, indigo and violet.

Yet the prism did not impose these colours on the white light; it simply enabled them to be discerned within it. What had hitherto been taken to be a simple colour – white – was shown to be a complex unity of different colours. The prism split the white light up into its constituent elements, so that the colours, which were already there in the beam of white light, could be separated and studied individually. In nature, they were combined; in the laboratory, they could be split up.

The same is true of Christian theology, which affirms the essential unity and coherence of the Christian faith while at the same time allowing us to identify its individual elements and study these individually. Theology does not invent these components; it merely uncovers them. They are not the product of some overactive theological imagination. All that the theologian has done is to isolate them, so that each can be admired and appreciated on its own, as well as in its interconnections with other theological ideas. The 'message of the cross' (1 Corinthians 1.18) is a unity – but it is a *complex* unity. It is by examining its individual components individually that the whole message can be better appreciated and understood.

In what follows, we shall try to weave together some core Christian ideas about the meaning of the death of Christ on the cross by following the trails left by the earliest Christians in the New Testament, as they tried to find words and images capable of expressing the new world of life and thought opened up by his resurrection. We may begin with one of the most dramatic themes of the New Testament – the victory of Jesus Christ over sin and death.

Victory over sin and death

'Thanks be to God, who gives us the victory through our Lord Jesus Christ' (1 Corinthians 15.57). The New Testament eagerly anticipates the final victory of God in Christ, when every knee shall finally bow to the one who is Lord (Philippians 2.11). God will subdue sin and death, and make all such hostile forces a footstool (Luke 20.43; Acts 2.35; Hebrews 1.13; 10.13). The cross and resurrection – both of which are explicitly referenced by the creeds – are the basis of the Christian hope of a final victory over sin and death, so that they need no longer be feared.

The early Church exulted in the triumph of Christ at Calvary over sin, death and Satan. The powerful imagery of the triumphant Christ rising from the dead and being installed as 'ruler of all' or 'sovereign' (Greek: *pantokrator*) seized the imagination of many Christian writers. The cross was seen as the site of a famous battle, comparable to those of the great Homeric epics, in which the forces of good and evil did battle, and the good emerged victorious.

Early Christian theologians were more interested in proclaiming Christ's victory over the enemies of humanity than in speculating as to precisely how this victory came about. Early Christian liturgies were saturated with the thought of the cosmic victory achieved by Jesus on the cross. His resurrection and triumphant opening of the gates of heaven to believers were proclaimed and celebrated rather than made the focus of theological debate.

This theme can be seen in the art of this early period and, more easily, in hymns such as the great Easter anthem written by Venantius Honorius Clementianus Fortunatus (c. 530 – c. 610):

> The royal banners forward go,
> The cross shines forth in mystic glow;
> Where he in flesh, our flesh Who made,
> Our sentence bore, our ransom paid.

Some Christian thinkers visualized the triumph of Jesus over death and sin through the cross and resurrection as a victory parade comparable to the triumphant processions of ancient Rome. In its Classical form, a general's soldiers, often leading the chain-bound leaders of the cities or countries they had defeated, went ahead of the victorious military leader through the streets of Rome, preparing the way for his triumphant arrival at the temple of Jupiter on the Capitoline Hill.

It was thus natural for Christian writers to encourage believers to think of the risen Christ triumphantly processing through the world, leading his conquered enemies – such as sin and death – behind him. Such powerful symbolism was firmly grounded in the New Testament, which spoke of the risen Jesus as 'making captivity a captive' (cf. Ephesians 4.8).

A further development of the theme of 'Christ the victor' depicts Christ as extending the triumph of the cross and resurrection to the realm of the dead. The medieval idea of 'the harrowing of hell' holds that, after dying upon the cross, Christ descended to hell and broke down its gates so that the souls imprisoned there might go free. The idea rests (rather tenuously, it has to be said) upon a biblical text (1 Peter 3.18–22) which makes reference to Christ 'preaching to the spirits in prison'. The dramatic power of this scene was such that, despite its slightly questionable theological foundation, it was picked up and incorporated into countless popular accounts of the significance of Easter.

The hymn 'You Choirs of New Jerusalem', written by Fulbert of Chartres (c. 970–1028), expresses this idea in two of its verses: Christ, as the 'lion of Judah' (cf. Revelation 5.5) has, by his death and resurrection, defeated Satan, the serpent (Genesis 3.15):

> For Judah's lion bursts his chains
> Crushing the serpent's head;
> And cries aloud through death's domain
> To wake the imprisoned dead.
>
> Devouring depths of hell their prey
> At his command restore;
> His ransomed hosts pursue their way
> Where Jesus goes before.

C. S. Lewis wove this thread of theological reflection into *The Lion, the Witch and the Wardrobe*. The White Witch rules Narnia not as a matter of right but by stealth and deception. The true ruler of the land is absent; in his absence, the witch has subjected it to oppression, imprisoning many of Narnia's inhabitants as stone statues in her castle.

As the narrative moves on, the rightful ruler of the land – the noble lion Aslan – advances into Narnia to reclaim his kingdom. The witch realizes that her power is beginning to fade, and puts Aslan to death on a stone table. Yet Aslan triumphs over death, and breaks down the gates of the witch's castle. He breathes upon the statues and restores them to life, before leading this liberated army through the shattered gates of the once great fortress to freedom.

The image of the cross and resurrection of Christ as victory over sin and death is deeply evocative. However, it raises a question which needs to be considered. If Christ defeated sin and death, why are they still present in our world? Christians still sin and die. It seems a somewhat curious kind of victory if the defeated forces are still present and active in the world.

There are several answers that can be given to this question. For me, one of the most helpful is to think of Christ's death and resurrection as marking a decisive turning point in the battle with sin and death, assuring us of a final victory in the future. As a result, we continue to struggle – but we struggle in hope. We need no longer fear ultimate defeat. Many theological analogies illuminating this point were developed around times of conflict, such as the Second World War. In June 1944 Allied forces succeeded in establishing a bridgehead in Normandy, which led to a decisive change in the direction of the war. The D-Day landings of June 1944 did not end the war in Europe, which went on until May 1945. With hindsight, however, they may be said to have inaugurated the final stage of the struggle. The outcome was assured; it was only a matter of time. To be a Christian is to live in this final phase of the struggle, knowing that victory will be achieved, and that death and sin will be defeated. Neither will be present in the new Jerusalem.

Entering God's presence: the cross as sacrifice

Some of the New Testament writings – especially the Letter to the Hebrews – describe the death of Christ on the cross as a sacrifice. What does this mean? To the modern age, the notion of sacrifice seems strange and distant, perhaps even culturally repulsive. We now use the language of sacrifice in a reduced and sanitized sense. A chess player might speak of sacrificing a pawn in order to gain a tactical advantage over his opponent. Or a busy manager might tell her colleagues that she would sacrifice her lunch break in order to finish a project on time. Yet in each case, the term 'sacrifice' really means (giving something up) The Old Testament, however, uses the word in a very different sense.

We must remember that many of the first Christians were Jews who were deeply immersed in the language, ideas and practices of Judaism. As we noted earlier (pages 122–3), Jesus Christ was seen as representing the fulfilment of the hopes and aspirations of Israel. For this reason, it made sense to see Christ's death as a sacrifice comparable to the sacrifices offered in the Temple at Jerusalem. Yet this was not about a repetition, or even an extension, of Israel's religious system. It was about bringing it to fulfilment so effectively that it was no longer required.

An example of the use of sacrificial ideas and images to make sense of the identity of Jesus is found in John the Baptist's declaration that Jesus is 'the Lamb of God who takes away the sin of the world' (John 1.29). This image calls to mind the great Passover celebrations, when a lamb would be slain as a reminder of God's faithfulness in delivering the people of Israel from captivity in Egypt (Exodus 12). Speaking of Jesus in this way suggests that the people of God are in captivity to sin, and need a new act of redemption and deliverance to set them free from its bonds.

The image of Jesus as 'the Lamb of God who takes away the sin of the world' also taps into the prophecy of Isaiah, who spoke of a coming suffering servant who would be slain like a lamb for his people (Isaiah 53). This suffering servant of God would be 'wounded for our transgressions, and crushed for our iniquities' (Isaiah 53.5). This prophecy of Christ compares him to 'a lamb that is led to the slaughter' (Isaiah 53.7), on whom the guilt and sin of the world is laid. (There may also be some connection with the scapegoat (Leviticus 16.21–22), which was sent into the wilderness bearing the sin of God's people.)

We see here a theme about the human predicament that plays an important role in Christian thinking about the meaning of the cross: exclusion from the presence of God. There is a fundamental breach in the relationship between God and humanity on account of sin. We need to be purified and sanctified before we can hope to see and approach God. Access to God depends on the purity of the individual; guilt and sin therefore have to be purged before it is possible to enter into the presence of God.

Two Old Testament passages may be noted in exploring this theme. The first is the Genesis account of the fall, which ends with the expulsion of Adam and Eve from Eden (Genesis 3.21). There would be no going back to the garden. Intimacy with God was a thing of the past. Yet writers such as Augustine of Hippo argue that we still retain a distant memory of Eden, and a hope that we might one day return – both to paradise and to fellowship with God. Frederick Buechner makes the same point in terms adapted to our own age: 'we have all lost Paradise; and yet we carry Paradise around inside us in the form of a longing for, almost a memory of, a blessedness that is no more, or the dream of a blessedness that may someday be again'.[2]

The second passage is the account of the 'Day of Atonement' ritual (Leviticus 16), which depicts Israel's high priest making an annual sacrifice on behalf of the nation. This solemn ritual reminded the people of Israel that God alone could cleanse them from their sin. We should not be surprised that the New Testament framed its understanding of the significance of Christ's death using language and imagery borrowed from the solemnities of Israel's worship – the 'holy of holies', the Temple, its altar and sacrifices, and the ritual washing away of sin through blood sacrifice.

Access to God was understood to require a state of purity. It is important to distinguish between 'being impure or unclean' and 'being sinful'. Burying the dead was seen within Jewish culture as a necessary and charitable action. Yet those burying a dead person would have to touch the corpse, which made them unclean (but not sinful). They would need to undergo a purification ritual before being admitted to the Temple. In the same way, 'being pure' is not the same as 'being without sin', even though the ideas are similar. The New Testament holds that the life, death and resurrection of Jesus Christ breaks down both barriers to entering the presence of God, by abolishing the need for ritual cleanliness on the one hand, and by purging the guilt of sin on the other.

What we find in the New Testament is not really an extended and detailed theory of Christ's death as a sacrifice. Rather, we see the language and imagery of sacrifice used to affirm that Christ actually achieved the ultimate goal of the Old Testament sacrificial system – the removal of guilt and impurity.

An extended discussion of this theme is found in the Letter to the Hebrews, which develops the illuminating and important idea that Christ is both a perfect high priest and a perfect sacrificial victim, so that his sacrifice is 'once for all' – that is, something that never needs to be repeated. Christ thus made the cultic system of Israel redundant by achieving what it promised but did not deliver.

There is therefore no longer any need for priests, sacrifices or temples in the Christian vision of life. Christ's perfect sacrifice obviates the need for the Old Testament religious cult, even if its language remains helpful in understanding the grounds and consequences of his triumph. Christians thus used – and continue to use – images from Israel's past to make sense of the Christian present.

Let's move on and look at another aspect of the death of Christ on the cross – the idea that his death can be thought of as a ransom. What does this mean?

Ransom

The concept of 'ransom' remains as familiar to us today as it was in the ancient world. People continue to be kidnapped and held to ransom, with money demanded to secure their freedom. The more important the captive, the greater the ransom likely to be demanded. It is probably not surprising that the New Testament should use this image as a natural and powerful way of expressing the significance of Christ's death on the cross. It is a 'ransom for all' (1 Timothy 2.6). Most significantly, the Gospels indicate that this specific word is used by Jesus himself to refer to the meaning of his own forthcoming death: 'For the Son of Man came not to be served but to serve, and to give his life a ransom for many' (Mark 10.45).

The concept of ransom appeals to our imagination, allowing us to explore its multiple elements and aspects. First, the implied context of the image of ransom is that someone has been imprisoned or kidnapped, and is unable to break free. This person's freedom depends completely on someone else being able and willing to meet the demands of the kidnappers. This parallels the Christian understanding of the human situation, and how it can be transformed. We are trapped in a web of sin. We are ensnared. We have fallen into a pit, and cannot get out. Someone has to do something which we are unable to do if we are to be set free.

Second, a ransom is the price paid to secure the liberation of this captive. This might take the form of money, possessions or territories. We have neither the power nor the resources to liberate ourselves. Someone else has to purchase our freedom as an expression of their love and commitment to us. This is a prominent theme in Paul's letter to the Christian church at Corinth. Christians, he declared, have been 'bought with a price' (1 Corinthians 6.20; 7.23). We have been ransomed 'with the precious blood of Christ, like that of a lamb without defect or blemish' (1 Peter 1.18–19). In other words, there has been a radical transformation in our status and way of life as a result of Christ's death on the cross.

And finally, the image of ransom speaks of liberation. When the ransom is paid, the prisoners regain their liberty. They are set free from bondage. The prison doors are thrown open. Once more, this chimes in with one of the great themes of the New Testament. Christ brings freedom from bondage to the law, bondage to sin and bondage to the fear of death. Through his sacrifice, Jesus is able to 'free those who all their lives were held in slavery by the fear of death' (Hebrews 2.15). 'The creation itself will be set free from its bondage to decay and will obtain the freedom of the glory of the children of God' (Romans 8.21).

(*The demonstration of divine love*)

What we do shows what we are like. The Christian gospel speaks of a God who loves us, and who shows this love by acting. Earlier, we noted C. S. Lewis's image of God as a diver who plunges the depths of cold, murky and muddy water to retrieve a precious object – namely, humanity. It's a memorable image of people doing something dangerous because they want to save someone who is important to them.

In his poem 'Dear Bargain', Richard Crashaw (1612–49) reflects on the astonishingly high value placed on people by Christ.

> Lord, what is man? Why should he cost thee
> So dear? What hath his ruin lost thee?
> Lord, what is man, that thou hast over-bought
> So much a thing of nought?

Crashaw here picks up a leading theme of the New Testament: 'God proves his love for us in that while we still were sinners Christ died for us' (Romans 5.8). A loving God acts in love to make salvation possible in and through Christ and invites us to return this love in response. 'For God so loved the world that he gave his only Son, so that everyone who believes in him may not perish but may have eternal life' (John 3.16).

At this point, we need to emphasize again the importance of the vital Christian insight that Jesus Christ is God Incarnate – that *God is Christ-like*. To appreciate the importance of this point, let us pick up a Latin phrase used by the eleventh-century theologian Anselm of Canterbury. To grasp the significance of Christ fully, we must try to think about God *remoto Christo* – 'apart from Christ' – and discover the limits this imposes on us. So what can we say about the love of God for us without making any reference to Christ? We could certainly say that this divine love is infinite, boundless and beyond human telling.

All of this is true, of course, but it is expressed in purely negative terms. We have explained what it is *not*, but failed to declare, what it *is*. In fact, we have come close to saying that we cannot really say anything meaningful about the love of God. We have spoken of it in very general, abstract and impersonal ways.

So let us now bring Christ back into our discussion, and consider how his reintroduction opens up new ways of thinking about the love of God. What can we now say? We might suggest that the love of God is shown in the story of Jesus Christ, who willingly gave up his life for others (John 15.3). Christ gave all that he had so that we might live. The gospel passion narratives tell us that the crowds standing around the cross mocked Christ, ridiculing his powerlessness and pain. 'Save yourself, and come down from the cross' (Mark 15.30). Yet Christ stayed there, and saved us instead.

Perhaps we could even say that until the coming of Christ, every image of God was ultimately an idol, in that it was something we ourselves constructed and worshipped. In Christ, we are given an image of God – something we can visualize, imagine in our minds, and relate to. Yet this is an *authorized* picture of God, rather than one we have invented or imagined. The dying Christ becomes a poignant image of the love of God embodying this love in his own life, and demonstrating it in his death. This is no abstract, impersonal notion of love; this is a heartbreaking affirmation of a death-defying love of such intensity and quality that early Christian writers struggled to find a word adequate to express it.

(*Forgiveness of sin*)

Finally, we turn to the great theme of forgiveness. The death of Jesus Christ makes forgiveness possible. Christ 'suffered for sins once for all, the righteous for the unrighteous, in order to bring you to God' (1 Peter 3.18). This theological insight is deeply embedded in popular Christian piety, as can be seen from the well-known Good Friday hymn 'There is a Green Hill':

> He died that we might be forgiven,
> he died to make us good,
> that we might go at last to heaven,
> saved by his precious blood.
>
> There was no other good enough
> to pay the price of sin,
> he only could unlock the gate
> of heaven and let us in.

The death of Christ is the basis of our forgiveness – a powerful reminder of both its costliness and reality.

The great theme of a loving God who forgives people is movingly portrayed in the parable of the prodigal son (Luke 15.11–35), with its vivid depiction of the waiting father who rushes out to greet his wayward child. But the story also raises an awkward question for many people. How can the father just forgive his son like that? It seems to suggest that the past can be forgotten as if it never happened or didn't really matter.

We are surely right to be worried here. It is fatally easy to cheapen forgiveness. I could say 'I forgive you' to someone who has deeply hurt me, and not really mean it. My resentment against that person would remain, and I would have 'forgiven' in word only, not in reality. Yet this parable only illuminates some aspects of God's forgiveness of our sins. There is clearly much more that needs to be said. The parable is not intended to be an exhaustive account of the theology of forgiveness, but a moving illustration of the transformative impact of forgiveness on the returning son.

But how, some will ask, can the cross be the basis of forgiveness? What is the inner logic of atonement? Here, we enter the realm of theological debate. My own view is that the primary concern of the New Testament is to tell us that the human situation has been potentially transformed by the death and resurrection of Christ, and that it invites us to accept and embrace this. We do not need to know how the cross works, any more than I need to know how antibiotics work if I am to be cured of a bacterial infection. Knowing how penicillin works will certainly deepen my understanding and appreciation of how I was healed, but it is not essential for my healing to take place.

Yet I fully concede that the discipleship of the mind invites us to reflect on the possible reasons for God's decision to redeem us in this way, even if we have to concede that there are limits to our understanding of this mystery. We need to grasp the inner 'logic of atonement' if we are to demonstrate and appreciate the coherence of the Christian 'big picture'.

A good example lies to hand in the eleventh-century writer Anselm of Canterbury, mentioned earlier in this chapter, who argued that the redemption of humanity must take place in a way that is consistent with God's own nature and purposes. Since sin is an offence against God, something needs to be done to restore the relationship between God and humanity, which has been damaged by sin. So how might this be done?

Anselm introduces the concept of a 'satisfaction' – a payment which compensates for the offence of human sin. Once this satisfaction has been made, the situation can revert to normal. Yet, Anselm observes, human beings do not have the ability to make this satisfaction. It lies beyond their resources. Humanity ought to make satisfaction for its sins, but cannot. And while God is under no obligation to make satisfaction, this is something that God could do, if it was appropriate.

Therefore, Anselm argues, if God were to become a human being, the resulting God-person would have both the obligation (as a human being) and the ability (as God) to make the necessary satisfaction. The death of Jesus Christ upon the cross demonstrates God's total opposition to sin, while at the same time providing the means by which sin could be really and truly forgiven, and the way opened to renewed fellowship between humanity and God. Anselm's analysis demonstrates the deep rationality of the atonement, showing the inner theological coherence of God's decision to redeem humanity in the first place, and to redeem humanity *in this specific way*.

While I treasure this insight, I sometimes wonder whether it runs the risk of turning the redemption of humanity into some kind of logical puzzle, offering an over-intellectualized approach to something that can never be properly and fully grasped by human reason. The important thing is that God has made redemption possible, and invites us to share in its joy and in the new life which follows. Understanding the inner logic of this is of real, but secondary, importance. Anselm's attempt to uncover this inner logic is a little speculative. However, it is important both to affirm and to appreciate the inner logic of Incarnation and atonement, and Anselm helps us begin to reflect on this theme.

This chapter has sketched some (and only some) of the main themes of Christian thinking about the atonement, offering snapshots of a rich and complex theological panorama. We have used a theological prism to separate out the individual colours of the rich Christian understanding of the meaning of the cross of Christ, and zoomed in on some of them. The New Testament, however, develops other lines of reflection to help us understand the meaning of the cross, which have not been discussed fully here. For example, the crucifixion was widely seen as placing Christ under a curse. For a Jew, anyone hanged upon a tree was cursed by God (Deuteronomy 21.23). This did not bode well for any Christian claim that Jesus Christ was the long-awaited Messiah. The idea of a 'crucified Messiah' was a contradiction in terms.

Paul realized the importance of this point, and its relevance for the meaning of the cross. 'Christ redeemed us from the curse of the law by becoming a curse for us – for it is written, "Cursed is everyone who hangs on a tree"' (Galatians 3.13). By being crucified, Christ did indeed bear a curse – *our* curse, which he willingly bore. In effect, Paul turned a criticism of Christianity into a theological virtue, expanding the vision of the saving work of Christ.

Yet while all these aspects of atonement can be studied individually, they are best seen as aspects of a greater whole. The Christian vision of salvation engages every facet of human nature. Humanity, the height of God's creation, is wounded, weak, disfigured, impoverished and emaciated. Christianity confirms this diagnosis, but gives us reason to hope that this masterpiece can be restored. It brings hope into our shadowy world. The darker we realize our situation to be, the more we can appreciate the difference that Christ makes.

Perhaps this is seen most clearly in the third aspect of the 'big picture' of Christ, which we shall explore in the next chapter – our experience of suffering and sorrow as we journey through this world.

12

Suffering: the shadow of the cross

————◆◆◆————

We now come to a region of the landscape of faith that many find troubling and distressing. Up to now, we have tended to think of the landscape of faith as constantly bathed in a soft and gentle sunlight, allowing us to see things relatively clearly, within the significant limits placed upon us as human beings. The Christian 'big picture' is like a lens that allows us to bring things into focus, or a window through which we can see a reality lying beyond and behind it. Yet not all aspects of that landscape of faith are so easily explored.

As we journey towards the interior of our island of faith, we find ourselves moving into a densely wooded region. The canopy of leaves above us casts shadows on the ground and filters the light so that only a few dim sunbeams pass through. Mists arise from the rivers and lakes, shrouding the paths and natural features around us. We find it increasingly difficult to see things clearly. Everything seems veiled in this shadowy region of the landscape, not least the disturbing enigma of pain and suffering in our world.

The problem of suffering goes beyond the fact that it is unpleasant to observe, and even more upsetting to experience. It causes distress for many at a deeper existential level. We cannot help but feel that suffering is an intruder into the world – something that shouldn't be there at all. Its presence seems to call into question the coherence of the world and the reliability of our theories about that world – including the trustworthiness of God.

So does the existence of suffering point to the failure or unreliability on the part of the Christian map of meaning? Up to now, this has sustained and guided us through the complexities of life. Yet what if suffering calls into question the reliability of this map of meaning? What if there is no meaning? What if the maps we have constructed are shown to be nothing but cruel inventions of our imaginations that have only a tenuous grasp on the realities of our world? Like the artist Stanley Smith, we find ourselves 'disturbed by a feeling of everything being meaningless'. It is a deeply troubling thought.

It is, however, not the only answer to the emotional distress and intellectual confusion that so often arise from suffering. In this chapter, we shall reflect on this question, which troubles many as they pass through the landscape of faith. We begin by considering the intellectual and existential fallout when a theory is shown to fail.

When theories fail

Like every good scientist, I make a point of studying the history of science. For a start, this discredits the ridiculous idea that science is a steady and simple pursuit of the truth. It reminds us how often science takes wrong turnings, and how slow it can be to recognize this. Perhaps more importantly, it brings home how some theories which once commanded wide assent were called into question by new observations, or a growing realization that a rival theory offered a better explanation of what was already known.

A good example is provided by the failure of the traditional model of the solar system developed by Ptolemy in the Classical era, which proposed that the sun, moon and planets all orbited the earth. As observations of the movements of the planets became more accurate, it grew obvious that the theory was struggling to cope with the new data. Attempts to modify some of its peripheral ideas did not solve the problem. In the end, the only solution was to abandon its core idea – that everything revolved around the earth. The rival approach of Copernicus, as developed and modified by Kepler and Galileo, proved far more successful.

Now some were doubtless saddened at the passing of the Ptolemaic model. Yet this was simply a theory about how the world worked. It did not touch on what is perhaps the most important question of all for human beings – the issue of *meaning*. Although Sigmund Freud famously asserted that the displacement of the earth from the centre of the universe caused people to have massive existential crises in the late 1500s, the evidence doesn't really support this. The problems really begin when our observations of the world call into question deeply held views about meaning, value and purpose.

The poet W. H. Auden (1907–73) was one of many in the 1930s who accepted the fundamental goodness of human nature and the ability of human reason to resolve crises. In 1939, however, he went to a cinema in a German-American district of New York and watched a newsreel depicting the Nazi attack on Poland. He was appalled when 'quite ordinary, supposedly harmless Germans' in the audience began shouting, 'Kill the Poles!'[1]

It was a traumatic experience for Auden. He realized that he could no longer believe that human nature was good. Furthermore, he realized that if he were to regard these actions as evil, he had to have some absolute standard by which he could defend this judgement. As the significance of this sank in, he realized that his liberalism was self-defeating: 'The whole trend of liberal thought has been to undermine faith in the absolute.' Auden's return to faith in God was triggered by his realization of the importance of the 'absolute', and the ability of the Christian 'big picture' to fit this in convincingly.

So does the presence of suffering cause us to abandon a core belief in God? Or the belief that there is meaning in life? A simplistic approach to the issue would certainly suggest so. If God loves us, we ought not to experience suffering. And if God is almighty, then suffering can be eliminated. The presence of suffering in the world is thus proof that God is either not loving or not almighty, or possibly both. In fact, there might be no God at all.

Discussions of the 'problem of evil' are often startlingly abstract and troublingly disengaged from the personal experience of the sufferer. Surely it is more important to be worried by evil than to try to explain it away neatly? I have a lot of sympathy for the approach I find in the American philosopher Marilyn McCord Adams, who argued that the real question was not 'Why did God permit all the evils that we know about?', but rather 'What can God do to make our existence a great good to us, without trivializing the experience of evil?' The emphasis here is not on theoretical abstractions, but on the realities of human experience.

In dealing with suffering, as with all deep existential questions, we have to learn and adapt to the limits of our rational capacities. It is easy and natural for us to believe that we can conquer the mysteries of life by rational assault. If something does not seem to make sense, there is no sense to it. The French philosopher Gabriel Marcel drew an illuminating distinction between a problem and a mystery which helps us to frame the issue here.[2] A problem is something we can view objectively, and to which we can find the single right answer without undue difficulty. A crossword puzzle is a good example of this – it can be solved totally and completely, and there is only one reasonable answer.

A mystery, however, is something more complex, and cannot be reduced to a simple right or wrong answer, partly because it overwhelms our capacity to make sense of it. The Czech philosopher Tomáš Halík was severely critical of an 'overcasual accumulation of certainties',[3] which he regarded as one of the worst vices of a facile atheism or a defensive religion. We have to come to terms with the depth and mystery of reality, including God and suffering. For Halík, we live in a post-optimistic age which can no longer be sustained by the discredited progressive ideologies of the past. We now realize that social and technological progress is not going to solve the human problem. We need to revisit alternatives.

When writing his books, Halík often withdrew to a hermitage deep in a Rhineland forest, and came to see the forest itself as an 'apt metaphor for religious mystery'. The forest is deep and broad, an 'unfinished symphony of nature', consisting of multiple layers of reality that cannot be reduced to a collection of individual trees. Our longing for simplicity means that we are tempted to see a grand mystery as if it were a cluster of small problems, each of which can be solved in terms of a single, simple answer, when in reality we have failed to grasp the depth, mystery and interconnectedness of our world.

It is helpful here to turn to the book of Job, which engages the place of suffering in the world. When I was younger, I hoped that the story of Job would give me some quick and easy answers to my questions about why God allowed suffering. I did not find any such simple answers; in fact, the bulk of the book of Job represents a sophisticated criticism of the neat little theories of suffering that are offered by Job's well-meaning 'comforters'. Each is shown to be inadequate.

As I grow older, I have come to appreciate the wisdom of this book. No theory is capable of answering the mystery of suffering. How can a mere mortal cope with such a vast mystery? Responding to Job's quest for an answer, God invites him to look at things in a very different way. Job is allowed to glimpse the 'big picture' which transcends what he can see from his own limited perspective. If I could put it like this, Job is allowed to ascend from the Road to the Balcony, and given the privilege of beholding the world from its perspective. It is as if a curtain is drawn aside and the vast panorama of the world is revealed.

By gaining a sense of the 'big picture' – which it is impossible for human beings to grasp fully or properly – Job is able to appreciate his own limited and somewhat self-centred view of things. He realizes that he is not in a position to understand things fully; that God's wisdom is deeper than his own and, finally, that he can cope with suffering simply because he knows God really is there.

Perhaps that is the deepest fear of many in our age of uncertainty and doubt – that the experience of suffering and pain points to an incoherent and meaningless world, and hence to meaningless human lives. The book of Job reassures us that we can live with unanswered questions about things that are too deep for us. Trusting that God is present in the midst of such uncertainty allows us to live meaningfully in what so often seems to be a meaningless world.

We cannot ascend to the Balcony and see the grand picture which makes sense of all that is going on. Our place is on the Road, and we have to learn to live with the limited vision of our human situation, while looking and hoping for some means by which that limit can be transcended. Suffering is part of life, whether Christian or secular. Yet Christians know that it is through the fire of suffering that we are healed and restored, even though we are never removed from its presence while we journey on the Road.

But if we cannot ascend to the Balcony, might God descend to the Road? Might God enter our world of suffering? The Christian understanding of the Incarnation sets out before us a mystery – something that we can never fully grasp, yet which reassures us sufficiently to help us continue our journey on that Road. How? First, it asks us to set to one side any notion of a detached, indifferent and uncaring God. God journeys to us so that God may journey with us along our *via dolorosa*. God suffered in Christ, and suffered for us.

Second, it affirms that suffering has become the means of our salvation. God enters into our world at the precise point of its most seeming incoherence and meaninglessness – and makes that the point of redemption, the fulcrum of transformation, the Archimedean point from which the world can be moved. It is as if God chose a place of despair, anxiety and bewilderment to reassure us that we are not alone in such places, and will not remain in such places. 'Even there your hand shall lead me, and your right hand shall hold me fast' (Psalm 139.9–10).

And third, we can see beyond the shadow of the cross to the dawn of resurrection. Those who share Christ's suffering will one day share his glory as well. I shall return to this theme presently, as it is such an important aspect of Christian life on the Road.

Why do we think that suffering is wrong?

The English poet John Keats was alarmed at the impoverishing 'touch of cold philosophy', which seemed inattentive to beauty and wonder. Yet perhaps there is another aspect to Keats's anxiety. Philosophers often seem unable to appreciate that discussions of the meaning of suffering are often driven by emotion and intuition, not cold reason. Our deepest intuitions tell us that things are not meant to be like this. The existence of suffering in the world is wrong. We feel it shouldn't be here – but when we are pressed to give evidence-based reasons for this judgement, we often struggle to provide anything that is even convincing, let alone compelling.

But why *should* we think this? Not everyone does. The atheist Richard Dawkins insists that suffering is as inevitable as it is meaningless and we simply need to get used to this. Human and animal suffering is precisely what we should expect in this meaningless world. It's a slick answer, but it leaves many unsatisfied. Deep down, we know things are not that straightforward. It is as if there is some hidden moral or aesthetic template embedded deep within us which causes us distress at the notion of suffering.

We don't just observe that suffering exists; we make the judgement that it ought not to exist. We bring an interpretative framework to bear on our experience, and judge that suffering is not merely unpleasant but is wrong. But where do we get this framework from? Both the framework itself and any judgements made on its basis go far beyond what experience discloses and confirms. So how do we get our deep intuition that the way things are is not the way they are meant to be? After all, that is the fundamental concern that leads us to talk about the 'problem of suffering'.

Some argue that the Christian 'big picture' makes suffering into a problem. The real truth, I would like to suggest, is much more interesting. The Christian 'big picture' *allows us to understand why we find suffering to be a problem in the first place.* Let's explore this important point further.

C. S. Lewis remarked that when he himself was an atheist, it seemed obvious to him that there could not be a God. Pain and suffering showed that either God did not exist, or God was pointless. Yet as he reflected on this position, he began to realize that it did not really make all that much sense.[4]

> My argument against God was that the universe seemed so cruel and unjust. But how had I got this idea of *just* and *unjust*? A man does not call a line crooked unless he has some idea of a straight line. What was I comparing the universe with when I called it unjust?

Lewis's point was simple and cannot be overlooked. Anyone who judges this world to be flawed or 'unjust' bases that judgement on an understanding of what the world *ought* to be like. But where does that norm come from? It is not something that we can observe or read off from the world around us.

For Christians, this sense comes from the biblical vision of a good creation that has gone wrong and which will be restored. Christianity's 'big picture' allows us to understand the present order as damaged and broken, and in need of mending and restoration. The narrative of creation, fall and final restoration permits us to say that this is not the way things are meant to be and this is not the way they finally will be.

Lewis found that Christianity provided him with a vision of justice and joy that enabled him to view this world as penultimate and provisional. It made sense – to the extent that this was possible – of our own world and experience, while at the same time proclaiming that something better lay ahead; something that was to be embraced and welcomed when the time came to enter it.

If we look through a Christian lens, we see this world of sorrow, pain and suffering set against the great vision of the new Jerusalem, in which 'mourning and crying and pain will be no more' (Revelation 21.4). This world seems flawed because we judge it against a higher standard – not a norm that we have invented or imagined, but one that is an integral part of the Christian 'big picture'. The good always seems inadequate when seen in the light of the best. If there were no new Jerusalem, this world would be unsurpassed. Because of the great Christian vision of a renewed creation, a transformed humanity and a place of dwelling in which we shall no longer experience suffering or death, we see our present world in the light of this future hope, and as a result judge it to be deficient or problematic.

One of the many intellectual failings of secularism is its seizing upon the problem of evil, which is invariably seen as disconfirming the existence of God, and failing to realize that there is a corresponding problem of *good*. G. K. Chesterton was alert to this point. From a Christian perspective, he argued, joy is the central feature of life, and sorrow is peripheral. 'Everything human must have in it both joy and sorrow; the only matter of interest is the manner in which the two things are balanced or divided.' How can we make sense of such a complex, varied reality which is neither one thing nor another?

Chesterton's answer is important. The world is not a meaningless jumble in which joy and sorrow are randomly thrown together. The dominant theme is that life is meaningful and joyful, though tinged with sadness and sorrow. 'Melancholy should be an innocent interlude, a tender and fugitive frame of mind; praise should be the permanent pulsation of the soul.' For, as Chesterton realized, this complex world is passing away, to give way to a world in which sadness and sorrow, pain and tears are no more. We can anticipate what is to come in the here and now.

Chesterton believed that the Christian 'big picture' offers answers to the fundamental questions of life, while leaving some minor issues unresolved. Given the limitations of the human mind, we cannot hope for any world view to make total sense of things. For the atheist, Chesterton suggested, sorrow becomes central and joy peripheral, because atheism can only engage with the peripheral questions of life, leaving the central ones unanswered. For Chesterton, it was a question of the perspective from which we see suffering. If there is no God then life is dark and gloomy, with occasional flashes of light. But if there is a God, we can see life as bright and good, even though shadows and shades remain for the present.

The 'how' and the 'why'

Many of my atheist friends blame God for the presence of suffering in the world. Why did God create a world like this? Why not make a world without pain, decay or death? It is natural for humans to want to attribute liability in this way. Yet it is a self-defeating argument. If there is no God – as atheists believe to be the case – then we are left with the continuing reality of pain, decay and death, but without anyone to blame, save the natural forces of an irrational universe that has not the slightest interest in us.

As Richard Dawkins rightly pointed out, an atheist universe has no place for notions such as goodness, evil or purpose in life. The sole characteristic of this faceless, godless and impersonal cosmos is a 'blind pitiless indifference'.[5] Dawkins would not speak of suffering and pain as 'evil', as they are simply natural, and there are no objective moral categories of 'good' or 'evil' to which they can be assigned.

Like gravity and entropy, pain and suffering are simply a 'given' in our world. The distress they cause is partly physical, yet arguably primarily existential. Why? Because they seem to point to an irrational and meaningless universe within which we are utterly insignificant. Atheists might well rage against such a meaningless universe and its indifference towards their personal wellbeing. I can understand their frustration and fury, but there is nothing for them to complain about. The same natural forces that brought them into existence in the first place are also the cause of their suffering and future personal extinction. What causes life in the first place also causes pain and death.

If we remove God from our way of thinking, pain and suffering still remain a baleful presence in our universe. There is no one to blame, apart from the blind forces of nature, which lie beyond human moral jurisdiction. Dumping this anger on what is, from their perspective, a non-existent God is little more than a rhetorical device, a diversionary tactic designed to distract attention from the vacuous intellectual circularity of their position. Why is there suffering and pain in the world? No meaningful answer can be given, apart from the catch-all 'that's just the way things are'.

That was certainly the view of the German philosopher Friedrich Nietzsche, who was convinced that the world had no intrinsic meaning. We could either be brave and learn to live with cosmic and existential meaninglessness, or invent our own ideas of meaning and impose them on the world and our lives. Nietzsche argued that the collapse of any belief in an objective truth about the world was liberating, in that it set human beings free to create their own ideas of meaning and value. For Nietzsche, there were no facts, just interpretations.

Yet Nietzsche recognized that having a framework of meaning allowed people to cope with profound uncertainty and suffering. 'If one knows the "why" of life, then one can cope with just about any "how".'[6] Nietzsche made this suggestion long before the emergence of the vast body of psychological research in recent years that has confirmed that this is indeed the case. People can cope with hardship and uncertainty if they believe these serve a purpose.

Viktor Frankl, who was interned in Nazi concentration camps during the Second World War, came to realize the importance of discerning meaning for coping with traumatic situations. Survival in concentration camps seemed to depend on maintaining the will to live, which involved the discernment of meaning and purpose even in highly demoralizing situations. Those who coped best with these appalling conditions were those who had 'big pictures' that enabled them to accommodate their experiences within their mental maps of meaning. They saw how those traumatic events could be opened up in new ways – perhaps by making them into better people.

Christianity teaches that suffering is real, not an illusion. Yet above all, it affirms that meaning may be discerned within its depths. The experience of suffering lies at the heart of the Christian faith, especially as seen in the death of Christ on the cross. Some might say that faith is about trusting that God will keep us from all the things we fear. As I read the New Testament, I see a very different picture: we must still face all the things we fear; yet the presence of God means that we are no longer afraid of them. We journey along the Road leading through the 'valley of the shadow of death' in the company of God as our shepherd.

Although we often focus on the cross of Christ as the basis of our salvation, this is only one aspect of its significance. We must never forget that God chose to use suffering as a means of salvation. The cross discloses a compassionate God – a God who suffers, as we suffer. *To know Christ is to know a compassionate God.*

> Praise be to the God and Father of our Lord Jesus Christ, the Father of compassion and the God of all comfort, who comforts us in all our troubles, so that we can comfort those in any trouble with the comfort we ourselves have received from God. For just as the sufferings of Christ flow over into our lives, so also through Christ our comfort overflows. (2 Corinthians 1.3–5, NIV 1984)

To know the crucified Christ is to know a God who gladly and willingly bore our sorrows on the cross of Calvary. 'In the pierced heart of the Crucified, God's own heart is opened up – here we see who God is and what God is like' (Joseph Ratzinger). God became caught up in a world in which the innocent are scapegoated and killed, and where we are all unwilling, to a greater or lesser degree, to face unwelcome truths about ourselves, preferring sugar-coated deceptions to the harsher medicine of truth-telling. God became personally acquainted with our grief. God has shared our sufferings, injecting the fragrance of his redeeming presence into the darker side of our existence. God is a fellow sufferer who understands us, not someone who views our situation clinically from a safe distance, uncomprehending and unaffected.

So how does this hope console us, and help us cope with the uncertainties and ambiguities of the Road? It allows us to see our present situation in its full context, by causing eternity to break into time and illuminate it. The 'big picture' of faith allows us to make a proper and empowering connection between the story of the crucified Christ and our own story. Just as Christ suffered and entered into glory, so shall we. The Christian life is lived under the dark shadow of the cross, yet illuminated by the hope of resurrection.

Meditating on the sufferings and resurrection of Christ as we journey along the Road reminds and reassures us that 'our present sufferings are not worth comparing with the glory that will be revealed in us' (Romans 8.18, NIV). So are we frightened by death? Faith assures us that to die is to gain – and to be with the Christ we long to know fully. Faith tells us of another country at the end of the Road – which is to be *our* country – where sorrow is no more, and where all tears have been wiped away.

Between Good Friday and Easter Day

Christians mark the death of Christ on Good Friday, and his resurrection on Easter Day. For most, these two days – along with Christmas Day, of course – are the highlights of the Christian year. Good Friday is marked solemnly in church services, often with readings of the gospel passion narratives, and reflections on the 'last words' of Christ from the cross. The mood of these services is dark and serious, focusing on Christ's pain and suffering, his cry of dereliction from the cross, and his final death and burial in a borrowed grave. We are left, as the first disciples were, in a state of shock at Christ's death, and uncertainty as to what happens next.

All of this, of course, is transformed and transfigured on Easter Day, which celebrates the resurrection of Christ and the dawn of a new hope among the disciples. The Church's Easter hymns are saturated with joy, delight and exuberance. We shall consider some of those great themes of joy and hope in a later chapter.

But what about the Saturday? What about the period between Christ's death and resurrection? This is often seen as an inconsequential interlude between two pivotal events. In fact, however, it offers us food for thought as we make our way through the uncertainty and shadows of the Road. How? By helping us realize that we live in a world primarily characterized by suffering and uncertainty – those two themes which converge so powerfully in the gospel narratives of the passion and death of Christ.

It can be helpful to think ourselves into the situation of the disciples on that Saturday, and use this as a lens through which to see the ambiguities and uncertainties we encounter as wayfarers through life. It is not simply that the full reality of the resurrection was something distant, beyond the horizon – it was something that was unexpected, even inconceivable to many. The disciples experienced the first Good Friday without knowing that there was to be an Easter Day. The anxiety, uncertainty and bewilderment of that special day resonate strongly with the spirit of our age today.

With this point in mind, let us revisit that first Good Friday and reconsider the haunting images we associate with Christ's lingering and painful death. The gospel narratives suggest the slow death of hope on the part of his disciples, as their world fell to pieces around them. Their hopes appeared to have been utterly and comprehensively dashed. They had to bury the one who should never have died in the first place. The sealing of the tomb in which the dead Christ had been laid seemed to mark the end of yet another false dawn in the long history of the hopes of humanity.

So where was God in all this? There is no hint of a consoling or empowering presence of God in the gospel accounts of the death of Christ. If anything, those narratives of the crucifixion and burial of Christ are saturated with a sense of the absence of God. Even the dying Christ seems to share that sense of abandonment. 'My God, my God, why have you forsaken me?' Here is the 'dark night of the soul' so familiar to readers of St John of the Cross, in which faith seems to be suspended without any support from reason or experience.

So often, that is *our* experience on the Road. We seem to be dealing with a 'hidden God' (Martin Luther). We journey through a shadowy world, in which God seems distant and remote. We are surrounded by pain, suffering and apparent divine abandonment, with no obvious sign of the presence of God. In this situation, we trust in God because of Christ. His faith in God sustains ours. Because we see in Christ a figure with whom we can identify, as well as one we feel compelled to follow, we step into his faith in God and try to make it our own, while carrying our own cross.

There are times for all of us who travel along the Road when we find it difficult to accept that God is present and active in the world. Yet those same thoughts were present on the first Good Friday. Because God was not *experienced* as present, some might have concluded that God was *not* present. Yet the resurrection challenged those thoughts and fears, exposing them as unreliable. Just as we now see Good Friday from the standpoint of Easter Day, so we must learn to see the same patterns of interpretation in present experience. What looks like a divine absence is better seen as a hidden divine presence.

Wayfarers on the Road thus look back to Good Friday and ahead to Easter Day. At the moment, however, they are in between, unable to achieve the clarity and assurance that comes with the resurrection, and instead struggling with the ambiguity and uncertainty of the cross. We have to accommodate the intellectual and emotional tension between the world as it is and our vision of the world as it ought to be, as this is disclosed in the new Jerusalem, when suffering and death will be things of the past.

This tension, mirrored in the theological landmarks of crucifixion and resurrection, can never be resolved under the limiting conditions of the Road. We cannot clamber on to a Balcony, and see the God's-eye view. Nor can we relocate ourselves to our journey's end, when we finally arrive at our destination, and view our journey from this perspective. We are in transit, walking by faith and not by sight, remembering and anticipating as we journey. When reflecting on suffering, our best 'understanding' is simply a 'standing under' the figure of the crucified Christ.

We are right to be suspicious of easy answers to deep questions. As C. S. Lewis and others have pointed out, the Christian 'big picture' does not bring everything into focus. There are parts of the landscape that are obscured by shadows and mists, obstinately refusing to come into sharp focus. Yet in this dark world, we perhaps ought to listen to the French religious writer Simone Weil, who compared her faith to a torch she used at night. Perhaps it was not bright enough to illuminate the whole landscape – yet it at least allowed her to find her way home. We dimly see something of an answer, even if its precise detail eludes us. We can learn to live with these questions if we sense that there is an answer to be had.

The core issue is how we *see* suffering – how we locate it on a map of meaning, in which we try to subdue our natural human tendency to make an emotional judgement about this matter, and see it in its proper light. Our secular age sees suffering as the serpent in paradise, something meaningless and pointless.

Christianity, however, deploys a significantly different map of meaning, which discloses Christ as the one who allows us to inhabit suffering meaningfully. We know he has been there before us, allowing us to follow in his steps. This insight does not remove suffering, but then neither does any intellectual solution, including abandoning faith in God. Suffering is a human given, independent of our world view. Yet our world view determines what we make of it, and how we cope with it.

The wisdom of our superficial age is that suffering negates belief in God. A wiser judgement is that the mystery of suffering draws some to God, just as it leads some away from faith. Yet the wisest judgement of all, evident to the trained eye of faith, is that trusting God gives us the strength and insight we need if we are to confront and cope with suffering in our lives.

Yet we have already begun to touch on some themes we shall be considering in more detail in the final part of this work. So let us turn to this section and consider more about the role of grace and the Holy Spirit as we journey on the Road.

Part 4

THE THIRD ARTICLE: THE HOLY SPIRIT AND THE CHRISTIAN LIFE

13

The Spirit of grace: being helped to flourish

I have often tried to find a visual analogy which captures my own transition from atheism to Christianity. The best that I have managed to come up with is island-hopping. I moved from one island of faith to another. As a teenager, I was a convinced atheist, and considered that no other way of thinking could be taken seriously. Although I began by thinking that atheism was self-evidently true, I gradually began to realize that it was a faith – a set of intellectual commitments that could not be proved to be true. I then began to wonder if there might be other islands of faith, and whether they might be rationally and aesthetically superior to the one I already knew. In the end, I migrated to another island, where I have now settled down and will spend the remainder of my days.

A number of factors sustained my early atheism – a sense of rebellion, a love of science (which I mistakenly supposed entailed rejecting God) and my general bewilderment about why anyone would want to believe in God in the first place. Although my main reason for rejecting Christianity was my conviction that it was utterly irrational, other factors clearly came into this – including a feeling that God was a total irrelevance, having no care for the world and no involvement within it.

At times, I thought of God as being like one of the deities of Classical Greek religion – enjoying nectar on the heights of Mount Olympus, indifferent to the pain and suffering of the human world. But most of the time, the God whom I considered irrelevant was the silent, distant cosmic architect who created the world and then lost interest in it – the so-called 'clockwork God' often (though unfairly) linked with the great British scientist Isaac Newton.

Many outside the churches read the creeds with such notions of God in mind. They imagine God as someone who is disengaged with the created world and with us; someone who makes the world, sets it going – and then walks away from it, leaving it to its own devices. God builds and winds up the cosmic clock, and then leaves it to tick, unaided and unattended. The creeds actively subvert these impoverished notions of God.

A gracious God

The creeds ask us to think of God in a certain way – a way that closes down unhelpful and unreliable accounts of the nature of God, such as the clockwork God of the 'Age of Reason', or the whimsical gods of Mount Olympus. The creeds invite us to speak of a God who chose to become incarnate in Christ, and who is present and active in the world through the Holy Spirit.

God actively and graciously enters into our world and our history in the great act of inhabitation and salvation that we call 'Incarnation'. As C. S. Lewis put it (page 135), God 'descended into his own universe, and rose again, bringing human nature up with him'. It is not difficult to realize that the God Lewis describes is much more interesting than the Age of Reason's disengaged and absentee God. As Lewis emphasizes, God *chose* to enter the world and bring about our redemption. God cared for us, and acted to show that love, long before we loved God or did anything that could conceivably deserve such a response.

Christianity uses the language of 'grace' to refer to the courtesy of God towards us, by which we are given things we do not deserve and could never hope to achieve. A clockwork god might be benevolent in its intentions, but is incapable of loving us in any meaningful sense of the term. Like the cold, distant and sullen gods of Olympus, this god does not – indeed, could not – give, does not care and does not act. Yet the Christian vision of God holds that God is – and always has been – present and active in the world and in human lives, in and through the Holy Spirit. God's graciousness towards us expresses itself in the person and work of the Holy Spirit, by which we are transformed, renewed and healed.

In this chapter, I shall explore this important aspect of the landscape of faith which is closely interconnected with the Christian understanding of human nature as broken, wounded, damaged and diseased. Our natural human capacities simply don't match up with what we know God wants of us. Yet God knows our strengths and weaknesses, and works with us, not against us. The Christian doctrine of atonement is about diagnosing our situation, and identifying what needs to be done to heal us, bind us up and set us free. We are helped to do something that we could never achieve by our own efforts.

One evening over dinner at my Oxford college, I fell into conversation with an Irish doctor who had worked in a clinic in East Africa just after the Second World War. Conditions were very basic, and the medical staff had only a limited stock of drugs at their disposal. Perhaps as a result of coming into contact with infected patients, the doctor developed a fever. He became confused, found it impossible to walk and couldn't think straight. His well-meaning colleagues did their best to relieve his symptoms, given their limited resources, but could do little to help him. They later told him that they had not expected him to live. After an anxious few days, however, the fever passed, and in due course he was able to return to work.

His close brush with death made a deep impression on the doctor, and led him to think hard about what to do with the rest of his life. But that wasn't the aspect of our conversation that I now remember. My new friend was musing about the impact of his infection back then. Normally an athletic man, he found he couldn't even get out of his bed; normally a quick-thinking person, he had become confused and unable to string thoughts together; normally a very fluent and eloquent speaker, he could only whisper and groan.

Wouldn't it be wonderful, he remarked, if there was some kind of infection that would make us more energetic, intelligent and articulate? Why did all infections have to have a negative impact on us? Surely someone could invent an infection that would make us wiser, stronger and nicer?

It was an interesting thought, and one that has remained with me. I had just been reading C. S. Lewis's chapter on 'Good

Infection' in *Mere Christianity*, in which he developed a distinction between simply existing at a physical level and coming to life spiritually.[1]

> Now the whole offer which Christianity makes is this: that we can, if we let God have His way, come to share in the life of Christ ... If we share in this kind of life we also shall be sons of God. We shall love the Father as [Christ] does and the Holy Ghost will arise in us. He came to this world and became a man in order to spread to other men the kind of life He has – by what I call 'good infection'.

Lewis's imagery is that of us becoming 'infected' – but in a good way. The Holy Spirit – God inhabiting us – is then able to begin the work of transformation within us, renewing our minds and hearts. As Lewis rightly saw, we are not merely told to become more like Christ, as if the Christian faith were a set of orders barked at us by some distant and uncaring general; we are enabled to become so by a God who enriches and graces our lives, redirects our wills and inspires us to do good.

What is grace?

Grace is God's favour, the free and undeserved help that God gives us to respond to his invitation to become children of God and share in the promise of eternal life. It counters our human recognition of our inadequacy, weakness and sinfulness with a vision of a gracious God who gives us what we need to break free from sin and embrace the hope of transformation and renewal. Grace brings *hope*. The Christian gospel could be summed up as the 'good news of God's grace' (Acts 20.24).

When I was young, I used to love reading fairy stories. One story in particular has stuck in my mind. It was about a king who wished to marry his daughter to her most eligible suitor. There was no shortage of men determined to win the princess's love and the king's approval, despite having to fight dragons and giants along the way. The moral of the story was clear: love is based on achievement. Not a very romantic idea, I admit, but one that seems to lie at the heart of Western culture. You don't get something for nothing.

This philosophy can find its way into the life of faith. Some Christians think and act as if God's favour is something that has to be earned, as if God were some mildly corrupt public official who needs to be bribed to get something done. It is natural for us to think of salvation in commercial terms. If you want something, you pay for it or do something to earn it. Yet the core meaning of grace is 'without cost'. God gives us what we could never afford to buy or hope to achieve. But that's not all. What we are given is a *transforming gift*.

God loves us as we are but does not leave us like that. God's gift to us is something that changes us into what our deepest instincts and longings tell us we are meant to be. This is one of the great themes of the Christian faith, expressed especially well in some of the psalms, which both lament the human sinful condition and long for its transformation. 'Create in me a clean heart, O God, and put a new and right spirit within me' (Psalm 51.10).

Perhaps the single best illustration of the transforming power of divine graciousness is found in the gospel encounter between Jesus and Zacchaeus, a much-disliked rich tax collector who made his money by collaborating with the Roman imperial authorities (Luke 19.1–9). On hearing that Christ was in his neighbourhood, Zacchaeus climbed a tree so that he could see Christ safely and anonymously from a distance. Yet Christ saw him, and invited him to draw near. 'Zacchaeus, hurry and come down; for I must stay at your house today' (Luke 19.5).

Those hearing Christ's affirming and welcoming words were startled that he should accept and welcome such a sinful person. Yet Christ's graciousness proved to be transformative. Zacchaeus was enabled to change; acceptance led to repentance. 'Half of my possessions, Lord, I will give to the poor; and if I have defrauded anyone of anything, I will pay back four times as much' (Luke 19.8). This moving story can be seen as affirming a major theological principle: *Salvation comes by grace, and ethics is about showing gratitude.* Transformation is the consequence, not the precondition or cause, of acceptance in the sight of Christ. God's grace comes first, and is followed by human obedience.

Yet some might want to raise a question here. Surely being loved can be seen as a reward for being beautiful or talented, rather than as an act of grace? Aren't we back in the situation of the fairy-tale I mentioned earlier? Martin Luther, perhaps one of the finest exponents of God's graciousness, did not think so. 'We are not loved because we are loveable,' he remarked, 'but are loveable because we are loved.'

The Holy Spirit

Christian theology has always seen a close connection between grace and the Holy Spirit. Ambrose of Milan spoke of the Holy Spirit as a 'river of grace', which refreshed and revitalized the exhausted human soul. One of the richest explorations of the relation between God's graciousness and the gift of the Holy Spirit is found in a later letter of the New Testament:

> When the goodness and loving kindness of God our Saviour appeared, he saved us, not because of works done by us in righteousness, but according to his own mercy, by the washing of regeneration and renewal of the Holy Spirit, whom he poured out on us richly through Jesus Christ our Saviour, so that being justified by his grace we might become heirs according to the hope of eternal life. (Titus 3.4–7, ESV)

This naturally leads us to think more about the Holy Spirit, and especially how this is linked with the great Christian themes of transformation, healing, renewal and refreshment. Many Christians find the idea of the Holy Spirit difficult to visualize. Christian art down the ages has had little difficulty in depicting God and Jesus Christ. But what about the Holy Spirit?

Early Christianity developed a rich use of symbols as a way of expressing its fundamental beliefs and values. Of those symbols, the most important was the cross. Christians were baptized with the sign of the cross, just as churches and other Christian places of meeting were often built in the shape of a cross. Yet other symbols emerged as important in the early Church, one of which was specifically linked with the Holy Spirit – the image of a dove.

The gospel descriptions of the baptism of Christ include reference to 'the Spirit descending like a dove on him' (Mark 1.10).

From the fifth century onwards, the image of a dove came to be used to represent the Holy Spirit, especially in the context of Christian baptism. This image was widely taken up in the Middle Ages, and is especially evident in the portrayal of the crucifixion of Christ. Many artistic representations of this event frame it in a Trinitarian perspective. Although the predominant image is a suffering Christ, the figure of the Father and a dove (representing the Spirit) are often incorporated into the background.

Yet the image of a dove is actually of relatively little help in visualizing the Holy Spirit, or grasping why the Spirit is of such theological significance. In trying to make sense of the person and work of the Holy Spirit, we need to begin by looking at some of the Old Testament. Here, the Hebrew term *ruach* is used widely to refer to the Spirit, helping us to grasp something of its significance and characteristics.

The Holy Spirit in the Old Testament

Most modern languages use at least three words – 'wind', 'breath' and 'spirit' – to translate the single Hebrew word *ruach*, which has a depth of meaning virtually impossible to capture and express using a single word. *Ruach*, traditionally translated simply as 'spirit', is associated with a range of meanings, each of which casts some light on the complex associations of the Christian notion of the Holy Spirit.

1 *The Spirit as wind.* The Old Testament writers are careful not to identify God with the wind and thus reduce God to the level of a natural force. Nevertheless, there was a clear parallel between the power of the wind and that of God. To speak of God as spirit affirms the power of the 'Lord of Hosts', and reminded Israel of the dynamic presence and action of the God who had called Israel out of Egypt. The idea of the Spirit as a specifically *redemptive* power is seen in the exodus from Egypt, when a powerful wind divides the Red Sea (Exodus 14.21). Here, the idea of *ruach* conveys both the power and the redemptive purpose of God.

The image of the wind also allowed the rich diversity of human experience of God to be accounted for and visualized in a genuinely helpful manner. Israel knew a hot wind which blew in from the deserts to the east, which scorched all the vegetation in its path. 'The grass withers and the flowers fall, when the breath of the LORD blows on them' (Isaiah 40.7). The western winds, however, brought coolness and rain to the hot dry land as they blew in from the sea. Similarly, God was understood to refresh human spiritual needs, like the rain brought by the western wind (Hosea 6.3), refreshing the land.

2 *The Spirit as breath.* The idea of spirit is associated with life. When God created Adam, God breathed into him the breath of life, as a result of which Adam became a 'living being' (Genesis 2.7). The famous vision of the valley of the dry bones (Ezekiel 37.1–14) also illustrates this point. The bones only come to life when breath enters into them (Ezekiel 37.9–10). The image of God as spirit thus affirms that God is the one who gives life, even to bring the dead back to life.

3 *The Spirit as inspiration.* The Old Testament often refers to the filling of an individual with the Spirit of God, by which individuals are enabled to perform tasks which would otherwise be impossible. The gift of wisdom is often portrayed as a consequence of the endowment of the Spirit (Deuteronomy 34.9). However, the most important role of the Spirit was in the inspiration of the prophets. A prophet was someone endowed with the gift of the Spirit (Isaiah 61.1; Micah 3.8; Zechariah 7.12), which authenticated the prophet's message – a message which is usually described as 'the word of the Lord'.

Each of these three aspects of *ruach* helps us both to understand what the Spirit does, and to visualize the person and work of the Spirit. It helps us to think of God as an active power within the world, like the wind. Like all analogies, this is helpful in some ways and not in others. It suggests that the Spirit is an impersonal force, for example, and does not really bring out the idea of personal agency. (For such reasons, many Christians feel uneasy about referring to the Holy Spirit as 'it'.) The personal aspects of the Holy Spirit are much more clearly identified in the New Testament. For example, John's Gospel describes the Holy Spirit as the 'comforter' or 'advocate', the one who consoles us, encourages us and stands by us in moments of doubt and despair.

This naturally leads us to reflect more on the New Testament's development of the Christian understanding of the Holy Spirit.

The Holy Spirit in the New Testament

The New Testament builds on the Old Testament witness to the Holy Spirit, emphasizing that God is active both within the created order and within human existence. The life, death and resurrection of Jesus Christ are clearly understood to mark a new phase in the presence and activity of the Spirit. The Old Testament spoke of the Spirit as a powerful wind blowing over the face of the waters, a shaping energy which gave life and direction to humanity. In the New Testament, this energy is understood to be focused on the person of Jesus Christ.

Perhaps the most dramatic description of this development is found in Peter's famous speech, delivered on the day of Pentecost in Jerusalem (Acts 2.1–29). His argument is simple: the great Old Testament prophecy of God pouring out his Spirit on all humanity is now fulfilled on account of Jesus Christ. A new day – the 'Day of the Lord' – has dawned.

One of the most important roles of the Spirit, according to the New Testament, is the empowerment of believers. Just as the wind fills a boat's sails, so the Holy Spirit gives direction and movement to the life of faith. Without the Spirit, we become spiritually becalmed. This idea is present in the Old Testament, but now it becomes clear that, far from being an impersonal force, the Spirit is an intensely personal manifestation of the power of God. The Spirit also brings to mind the words and deeds of Jesus Christ. 'The Holy Spirit, whom the Father will send in my name, will teach you everything, and remind you of all that I have said to you' (John 14.26).

A second role of the Holy Spirit is that of illuminator. How are we to make sense of the Bible and apply it to our lives? Many of the New Testament letters emphasize that we are not left on our own to wrestle with such questions: God somehow equips, enables or guides us throughout the journey of faith.

> I pray that the God of our Lord Jesus Christ, the Father of glory, may give you a spirit of wisdom and revelation as you come to know him, so that, with the eyes of your heart enlightened, you may know what is the hope to which he has called you, what are the riches of his glorious inheritance among the saints, and what is the immeasurable greatness of his power for us who believe.
>
> (Ephesians 1.17–18)

Most Christians would hold that the Spirit does not provide Christians with a new revelation of God, but rather with a deeper understanding of what has already been revealed, and a sense of how this might affect the way in which we live, or help us reach a decision about what we ought to do.

A third aspect of the work of the Spirit is dwelling within believers. 'Do you not know that you are God's temple and that God's Spirit dwells in you?' (1 Corinthians 3.16). The gift of the Holy Spirit is seen as a 'pledge' of our salvation, a 'seal' which confirms our relationship with God. Both of these ideas are borrowed from the commercial world of the first century in which the New Testament letters were written.

For Paul, God has confirmed our salvation by 'putting his seal on us and giving us his Spirit in our hearts as a first instalment' (2 Corinthians 1.22). The Greek term *arrabōn*, usually translated as 'pledge' or 'first instalment', refers to a deposit paid in advance to secure the purchase of an item. Legally, the item now belongs to the buyer, who is under an obligation to pay the remainder of the price at an agreed time. The granting of the Holy Spirit is seen as a portion of the full riches of God to keep us going until we enter the new Jerusalem. God's greatest gift to us is not some commodity which bears no relation to the one who gives it, but is rather the living presence of God in our hearts and souls.

The image of a 'seal' refers to an imprint, often in wax, which proved the authenticity of a letter or document (such as a contract) in Roman times. The seal was a sign of trustworthiness, a reassurance that promises made would be honoured. In Chinese culture, the 'chop' serves as a pledge of commitment which will

182

be fully honoured in the future. The 'chop' is a personal seal, usually crafted from stone, which is dipped in red paste and stamped on documents or artwork as a mark of their authenticity.

The theologian John Calvin emphasized this point in his definition of faith, which some regard as one of the most comprehensive and helpful to have been developed by a Christian theologian:[2]

> [Faith] is a steady and certain knowledge of the divine benevolence towards us, which is founded upon the truth of the gracious promise of God in Christ, and is both revealed to our minds and sealed in our hearts by the Holy Spirit.

This richly Trinitarian understanding of faith focuses on the 'gracious promises' of God, revealed and confirmed by the life, death and resurrection of Jesus Christ, which the Holy Spirit plays a critical role in *appropriating* and *applying*. The Holy Spirit acts upon us, illuminating our minds and opening our hearts, so that we can receive and be transformed by the truths of faith.

For Calvin, Christian faith is not just about understanding; it is about renewal and transformation through the power of a God whose trustworthiness is shown in and through Jesus Christ. The Holy Spirit is understood as the agent of both illumination and transformation, opening us up to the truth and presence of the living God.

This theme of the Spirit as the one who enables us to trust God and grasp the promises made to us in Christ plays an important role in the devotional life of many Christians. It is, for example, an important aspect of a Christian understanding of prayer. 'The Spirit helps us in our weakness; for we do not know how to pray as we ought, but that very Spirit intercedes with sighs too deep for words' (Romans 8.26). Prayer is about being in the presence of God, laying out what is on our hearts. In the end, prayer is a recognition of our dependence upon a dependable God, and a challenge to the illusion that we are autonomous and self-sufficient.

The Pelagian controversy

The Christian Church has had more than its fair share of controversies down the ages. For some more critical observers, these often seem to amount to petty bickering over pedantic questions. Yet some of those debates are genuinely important, in that they open up deep questions about the nature of faith, and help us to understand some points more fully. The Pelagian controversy of the early fifth century is one such debate and helps us to clarify our thinking about the nature of God's grace.

The controversy centred on two individuals: the British theologian Pelagius, who was based in the great imperial city of Rome, and Augustine, the bishop of the Roman colonial town of Hippo Regius in North Africa. Following his arrival in Rome, Pelagius became concerned about the moral and spiritual shortcomings of the Roman church. Christians did not seem to be taking the idea of personal holiness seriously. Like any religious reformer, Pelagius tried to do something about this, urging believers to lead better lives.

So far, so good. The difficulty was that Pelagius developed a form of moral and religious rigour which demanded that believers should take control of their lives, and become perfect. God had graciously given Christians the Ten Commandments and the moral example of Christ. It was now up to Christians to live their lives in perfect accordance with these norms. By giving us these standards in the first place, God had made it clear that we were capable of achieving them. Failure to become holy was simply not an option for believers.

Augustine, however, regarded Pelagius as being inattentive to the reality of human sin and the gift of divine grace. Human beings were wounded and damaged by sin, and were simply not capable of total obedience to God's standards. In fact, one of the reasons that we were given the Ten Commandments and the moral example of Christ was to force us to realize our inability to achieve them through our own strength, and thus to discover the empowering grace of God.

Augustine also wrestled with a question that troubles many – the interconnection of our troubled past with our present life. Pelagius thought we could break free instantaneously and completely from the influence of the 'Old Adam'. Augustine knew better. He himself discovered Christianity relatively late in life, after living a somewhat exotic life in Rome. So did his new faith allow him to turn his back on the past, making a clean break with his history? No. For Augustine, our past shadows our present. We never entirely escape from the personal demons of our past. They can indeed be forgiven; yet they still linger as embers, capable of being rekindled.

Human nature may indeed possess a 'homing instinct' for God, through bearing the 'image of God'. Yet there seems to be another force, pulling us in another direction, reasserting the claims of the 'Old Adam', and trying to drag us down. There is certainly a disjuncture between the old life and the new, but not an absolute separation. For Augustine, the grace of God means that while the grip of our past endures, it does not control us. The present may not cancel out the pain or distress that has come before it, but it allows us to break free from its capacity to enslave us.

Although Pelagius was right to challenge any moral and spiritual laxity on the part of Christians, it seems to me that he risked reducing Christianity to external conformity to a religious code of conduct. Augustine's view of human nature is far more biblical, attentive to the impact of human frailty and sin on our capacity to change ourselves for the better. It is as though we had an illness that diminishes our ability to do the things we know we ought to be doing yet find we simply cannot achieve. For Augustine, God's graciousness is evident in the divine willingness to accept us, even though we are still broken and damaged, and to heal and renew us. The Church, for Augustine, was thus not a collection of people who had achieved moral and spiritual perfection, but a community of people who were recovering from the wounds of sin.

We shall consider this point in more detail later in this work, as we reflect on the role of the Church in the Christian life. But first, we will move on to consider how the ideas we have been exploring in this chapter feed into our thinking about God. It is time to think about the doctrine of the Trinity.

14

When words fail: exploring the Trinity

When I was an atheist, I took a rather condescending and smug pleasure in regarding religious people as deluded and irrational souls who believed all sorts of ridiculous nonsense. If I had then been asked to single out what I regarded as the most absurd aspect of Christian belief, I would have pointed to the doctrine of the Trinity. How can God be three and one at the same time? It was incomprehensible nonsense, violating all the categories of human logic. It seemed to be on the same level as the ideas of one of P. G. Wodehouse's more brilliant literary creations – the empty-headed Madeline Bassett, whose personal creed included items such as: 'every time a fairy blows its nose, a baby is born'.

My own later decision to embrace Christianity was fundamentally an issue of intellectual trust, as I began to see that this way of looking at the world made more sense of things than atheism. The early maps of Africa and South America developed by European explorers offered detailed renderings of coastal regions; the interior regions of these vast continents, however, were often uncharted, precisely because they were unexplored. I was conscious that I had yet to engage fully with Christianity. There were aspects of the Christian landscape of faith that were unknown and unexplored. In stepping into the Christian 'big picture', I was taking certain things on trust, hoping that they would turn out to have a rationality which at the time was not entirely clear to me. The most significant of those was the doctrine of the Trinity.

Intellectual integrity demanded that I gave this attention. One classic way of evaluating a scientific theory was set out by Charles Darwin: the theory 'must sink or swim according as it groups and explains phenomena'.[1] How well does it map on to what is actually observed? Aristotle held that 'saving the phenomena' was of critical importance. A theory which forced us to disregard certain observations, or which seemed to force them into its template using intellectual violence, was likely to be wrong. I had been impressed by the capacity of the Christian vision of reality to fit in both observation and experience. Yet there was another way of evaluating a theory – identifying its vulnerabilities, and using these to try to falsify it. Falsifying a theory does not tell us what is right; it does, however, at least tell us what is wrong.

Looking back on my reflections on the doctrine of the Trinity in my first few years of faith, I can now see how they illustrate the importance of the discipleship of the mind. I asked some clergy to help me make sense of the Trinity, and received responses which ranged from the superficial through to the embarrassing. I make no judgement on how the churches educated their clergy back then, but my experience suggested that these public representatives of Christianity were incapable of explaining either *why* Christians should believe in the Trinity in the first place, or *how* best to make sense of this. I was offered hopelessly simplistic and generally pointless analogies – such as water, ice and steam – without any serious attempt to explore the inner logic of the Christian faith.

Then I started the serious study of Christian theology. It was like a second spiritual birth, bringing a new quality and focus to my faith. I found theology to be invariably demanding and occasionally infuriating. Yet it forced me to expand my mind to develop a principled attentiveness towards the rich Christian vision of reality, and force myself to take it to pieces and uncover its inner logic. Some suggest the study of theology is destructive of faith. Perhaps it destroys a simplistic faith; but if so, it is merely to replace it with one that is more intellectually rigorous, apologetically informed and spiritually engaged.

In this chapter, we will reflect on the implicit Trinitarian logic of the Christian faith, aiming to work out both *why* this doctrine is part of the landscape of faith, and *how* it can best be understood and represented. Let's begin by making a point that's essential to a right understanding of this issue.

The concept of mystery

One of the most fundamental insights of faith is that God cannot be fully and reliably grasped by human reason. God simply overwhelms our mental capacities. The vastness of the reality we inhabit simply cannot be grasped in anything other than a partial and limited manner by the human mind. That's one of the reasons why the idea of 'mystery' is so important, both scientifically and theologically. A mystery is not an irrationality; it is something which overwhelms the capacities of human reason.

Augustine of Hippo set out our inability as human beings to capture God in a famous aphorism: 'If you think you have grasped God it is not God you have grasped.' *Si comprehendis non est Deus.* If you can get your mind around it, it cannot be God. It is something else, which you might incorrectly think is God, but is really something you have created and invented, and have improperly labelled as God.

Anything that we can grasp fully and completely simply cannot be God, precisely because it would be so limited and impoverished. It is easy to create God in our own likeness – a self-serving human invention that may bear some passing similarity to God, but actually falls far short of the glory and majesty of the God that stands at the heart of the Christian disclosure. In the end, our words are just not good enough to cope with the conceptual majesty of God so splendidly expressed in the theological notion of glory.

We cannot overlook the importance of this point for Christian apologetics. In attempting to defend the rationality of faith, we run the risk of impoverishing the gospel, offering a mess of rational pottage instead of a grand vision of the mystery of God. As Marilynne Robinson once noted, 'the attempt to defend belief can unsettle it, in fact, because there is always an inadequacy in argument about ultimate things'.[2] Reason can only find its way to a diminished divinity, a rational principle or impersonal first cause which lacks the depth and detail of the mystery of God as disclosed in Christ. Reason may indeed be a portal through which we enter the Christian faith; what we find within, however, overwhelms reason, and forces us to expand our vision of God rather than remain content with the thin and shallow preconceptions with which we first arrived.

Human reason is a good critical tool for exploring reality; it is, however, unreliable in determining in advance the form that reality must take. The first question a natural scientist will ask about any theory or hypothesis is not going to be whether this is *reasonable*, as if human reason can tell us in advance what the universe ought to be like. The key question is this: what reasons could be given, what evidence produced, for believing that it is right? Science is about trying to work out the rationality of the universe, not about forcing the universe to fit into our preconceived notions of what form that rationality should take.

All too often, the rationalist dismissal of a rival approach as 'irrational' simply means that it does not accept the supremacy of the Age of Reason's distinct and very limited notion of rationality. Science has forced revision of this diminished and impoverishing approach to human reason, partly because of its recognition that our universe is a mystery – something with so many impenetrable and incomprehensible dimensions that our minds struggle to take it in. We can only cope with such a mystery either by filtering out what little we can grasp, and hoping that the rest is unimportant, or by slimming it down to what our limited minds can accommodate, and thus simply reduce it to the rationally manageable. Yet both these well-intentioned strategies end up distorting and disfiguring the greater reality we are trying to engage.

The physicist Werner Heisenberg once argued that scientific thinking 'always hovers over a bottomless depth'.[3] We are confronted with the 'impenetrable darkness' of the universe, and are forced to realize our acute difficulties as we struggle to find a language that is adequate to engage and represent this opaque world. Those of us who have studied quantum theory know how it was forced to develop its own rationality to cope with our fuzzy world which calls into question inadequate common-sense conceptions of what is reasonable, shaped by our limiting experience of reality. Human rationality must adapt to the structures of the universe, rather than prejudge what these ought to look like, on the basis of some naïve predetermined notion of what is reasonable.

Similarly, the Christian faith recognizes that it is utterly impossible to represent or describe God adequately using human language. Christian theology rightly uses the term 'mystery' to refer to the vastness of God, in that human images and words falter – if they do not break down completely – as they try to depict God fully and faithfully.

A mystery is not a flawed concept whose inner contradictions are cruelly exposed by human reason, but something that exceeds the capacity of human reason to discern and describe. To speak of some aspect of the natural world or of God as a mystery is not to try to shut down the human reflective process, but to stimulate it – by opening the mind to an intellectual vision that is simply too deep and broad to be fully apprehended through our limited and impaired capacity for vision, and challenging us to do our best to represent it within these limits.

For many critics of Christianity, the doctrine of the Trinity demonstrates that faith is basically irrational. Yet the real issue here is the fundamental incapacity of the human mind to cope with something as vast as God, paralleling comparable failures within the scientific domain to grasp the complexity of our universe. The risk is that we reduce our thinking about God to what our minds can manage, and in doing so reduce God to our level.

This framework of 'mystery' helps us to understand the creative tension between theology and worship. It helps us celebrate the fact that so much of God can be grasped, however inadequately, by the human mind – and this leads to theology. Yet at the same time, we have to recognize that so much remains beyond the human capacity to understand – and this leads to worship, in the sense of acknowledging that the greatness and majesty of God eludes verbal analysis, and is best expressed in praise and adoration.

The doctrine of the Trinity is the outcome of the Christian community's principled stand against reducing God to manageable banalities or rational platitudes. It aims to tell the truth about God, no matter how difficult this might be to capture or represent. Some theologians seem to think they are doing God a favour by revising Christian belief to make it more rational. In fact, they are simply making themselves the 'measure of all things' (to use a phrase from the pre-Socratic philosopher Protagoras). We try to reduce God to what we can cope with. God, however, wants to expand our minds instead.

The doctrine of the Trinity aims to stop us reducing God to something inadequate – to something that might resemble God, but is actually very different. It prevents us from diminishing God's majesty and glory. The doctrine of the Trinity is not meant to be *understood*; rather, it aims to preserve the rich Christian vision of God against those who want to limit God to the comfortable ideas of armchair philosophers. The Trinity is not something that we can master and subdue intellectually; in the end, it is something that masters us.

The Trinity: preserving the mystery of God

The Swiss theologian Emil Brunner argued that the Trinity is to be seen as a 'theological security doctrine', designed to protect the glory and majesty of God from our well-meaning attempts to scale these down to something that is easier for us to handle. As the Church reflected on the rich biblical witness to the words and deeds of God in Scripture, and her experience of God's presence in her life and worship, it became clear that the neat, simplistic philosophical slogans of the past were not going to be good enough to do justice to its majestic and glorious vision of God. A new way of thinking was needed.

And so the concept of the Trinity began to emerge – always slowly, initially tentatively, and finally conclusively. No better solution could be found, and subsequent theological reflection has yet to come up with anything better. In the end, we are forced to recognize that human words are simply inadequate to express the glory and wonder of God. When John Donne spoke of the 'exceeding weight of glory', he was trying (among other things) to articulate the intellectual difficulty of expressing the immensity of God. Similarly, Charles Gore wrote of the Christian doctrine of God, recognizing 'an awful sense of unfathomed depths beyond the little that is made known'. As recent studies of the psychology of human awe have emphasized, awe is the human response to something that exceeds our capacity to comprehend. Divine glory elicits our joyful adoration, yet eludes our total comprehension.

So what pressures led to the emergence of this way of thinking and speaking about the richness of the Christian vision of God? In what ways does the doctrine of the Trinity help preserve the mystery of God?

Both the Old and the New Testament writers are emphatic that there is only one God, who is the God of Abraham, Isaac and Jacob. 'Hear, O Israel: the LORD our God, the LORD is one' (Deuteronomy 6.4, NIV). This theme is taken up, endorsed and echoed by the New Testament writers. For New Testament writers, there is no God other than the one who created the world, led Israel to freedom and gave the law at Sinai. The God who liberated Israel from captivity in Egypt and the God who raised Jesus Christ from the dead are one and the same.

The most significant factor leading to the emergence of Trinitarian ways of thinking is the basic Christian insight that Jesus is God Incarnate – that in the face of Jesus Christ, we see none other than the living God himself. The New Testament even hints that he was active in the process of creation itself (John 1.3; Colossians 1.16; Hebrews 1.3). Jesus is the one who can be called God and Lord, who acts as our Saviour and judge, who is worshipped, and to whom prayers are addressed.

Yet New Testament writers do not *identify* God with Jesus Christ. Jesus clearly refers to God as someone other than himself; he prays to God; and finally he commends his spirit to God as he dies. At no point does the New Testament even hint that the word 'God' ceases to refer to the one who is in heaven. Christ is God Incarnate; yet Christ prays to God as one who is distinct and beyond him. In one sense, Jesus is God; in another, he is not. It is a paradox captured – yet not resolved – by early Christian writers such as Germanus of Constantinople:

> The Word becomes incarnate,
> and yet remains on high.

The situation is made still more complex, rather than resolved, through the New Testament's insistence that the Holy Spirit is somehow involved in our experience of both God and Jesus, without being identical to either of them (see, for example, John 16.14). In some sense, Jesus Christ gives, or is the source of, the Spirit. Yet the Holy Spirit and Christ cannot be directly identified. The Spirit of God, which the Old Testament recognized as being present in the whole of creation, is now experienced and understood afresh as the Holy Spirit of the God and Father of our Lord Jesus Christ.

The Christian Bible thus offers a rich and complex picture of the nature of God, and especially the way in which God relates to the created order in general and human beings in particular. The doctrine of the Trinity aims to preserve this mystery by insisting that this grand vision of God in its totality is apprehended by faith, despite the mental discomfort that this causes – not because this vision of God is irrational, but because it is so overwhelming in its scope and depth.

History suggests that there are two main ways in which we can deal with this complexity. First, we can accept this rational challenge, interpreting it as a sign of the fundamental inability of fallen human nature to comprehend and enfold God fully and reliably. Second, we can take this discomfort as evidence of irrationality, and hence seek to reframe or reformulate the Christian faith in ways that are seen to resonate with human reason.

Yet this second approach, though doubtless admirable in its intentions, is disastrous in terms of its outcomes. The doctrine of the Trinity affirms a coherent vision of God as creator, redeemer and sanctifier, insisting that these three functions or roles of God are all to be seen as integral to the nature and identity of the 'God of the Christians' (Tertullian). The theological challenge is to allow us to visualize such a notion of God, deploying our imagination to help us grasp what we know to be true yet find difficult to see.

A rationalist approach, however, argues that such a complex vision of God is intellectually compromised, and demands simplification as a precondition for rational acceptance and cultural plausibility. Historically, the best example of this is Deism, a truncated concept of God which gained cultural traction during the 'Age of Reason'. For Deism, God was essentially to be conceived as the creator of the world, but without any further involvement with it.

But what sort of God is this? The idea may be easy to understand, but can it bear the weight of the biblical witness and Christian experience? This is a static God who is outside space and time, whom we have to discover. It is an absentee landlord, a God who is always beyond us, and not a God who comes to meet us where we are. This view of God bears little resemblance to the God who makes himself known to us through Scripture, through the death and resurrection of Jesus Christ, and in Christian experience.

Deism is thus eminently rational; it is, nevertheless, a thin and emaciated concept of God in comparison with the rich and complex vision of God which is characteristic of Christianity. This notion of God is not an acceptable, or even a recognizable, version of the Christian God. The doctrine of the Trinity articulates the distinctively Christian concept of God in order to safeguard its integrity and ensure that we do not confuse this distinct vision of God from its alternatives in the cultural and religious marketplace.

We could say that thinking of God as 'Father, Son and Holy Spirit' identifies the three essential building blocks or models that we must use if the full depth of the Christian experience and understanding of God is to be expressed adequately. No one picture, image or model of God is good enough. The first model is that of the transcendent God who lies beyond the world, as its source and creator; the second is the 'human face of God', revealed in the person of Jesus Christ; the third is that of the Holy Spirit, an immanent God who is present and active throughout the created order.

The doctrine of the Trinity affirms that these three models come together to disclose a coherent understanding of God which incorporates, naturally and plausibly, the essential Christian insights into the God who raised Jesus Christ from the dead. None of them, taken on its own, is adequate to capture the richness of the Christian experience of God.

If God were only 'Father', we would have to think of him as the distant and far-removed creator of this world who never becomes directly involved in its affairs. He would govern it from the safety of heaven, far removed from its problems and dangers. If God were only 'Son', God becomes identical with Jesus Christ, so that Christ is God, and God is Christ. Yet the New Testament insists upon a genuine *distinction* between Father and Son. Again, if God were only 'Spirit', we would have to think of God as located within the flow of the natural, perhaps expressing this idea in terms similar to those used by nineteenth-century idealist philosophies. But Christians know that God just isn't like this. God is not reduced to being part of the natural process, but stands over and above it.

And so we are forced to recognize the need to bring together these three models or ways of visualizing God if an authentically Christian view of God is to result. Any one of these three models is only a starting point; the other two add a necessary perspective and depth. Good theology is about unfolding and unpacking – not reducing and distorting – our vision of God, as we realize how much we limit God by our preconceptions and misunderstandings. The doctrine of the Trinity helps us recapture the vibrant reality of God in our minds and in our hearts. It liberates us from our scaled-down and domesticated half-truths about a God who can never be confined to formulae or theories.

Going deeper into reality: the Trinity and a 'surface faith'

The Trinity is our attempt to put into words – however faltering and inadequate – the full wonder of the Christian God, who created us, knows us, loves us and enters into history to find and meet us. Now some might rightly wish to raise an objection at this point. They trust in God, and believe firmly that they have been redeemed through Christ. So why do they need to believe this complicated stuff about the Trinity? Isn't their simple faith good enough? These are reasonable concerns, and they deserve a thoughtful answer.

No, we don't *need* to believe in the Trinity. But when we start to reflect on our faith, we find that – perhaps without realizing it – we already *do* believe in the Trinity, in that this is *implicit* in what we already believe. We discover that a Trinitarian grammar or logic underlies the way we speak about our faith in God. The Trinity is the bigger picture of God that results from teasing out the implications of what we know about God from the Bible and our experience. Christians pray and worship; they talk about being saved by Christ; they talk about being guided by the Holy Spirit. The doctrine of the Trinity makes explicit the concept of God that is implicit in these beliefs. It helps us grasp what must be true about God if all of these simple statements of faith are true and trustworthy.

A 'surface faith' is about what we see and experience. It involves prayer and worship. It's about affirming the articles of the creeds, and talking about Christ as our Saviour and Lord. But beneath this is a 'deep faith' – a set of more profound beliefs that are implied by our 'surface faith'. The doctrine of the Trinity is like the part of the iceberg that is under the water. It's there, and it needs to be there. But for everyday purposes, you don't have to worry about it. You can live out the Christian life without explicitly talking about the Trinity! What you must realize is that there is a deep Trinitarian logic to the language of our faith. When we *declare* that Jesus is Lord, we *imply* that God is Trinity.

Think of Claude Monet's paintings of water lilies in his garden at Giverny in northern France. Their great leaves and elegant flowers seem to float on the surface of the water, creating an impression of tranquillity and harmony. But what is going on beneath the surface? What is the bigger picture? The surface appearance turns out to be sustained by a complex root system. The water lilies grow on stalks that are embedded in the ground at the bottom of the pond. These roots provide both physical support and biological nourishment for the leaves and flowers. They're part of a bigger picture that is not fully apparent to the observer delighting in the delicate ornamental blooms on show.

Theologians tend to approach the Trinity in two main ways. Some argue that it is the Christian faith's last word about God. It's like the keystone in an arch. When engineers built arches in ancient Rome, they began by constructing a curved wooden frame to hold together the stones. But when the keystone was put in place at the top of the arch, the wooden frame could be taken away. The keystone was the final element of the arch, and once it was in place, it held the whole structure together without the need for any external support.

That's the view I take. I see the doctrine of the Trinity as the conclusion of a long process of reflection about faith. It is the keystone in the arch of Christian beliefs, the final piece in the jigsaw of faith, holding everything together in a coherent whole.

Others argue that the Trinity is the foundation of faith – the cornerstone rather than the keystone. Instead of being the last stone put in place to hold a structure together, it is the first stone to be put in place, around and upon which all the remaining stones are arranged and laid. If this stone is correctly in position, everything else falls into place naturally.

But whichever view you decide to take yourself, the important thing to remember is that you can live in a building without needing to think too much about how it was constructed. We can get on with the Christian life without losing sleep over the fine details of Trinitarian theology. But it certainly helps to know that the building is stable and rests on a secure foundation.

C. S. Lewis on the Trinity

After an initial period as an atheist, Lewis developed a faith in God in 1930, and moved towards a definite Christian commitment late in 1931. As he began to explore his faith, he realized that the doctrine of the Trinity allows us to affirm the transcendence of God without implying that God is 'the immobile, the unanswering'. He believed 'the huge historic fact of the doctrine of the Trinity' sets out a vision of an eternal and perfect God who enters history as 'a purposing, feeling, and finally crucified Man in a particular place and time'. It is an appropriate and helpful way of expressing the core intuitions about God which lie at the heart of the Christian faith.

Lewis also offers us approaches to the Trinity which allow us to look at this abstract doctrine in a visual way. First of all, he makes the point that the doctrine of the Trinity makes sense of the Christian experience of prayer.[4] Imagine 'ordinary simple Christians' – that is, believers who would not think of themselves as theologians – kneeling down to pray. What do they experience?

Well, perhaps most obviously, prayer is about getting in touch with God. But as Lewis points out, Christians are aware that it's more complicated than that. For a start, it's as if someone is helping us to pray. More than that: it's as if someone is acting as the channel for those prayers.

> You see what is happening. God is the thing to which [the Christian] is praying – the goal he is trying to reach. God is also the thing inside him which is pushing him on – the motive power. God is also the road or bridge along which he is being pushed to that goal. So that the whole threefold life of the three-personal Being is actually going on in that ordinary little bedroom where an ordinary man is saying his prayers.

Lewis's point is that the believer's experience of prayer fits into the 'big picture' provided by the Christian faith. The doctrine chimes with our experience and helps us make more sense of what is going on.

Lewis has two more helpful things to say. First, he reminds his readers that a religious 'theory' or 'doctrine' is always secondary to the reality to which it refers. The doctrine of the Trinity is an attempt to capture the experience of God. It makes no sense in isolation from that experience, and can never hope to capture its imaginative or emotional power.

Second, Lewis points out that we see things from a limiting and constrictive human perspective. He suggests that we think of ourselves as 'Flatlanders', two-dimensional people who are trying – and failing! – to visualize three-dimensional objects.[5]

> Flatlanders, attempting to imagine a cube, would either imagine the six squares coinciding, and thus destroy their distinctness, or else imagine them set out side by side, and thus destroy the unity. Our difficulties about the Trinity are of much the same kind.

Lewis doesn't really offer his readers a defence of the doctrine of the Trinity or any new evidence for believing in it. Instead, he provides a visual framework that allows us to perceive things in a new way and to realize that our previous difficulties arose from seeing them from a limited (and limiting) perspective.

Analogies for the Trinity

One of the reasons why so many Christians find the Trinity problematic is that it is difficult to *visualize*. Patrick, the patron saint of my native Ireland, is believed to have used the leaf of a shamrock to illustrate how a single leaf could have three different elements. Gregory of Nyssa used a series of analogies in his letters to help his readers grasp the reality of the Trinity, including the analogy of a chain. There are many links in a chain; yet to be connected to one is to be connected to all of them. In the same way, Gregory argued, someone who encounters the Holy Spirit also encounters the Father and the Son.

Gregory also unpacked the idea of a revealing God, and teased out its rich implications using appropriate images. It allowed him to distinguish – without separating – God as Speaker, Word and Breath. The speaker, the speaker's word and the speaker's breath parallel the Trinitarian structure of Father, Son and Holy Spirit. God's spirit 'cannot be separated from God in whom it exists, or from God's Word which it accompanies'. Gregory's key point here is that God does not use delegates or intermediaries to speak to us. God speaks *directly* to us. In one sense, the doctrine of the Trinity represents an unfolding of the inner logic that lies within this statement.

The analogy that I find most helpful focuses on the idea that the Trinity is the personal name of the Christian God. In other words, when we use the phrase 'Father, Son and Holy Spirit', we are *naming* God, identifying the God that we are talking about.[6] The Old Testament often identifies God with reference to turning points in the history of Israel – the great stories of Abraham, Isaac and Jacob, of the exodus from Egypt, and so on. This is made clear in a number of Old Testament passages (e.g., Exodus 19.4–5; Deuteronomy 26.5–9; Ezekiel 20.5–26). Question: who is our God? Answer: God is the one who made promises to Abraham, who delivered us from Egypt, and who led us into the promised land.

Now we turn to the New Testament. Who is the God whom Christians worship and adore? To answer this question, the New Testament tells the story of Jesus Christ. Question: who is the God whom Christians worship and adore? Answer: the one who 'raised Jesus our Lord from the dead' (Romans 4.24). Of course, the New Testament writers make it clear that the God who 'raised Jesus our Lord from the dead' is the same God who delivered Israel from Egypt. This approach to the Trinity is strongly dynamic, appealing to the *acts* of God rather than the static *being* of God.

The doctrine of the Trinity can thus be seen as a summary of the story of God's dealings with us. It tells the story of how God created and redeemed humanity, emphasizing that this is not a story about three different divine agents, but is the story of one and the same God throughout. It spells out exactly which God we are dealing with. Who is the God whom Christians know and love, and who in turn knows and loves them? The God who created the world, who redeemed us in Christ, and who is present with us now through the Holy Spirit. The Trinity is a proper name for the Christian God.

This distinct Trinitarian logic lies behind so much of Christian life and thought, safeguarding its distinct identity and its inner coherence. As C. S. Lewis pointed out, Christians naturally work within a Trinitarian perspective when they pray. Similarly, when they gather together for worship, they find themselves adoring the Father through the Son in the Holy Spirit. This naturally leads us to think more about the Christian community of faith often known as 'the Church'. How does this fit into the landscape of faith? We shall consider this in the following chapter.

15

The community of faith: why the Church matters

━━━◆◆◆━━━

The New Testament is clear that the death and resurrection of Christ make possible a new way of life and thought. A new age has dawned, opening up new possibilities for human existence, breaking down traditional ethnic and social barriers. Yet new ideas lead to the creation of new communities concerned to convey and consolidate such new visions of life. The Christian Church is the community of this new epoch in human history, called into being by God to support and sustain those who have been drawn into this 'new creation'.

Christians are the wandering people of God, sojourners and wayfarers in our strange world, whose shared vision of the meaning of life and the hope of glory keeps them going as they travel along a Road which is so often shrouded in mist and darkness. They travel together, offering each other support and mutual comfort as they try to grow in their faith while they journey on the Road, passing through what often seems to be an indifferent or hostile world. They explore the landscape of faith together, encouraging each other as they uncover its mysteries.

The Greek word *ekklēsia*, traditionally translated as 'church', refers to an assembly of people convened for a purpose. During the Golden Age of ancient Athens, an assembly of citizens was summoned in times of need – for example, at moments of political crisis, when a decision had to be made about whether to go to war, or to elect representatives.

The New Testament sees the Church as such an assembly of Christians, which God called out of darkness into a marvellous light (1 Peter 2.9). Initially, Christians seem to have used the word 'church' to refer simply to a gathering of believers, likely to have met in a private house for prayer and worship. Paul's letters to the church at Corinth or Philippi are addressed to relatively small groups of people, who probably met together secretly in homes.

Once Christianity became a legal religion following the conversion of the emperor Constantine in 313, a major change in its public profile began to take place. As they were no longer forced to meet in secret, Christians could begin to construct their own buildings for public worship. Gradually, the word 'church' came to refer to a specific building in which Christians assembled, rather than the assembly of believers itself.

At its heart, the Church is the community of people who gather around Christ. We can see anticipations of this idea in the New Testament. For example, Christ speaks of his coming death as creating a gathering point or focus of attraction for world-weary people seeking meaning, transformation and fulfilment. 'I, when I am lifted up from the earth, will draw all people to myself' (John 12.32). The Church is the community that gathers around the crucified Christ, anticipated in those who assembled around the cross at Calvary on the first Good Friday, and developed further in Paul's proclamation of the gospel in terms of the 'message of the cross'.

Some theologians have compared the Church to a walled garden, similar to the Garden of Eden. Isaac Watts, best known for his hymn 'When I Survey the Wondrous Cross', also wrote other hymns which expressed this idea, emphasizing that the Church was a place of safety within which believers could grow in their faith:

> We are a garden walled around,
> Chosen and made peculiar ground;
> A little spot enclosed by grace
> Out of the world's wide wilderness.

A similar point is made by the traditional idea of the Church as a boat, ferrying its passengers to safety across a tempestuous ocean. Just as Noah's ark bore people (and animals!) through the floods to safety, so the Church, like a boat, represents a place of security in the face of chaos, and a mode of transport to a safe haven. This idea is reflected in the architecture of many churches. The nave, the central part of the church in which the congregation sits, takes its name from the Latin word for ship, *navis*, in that the vaulted roof of the nave looks rather like an inverted ship's keel.

The Church is the group of people who are drawn to Christ, believing that they have found in him the answers to life's deepest questions. It is the crystallization of a community around the focal interpretive story of Christ – a way of seeing God, ourselves and the world in the light of the life, death and resurrection of Jesus Christ.

The Church and the discipleship of the mind

As we have seen, the discipleship of the mind is the process through which Christians develop habits of thought which allow our world to be seen, understood and evaluated in new ways. For Augustine of Hippo, the human eye must itself be healed by God's grace if we are to see the landscape of our world properly, and lead meaningful lives within it:[1]

> Our whole business in this life is to heal the eye of the heart in order that God may be seen. It is for this reason that the holy mysteries are celebrated and the word of God is preached.

Augustine's phrase 'healing the eyes of the heart' (borrowed from Ephesians 1.18) suggests that the acquisition of these new habits of thinking may be compared to a blind person being enabled to see the world for the first time. The reality of the world is hidden from us until we are enabled to see it properly. Yet Augustine develops a point which will be of central importance in this chapter: the discipleship of the mind takes place within the community of faith. The Christian habit of thought that we call the discipleship of the mind is both generated and sustained by the Christian gospel, especially as this is proclaimed and embodied in the life of the Church.

The discipleship of the mind is not about an instantaneous illumination of our minds through which we suddenly find ourselves in possession of answers to all of life's questions. Through faith, we enter into the rich pasturelands of the Christian world, and begin to feed and grow. The discipleship of the mind is a process of reflection, discernment and growth. We learn from those around us, as they share what they have found helpful in the hope that it may help us as well. Wisdom is acquired over time, through the reflective inhabitation of the community of faith, as the core themes of faith are grasped, digested, absorbed and assimilated into a coherent way of thinking in dialogue and debate with others. These habits of thought, acquired and tested over time, can be thought of as the 'mind of Christ'.

C. S. Lewis, reflecting on his own experience of spiritual growth and theological reflection, remarked that 'the one really adequate instrument for learning about God is the Christian community'.[2] It is within such a community of people 'united together in a body, loving one another, helping one another, showing [God] to one another' that the life of faith takes root and develops. Although Lewis found his faith stimulated and enriched in other ways – most notably, through the group of colleagues that we know as 'the Inklings' – there is no doubting the importance he attached to the Church as a means of grace.

And what did Lewis mean by the Church? There is no doubt that his faith was stimulated and supported by two worshipping communities that he attended in the first phase of his journey of faith: the chapel of his Oxford college, and the local parish church of Holy Trinity, Headington Quarry, Oxford. Yet Lewis also found enrichment and encouragement from the witness of Christian writers of the past – such as George Herbert – who helped him to grasp his faith at the imaginative, not merely the rational, level.

Lewis realized that the Christian community of faith, past and present, gave him a way of understanding his faith which affirmed his individuality while at the same time connecting him with others, and thus opening him up to deeper and richer ways of seeing things. The rich resources of sermons and spiritual writings of both the past and present enable us 'to see with other eyes, to imagine with other imaginations, to feel with other hearts, as well as our own'.

This same point can be made in other ways. In 1159, the English theologian John of Salisbury used an analogy to explain how we can learn from the wisdom of the past.

> Bernard of Chartres used to compare us to dwarfs perched on the shoulders of giants. He pointed out that we see more and farther than those who went before us, not because we have a sharper vision or greater height than them, but because we are lifted up and held high by their gigantic stature.[3]

That's why I read people like Augustine of Hippo, Athanasius of Alexandria, Thomas Aquinas, Martin Luther and C. S. Lewis. I gain wisdom and insight by standing on their shoulders. I don't have to agree with them – but they provide me with good responses to the questions of our world, and challenge me to try to do better.

Although the Church is often seen as the repository of a fixed and unchanging faith, it is better seen as a 'laboratory,' in which the community of faith wrestles with how best to understand the gospel and bring it into creative dialogue with contemporary culture. The Church is both a grateful recipient and active interpreter of the Christian faith, seeking to be both faithful and effective in its reflections. Each generation needs to forge its own distinct visualization of the gospel, realizing that this is a temporary implementation of the Christian 'big picture'. The creeds create space for facilitating this process of imaginative interplay between the community of faith and its context, emphasizing the need to be firmly rooted in the Christian tradition, while liberating us from the tyranny of traditionalism.

The Christian vision of faith: one holy, catholic and apostolic

Christian theologians sometimes speak of the 'four marks of the Church', picking up on a section of the Nicene Creed which affirms belief in 'one holy, catholic and apostolic Church'. So what do these four words mean? And how do they help us make sense of the landscape of faith as we journey along the Road?

The 'four marks' are often discussed in terms of the institutional agendas and concerns of the churches. I shall depart from this practice. Instead, I shall focus on how these four categories help us to grasp the coherence and function of the Christian 'big picture'.

To start with, there is *one* Christian 'big picture', which allows us to grasp the coherence and intelligibility of our lives and our world. The Christian 'big picture' – to borrow some words from the novelist Henry James – represents 'the effort really to see and really to represent' our God, our world and ourselves. Christianity invites us to see our apparently fragmented and muddled world as having an underlying unity, hidden beneath the surface of things. The point to appreciate is that this unitary vision of reality allows us to recognize the irreducible many-sidedness of our world, and the kaleidoscopic variety of human experience, while seeing these as held together by the grander sense-making vision of faith.

We find this theme especially in the later writings within the New Testament, such as the Letter to the Colossians, which speaks of Christ as the one in whom 'all things hold together' (Colossians 1.17). We live in and know a variegated world, and can celebrate that diversity – while at the same time knowing that there is a hidden unity beneath its surface. Christianity gives us an expansive vision of our world, helping us realize how much more there is to discover and appreciate.

The Christian 'big picture' is also *holy.* Many automatically translate 'holiness' as 'morality' or 'goodness'. While there is indeed a correspondence here, it is not an identity. To be holy is to be set apart, called to be distinct, to reflect the character of God rather than passively endorse what the German poet Hermann Hesse once called the 'intellectual fashions and transitory values of the day'. To be holy is to be Christ-like. The Christian vision of faith helps us grasp what is distinctive about Christian thought and life, so that we sing the Lord's song in an increasingly strange land (Psalm 137.4). We are the 'salt of the earth' (Matthew 5.13), but can too easily lose that saltiness.

Yet holiness does not entail separation from the world, or the cultivation of isolation in order to avoid contamination or impurity. Some Christian writers and groups do consider holiness as demanding a distancing of the Church from the world, or an isolation of believers from the complexities of everyday life. Yet Christ himself chose to avoid distance or separation from the world, and actively – even scandalously – associated with those who were seen as sinners and outsiders by the religious authorities of his day.

The creeds help us to see why it is Jesus Christ – and not someone else – that we place at the centre of our moral universe. Christian ethics is not simply a code of moral values. It is a way of behaving which emerges from the 'big picture' of faith, focusing on Christ as the image and embodiment of God. The Christian faith gives us a lens through which we see the world, ourselves and other people. It invites us to strip off our layers of illusion and defensiveness, so we can see things – and ourselves – as they really are. We now see the world as God's creation – something that belongs to God and matters to God, and has been entrusted to us. A changed understanding of the world thus leads to a changed attitude towards the world.

We are also invited to think of the Christian faith as *catholic*. This term is not easy to translate. It means something like 'embracing in its totality' or 'conveying the whole'. Some translations of the creeds use the word 'universal' for this technical term, probably because of a fear that 'catholic' is too easily confused with 'Roman Catholic'. The emphasis here is on the coherence and comprehensiveness of the Christian 'big picture'. This does not mean, however, that it engages *everything*.

I do not for one moment think that Christianity tells me the distance to the nearest star, or the density of the moon. Rather, it discloses everything I need to know to lead a meaningful human life. It helps me see what is wrong with the world. It allows me to grasp what God has done to change things, and what I need to do to benefit from this, and be part of this renewed and redeemed way of living. And it reassures me that the Road is actually going somewhere, rather than petering out in a meaningless wilderness.

Yet the catholicity of faith also issues a challenge to individualist accounts of faith, which limit the scope of belief to what we personally find meaningful. Occasionally, I meet people who tell me that they disregard sections of the creeds because they are 'not important' or 'not relevant to my concerns'. Yet the creeds invite us to explore the whole landscape of faith rather than limit ourselves to the places we know and like. They suggest that ours might be an impoverished faith, confined to the familiar. Might our faith be enriched by exploring a fuller landscape of faith? Might there be facets of faith that we have yet to discover?

Finally, we must think of the Christian faith as *apostolic*. It articulates the attitude of the apostles. The word 'apostle' is derived from the Greek verb *apostellein*, 'to send out', and means something like a 'messenger' or 'emissary'. In the New Testament, it has the developed sense of 'someone who is commissioned to preach the good news', or 'someone whom Jesus Christ authorized to preach on his behalf'.

Christian writers of the late second and early third century – such as Irenaeus of Lyons, Tertullian and Clement of Alexandria – emphasize the importance of 'sound teaching' in keeping the churches. These writers speak of a 'canon of truth' or 'rule of faith', meaning a framework of faith, professed and taught in the churches, which is understood to have been passed down from the apostles.

The Christian vision of reality is thus understood to be founded on the teaching of the apostles, and to be continuous with them. This grand vision is not something that we have invented, but something that has been entrusted to us through an unbroken line of witness stretching back to the apostles themselves. Yet this view of reality is also 'apostolic' in the sense of being *missionary* – that is, capable of drawing people to itself through the luminosity of its clarity and the capaciousness of its vision.

These four ways of thinking about the Christian 'big picture' are helpful in themselves, but also feed into our thinking about the place of the Church in the life of faith. In the remainder of this chapter, we shall focus on the roles that the Church plays in sustaining and developing Christians as they travel along the Road.

The Church as a community of learning

The Church is a community of learning – a school of discipleship. The later letters of the New Testament emphasize the importance of teaching, both for the transmission of faith to later generations, and as a means of helping present-day Christians to develop maturity in their faith. In the early Church, the bishop was often seen as having a significant teaching role. Cyril of Jerusalem is widely regarded as one of the finest teachers of this period: his 'catechetical lectures' were delivered at Jerusalem around the year 350 to those preparing for baptism. The early Church took this public demonstration of Christian commitment very seriously, and used the period of Lent to teach those who wished to publicly acknowledge their faith through baptism about the Christian faith and life. The ceremony itself took place on Easter Day in order to celebrate the new life it brought.

Instruction is an important aspect of the Church's identity and mission. Christianity is not an uninformed trust in God, or a blind faith in certain doctrines. It is a coherent set of ideas linked together to enable believers to make sense of life, and live it to the full. As the recent rise of the 'New Atheism' has made clear, Christians need to know what they believe, and why they believe it.

In the intensely secular culture of the twenty-first century, the assumptions of faith are regularly challenged, if not actually ridiculed. Christians can easily feel demoralized and intimidated, tempted to 'go with the flow'. But the Christian community offers an environment which allows the growth rather than the withering of faith.

Like a tender plant, our faith needs to be protected if it is to grow. The sociologist Peter Berger spoke of the importance of what he called 'plausibility structures' – a community within which certain beliefs are accepted and affirmed, and within which people are supported and encouraged as they grow into this faith. In its worship and teaching, the Church shows its excitement at the extraordinariness of God, and its passionate longing to talk about the beauty and splendour of

God. It helps us realize how much more there is to discover, how much more to appreciate, as we journey in faith.

To protect faith in this way is not to disengage from the world, nor from the deep questioning and intellectual unease of our age of uncertainty and doubt. It is to create an environment in which believers can wrestle with questions without being overwhelmed by them, and so discover answers that they find to be satisfactory. Too often, believers are not sufficiently familiar with their faith to know how such questions might be answered. An integral part of the discipleship of the mind is becoming familiar with the deep inner logic of faith, and the approaches and insights of the leading representatives of Christianity down the ages.

Christianity is not simply about acquiring information on the beliefs, history and practices of the churches. It is about our personal assimilation of faith, which requires engagement with the Bible and the long Christian tradition of biblical interpretation. It means listening to those who have already been through this process of reflection and assimilation, and finding out what we can learn from what they have learned.

The Church – as a community of believers – helps us to grasp the Christian story, and learn to *inhabit* it, not simply to understand it. The Church provides a community which is nourished by this way of thinking – for instance, through preaching which illuminates our minds, transforms our hearts and inspires us to take action. Preaching helps us to make connections between the horizontal and vertical dimensions of life.

This teaching role of the Church does not simply concern what Christians believe; it's about inculcating values, and exploring how these can be put into practice in life. At its best, the Church is a community of wisdom, in which guidance can be given about how best to live out the Christian faith in an increasingly complex world where many of the old certainties are called into question.

The Church as a community of support

The Church is a community which enfolds us, protects us and encourages us as we grow in our faith. It is like a nursery which helps us set down roots and grow. One day, we can look after ourselves. Yet we need a place in which we can explore our faith and test its limits, make mistakes and learn from them. It's no accident that many Christians find it helpful to talk about the Church as a mother. It's an image that can be traced back to Cyprian of Carthage in the third century. 'You cannot have God as your father', he remarked, 'unless you have the church as your mother.'[4]

I learned to play chess when I was about 6. To begin with, I wasn't much good at it. I had no idea about making strategic moves, and tended to rely on my opponents having even less experience of the game than I did. At 13, I moved to a new school, which had a well-established chess club. I suppose it was inevitable that I would join it. For the next four years, I was an active member, and over time I noticed two things happening.

First of all, I got much better at playing chess. It wasn't just because I had more practice at playing; it was because I could talk to older students who took chess seriously and had devoured books by grand masters. I found myself beginning to grasp the game at a deeper level than before. Previously, I had just moved pieces around according to the rules; now, I played strategically.

Second, I was supported by others in thinking that chess was interesting and worthwhile. My school had a very strong sporting tradition and an outstanding reputation in rugby, cricket and rowing. Chess was seen by most of my peers as a game played by socially backward students who were incapable of doing anything more interesting or worthwhile. So we chess enthusiasts huddled together for comfort. Within the club, there was a sense of shared values and friendship, and this helped us cope with the gently critical attitude of others. It's much easier to handle marginalization in company than on your own.

I gave up playing chess when I went to university at Oxford, partly because my academic work was so interesting that it displaced the game. But after I discovered Christianity, I found the same pattern repeating itself. Going to church in Oxford helped me in two ways. First, it introduced me to people who knew a lot more about their faith than I did. Personal friendships opened the way to a deeper understanding of what the Christian faith was all about, and how best to live it out. Every now and then, a sermon might prove especially exciting and help me to grasp something that had hitherto eluded me. The church was a community that stimulated my growth in faith.

But there was more to it than that. In the 1970s, Oxford students were fascinated by Marxism, and tended to see any kind of religious belief or involvement as outmoded and reactionary. Why read about Jesus Christ, when you could read Mao Tse Tung's *Little Red Book*? Churches provided intellectual and moral support to Christian believers in the face of hostility, indifference and cynicism. They were like spiritual oases in the midst of a wilderness or desert, offering refreshment and revitalization. Of course, we all know that churches can go wrong, and end up becoming inward-looking, suspicious and oppressive. But it doesn't need to be like that, and it's not meant to be like that.

The Church is a community of faith – an idea that is often expressed in terms of Paul's powerful image of the 'body of Christ' (see especially 1 Corinthians 12), which suggests an interconnected body of people, each of whom has a role to play in sustaining the ministry of the Church. To speak of the Church as the 'people of God' (cf. 1 Peter 2.10) is not to deny the importance of individuals or human individuality; it is to recognize that individuals are enabled to grow in wisdom and to overcome their limitations through belonging to a community. As Dietrich Bonhoeffer realized, other people are good for us – no matter how irksome and difficult we may at times find them. They help us identify and face up to our pride, weaknesses and vanities. And as others accept us, so we come to accept others. We journey on the Road in company, helping and supporting each other as we travel.

The Church as a colony of heaven

The Church is a community of believers, a colony of heaven on earth, a place in which the 'Spirit of grace' (Zechariah 12.10, NIV) dwells. In its worship and prayer, the Church speaks the language of heaven. Though we live on earth, we observe the customs and values of our real homeland. Christians thus live in two worlds, and must learn to negotiate their boundaries. In one of his letters, Paul develops the idea of the Church as a 'colony' of heaven. What might he have meant by this?

Modern Western ideas of 'colonies' are largely shaped by the legacy of European imperialism in the nineteenth century, when overseas territories were in effect annexed as belonging to a European state, such as the UK or France. The Roman idea of a colony was very different. For a start, the term referred not to a territory, but to a city or township. When a city was conquered, its administration was handed over to Roman settlers. Typically, a city would be populated by Roman citizens, or by inhabitants of the region around Rome ('Latins'). These colonies would be seen as extensions of the mother city abroad, with citizens enjoying the right of return to Rome. During the New Testament period, Philippi was a Roman colony.

This historical fact illuminates one of the most interesting features of Paul's letter to the church at Philippi: its use of the Roman colony as a way of understanding the place of the church. Paul assumes that his readers in Philippi, already familiar with this political model, will understand his allusion to the situation in the colony and its implications for thinking about the Christian life. 'Our citizenship is in heaven, and it is from there that we are expecting a Saviour, the Lord Jesus Christ' (Philippians 3.20). What did he mean?

The immediacy of Paul's analogy is now lost on us, and we must therefore reconstruct and unfold what would have been intuitive and obvious to Paul's original readers. Just as Philippi saw itself as an outpost of Rome in the distant province of Macedonia, so Christians must see themselves as a colony of heaven on earth. The idea of Christians being 'citizens of heaven' came naturally to Paul, since he himself held Roman citizenship and was aware of the privileges this brought. There are probably three ways in which Paul's analogy would have connected with his readers in Philippi.

First, and perhaps most importantly, Roman citizens residing in Philippi had the right to return home to the metropolis after their service in the colony. Philippi was not where they really belonged. Paul's point is that one of the 'benefits of Christ' – that is, what Christ won for believers by his obedience, death and resurrection – was the privilege of being a citizen of heaven, including the right to live there.

Second, the Roman colony at Philippi spoke Latin, the language of their native Rome, in addition to the other languages that were called for as a result of living in Macedonia (Paul, remember, wrote in Greek to the church at Philippi). And third, they observed the laws and customs of Rome at Philippi. Through language, laws and customs they maintained their identity as Roman citizens. One day they would return to their homeland. In the meantime, they kept alive its memory through something akin to imaginative inhabitation – partly to recall the past, yet partly also to anticipate the future.

These themes of recalling the past and anticipating the future are also linked with the Christian understanding of sacraments, to which we now turn.

16

Signs of God's presence: reassurance and affirmation

———— ▪◦▪ ————

As we journey on the Road, we often use symbols to remind and reassure ourselves of our history, identity and destiny. Many – but not all – Christians use the word 'sacrament' to refer to actions and signs which are seen as possessing special importance in maintaining and developing the Christian life. At its heart, a sacrament is a visible sign and reassurance of God's grace. The term comes from the Latin word *sacramentum*, which originally meant 'a sacred oath', such as the oath of obedience that a Roman soldier might swear to the people and Senate of Rome. The third-century theologian Tertullian used this analogy to bring out the importance of sacraments in relation to Christian commitment and loyalty within the Church. Baptism, for example, can be seen as a sign both of allegiance to Christ and of commitment to the Christian community.

My concern in this chapter is not to resolve long-standing theological debates about the definitions of sacraments, but to reflect on their role in helping us journey through the landscape of faith. I know that many readers will regret that I have not engaged more fully with some of the classic theological debates about the definition and function of the sacraments. I am aware of these problems, and wish there were some other way of dealing with them in such a brief space. In the end, I decided that it was best if I simply set out some approaches that have helped me, while making it clear that there is much more that needs to be said.

So what is a sacrament? The old Prayer Book catechism (1662) tells us that a sacrament is 'an outward and visible sign of an inward and spiritual grace given unto us, ordained by Christ himself, as a means whereby we receive the same, and a pledge to assure us thereof'. These physical signs engage both our physical senses and our imaginations, opening up new ways of thinking, and calling to mind important moments in our past history. So what role do these outward and visible signs play, either as a means of grace, or as an assurance of God's love and care for us?

To explore these questions, I shall focus on one aspect of the Christian life: our identity as members of the family of God. We cannot know who we are without first discovering whose we are. Our true identity is not something we create, earn or discover; it is rather something that is given to us through adoption.

Adoption: gracious acceptance into a community

In an earlier chapter, we looked at a range of New Testament images or models of salvation. One model that we did not discuss there is of particular relevance to thinking about the place of signs in the Christian life: *adoption*. The image is drawn from the sphere of Roman family law, with which Paul (and many of his readers) would have been familiar. The image of adoption is used by Paul in several of his letters to express the distinction between believers as 'sons of God' and Jesus Christ as 'the Son of God' (Romans 8.15, 23; 9.4; Galatians 4.5).

Under Roman adoption law, the head of a family (*paterfamilias*) was free to adopt individuals – almost invariably males – from outside his natural family, and give them the legal status of adoption. This had three consequences for the adopted person. First, it meant that all his existing debts would be cancelled; second, he would be granted the same inheritance rights as the natural children of the *paterfamilias*; and third, he would take on the name of the adopting family and have the same social status as its other members.

Paul found that this Roman legal procedure was a helpful analogy in expressing the changed status of believers. To be adopted is to become a full member of a new family. Through faith, believers are adopted into the family of God, with all the benefits that this brings. Most importantly, Paul sees adoption as an act of grace, something that is wrought by the Holy Spirit working within us. Adoption is about the conferring of the three privileges noted above – privileges that we do not deserve, yet which God graciously bestows upon us. Let us consider each of these three benefits in more detail.

First, adoption involves the cancellation of our debts. In the Roman context, an adopted son would often come from a poorer family, and might even have been sold into some form of slavery – typically as a 'bondsman', whereby he would have agreed to serve a household for a period of several years for a certain sum. The process of adoption involved the *paterfamilias* settling all debts, effectively liberating the son from his obligations by buying his freedom. Paul hints at this in speaking of the 'freedom of the glory of the children of God' (Romans 8.21).

Second, adoption involves receiving inheritance rights. To be a member of the household of faith is to be an heir of God. Believers are thus 'heirs of God' and 'co-heirs with Christ' (Romans 8.17, NIV), in that we share in the same inheritance rights as Jesus Christ. All that Christ has inherited from God will one day be ours as well. For Paul, this insight helps us cope with suffering. Christ suffered before he was glorified; believers must expect to do the same.

Third, adoption into the family of God brings a new sense of belonging, as we enter into a relationship with the God 'from whom every family in heaven and on earth derives its name' (Ephesians 3.15). We are now part of a new household and family, and we take on a new name which reflects this new identity. All people need to feel that they belong somewhere. Social psychologists speak of the necessity of a 'secure base', a community or group which gives people a sense of purpose and an awareness of being valued and loved by others. In human terms, we have the family unit; in Christian terms, we are adopted into the family of God. We can rest assured that we are valued within this family, which gives us the self-confidence to work in and witness to the world.

This third aspect of adoption has become increasingly important in more recent times, as social fragmentation within Western culture leads many people to feel they do not belong anywhere. There is a pervasive sense of being lost, displaced, adrift, and a yearning to belong somewhere, to have a place that can be called our home. To be adopted into the family of faith is to be welcomed into a grand household which becomes our home – a place where we belong, not merely a place where we live.

While adoption can be expressed as the transfer of parenting rights from one's biological parents to others, this fails to do justice to the existential transformation that the process brings. Within Roman society (which determines how Paul's model is to be interpreted), adoption was about someone enjoying the benefits of belonging to an influential family, with the change in social and financial status that this entailed. Paul is likely to have had the example of the first Roman emperor Augustus in mind. Born into a plebeian family, Augustus was adopted into the family of Julius Caesar. Caesar's family connections ensured Augustus's subsequent rise to fame and fortune.

The Christian Church is a community of believers, the family into which believers are adopted. Believing and belonging are intimately connected, so it is not always clear which is cause and which is effect. Both are core aspects of Christian identity. There is, of course, a perfectly sensible discussion that needs to take place here – namely, which specific Christian denomination or group is to be preferred. However, this is not my agenda here. Like C. S. Lewis, I am happy to commend Christianity in general, and leave it to my readers to determine their own denominational commitments. For my purposes, Christians are those who are part of the family of faith whose ancestry can be traced back to Abraham, Isaac and Jacob at the dawn of civilization.

This being the case, a series of important questions arises. How can I know that I am a member of this family? How can I be reassured of my identity? How can I know my family history, and feel that I am truly one of its members? We shall consider questions such as these in what follows.

Belonging to the family of faith

Remember! This theme of remembering resonates throughout the history of the people of God. They are called to remember who they are, and how they came into being. And they are to remember the words and deeds of the creator and Saviour God who has called them, and remains their comforter and guide to this day.

Everyone knows how important it is to keep memories alive. Physical objects can help us remember people and events in our family history. That's why we keep photographs of family members and friends. I have an old brass microscope on my office desk, given to me by my great-uncle in the early 1960s. He was a pathologist, and hoped that I might come to share his interest in the natural world. That microscope now reminds me of my early love of the natural world which led me to want to become a scientist. But it also reminds me of my great-uncle, who died a few years after giving me the microscope. I'm sure every reader of this book can point to something that plays a similar role in their lives.

One of the best ways of preserving important memories is to tell stories. We use 'grand stories' or metanarratives to help us understand who we are and how we should live – to tell us what things mean and what we are meant to be doing. Yet we also use stories to help us to remember people and events that lie in the past yet are important to shaping and maintaining our identity as individuals and communities.

We live in a world that is shaped by stories – by narratives which tell us who we are and what really matters. But which story can we trust? One of the dominant narratives of Western culture goes something like this. 'We are here by accident, meaningless products of a random process. We can only invent meaning and purpose in life, and do our best to stay alive – even though there is no point to life.' But is it right?

There is, however, another narrative, which takes a very different approach. 'We are precious creatures of a loving God, who has created us with something special in mind.' This is the master story that we find in the Bible, and which is echoed in great Christian writers down the ages.

These two stories are totally incompatible. They can't both be right. So which do we trust? In the end, we have to decide which is right. And having made that decision, we then need to inhabit the story we trust. Faith involves two decisions. First, we have to decide which story we can trust. And then we have to enter that story, becoming a participant, not an observer. We live inside that story. And by doing so, we become a member of the family of faith.

Symbols and signs – such as bread, water and wine – do not possess meaning in and of themselves. They need to be set within the context of an informing story, which attaches the sign to a story. Christians have become so used to seeing the imaginative link between bread and the death of Christ that they sometimes forget that this link is created and safeguarded by the eucharistic narrative (1 Corinthians 11.26). Yet bread is also linked with other narratives. We too easily forget that while the people of Israel were captive in Egypt, they were fed bread by their oppressors in order to ensure their continued capacity to work. This bread of affliction may have been physically nourishing, but its purpose was sinister – to enslave, to oppress and to exploit. Yet while wandering in the wilderness, the people of Israel remembered the bread but forgot its purpose (Exodus 16.3). They had ample bread in Egypt, but none in Sinai.

For Christians, it is important to recall and savour the foundational stories of faith – the exodus from Egypt and entry into the promised land, and the death and resurrection of Jesus Christ. Those are the stories which shape our identity, and which give meaning to the signs and symbols we use as we journey on the Road. We hear these stories read again and again, and absorb their details. They mingle historical narration and theological interpretation, telling us both what happened and what this means. These stories are generative, in the sense that they both undergird and give rise to beliefs and moral values. And we are reminded of them by signs – by physical objects and human actions which call to mind the formative events of our past, which are to be remembered, treasured and turned over in our minds and imaginations, so that we can extract every morsel of spiritual significance from them.

Consider the 'exodus narrative' – the story of how the people of Israel were delivered from their harsh bondage in Egypt and led through the wilderness into the promised land of Canaan. It was a formative era for them, during which they had to learn the privileges and responsibilities of being the people of God.

During this period, they were able to reflect on the nature and character of their God. It led to the renewal of a sense of identity as the people of God.

The Passover celebration was about remembering the exodus, and became a focus for Israel's memory of its past and hopes for its future. When future generations asked why the Passover was being celebrated, they would be told about the deeper meaning of the event (Exodus 12.26–27). The Passover ritual recalled the history of the exodus from Egypt. Each household was to sacrifice an unblemished male lamb, and brush some of its blood on to the door frames as a mark of identity. The distinctively Christian idea of Jesus Christ as the 'lamb of God' reflects this theme, linking the death of Jesus on the cross with the Passover lamb. The families would then roast the lamb and eat it, accompanied with bitter herbs and unleavened bread. So what was the point of this Passover ritual?

First, it reminded Israel of the great events in history that brought it into being. The festival of Passover was to be a permanent memorial of the mighty acts of God that led to Israel being liberated from bondage in Egypt: 'Remember this day on which you came out from Egypt, out of the house of slavery, because the Lord brought you out from there by strength of hand' (Exodus 13.3). Once Israel had settled in the promised land, it was to continue the Passover ceremony as a way of remembering this act of divine deliverance.

Israel spent 40 years in the wilderness of Sinai, journeying from Egypt to the promised land. The period of wandering in the wilderness was seen as a time of preparation – a period in which Israel could discover more about the God who loved, called and liberated it. Israel's long period of wandering in the wilderness was no easy time. At points, it was a time of doubt, rebellion and restlessness. Yet on other occasions it proved to be a time of dedication and purification – a period in which Israel was able to discover its identity as a people, and the reasons for being called into existence by God.

As the people of Israel wandered through the wilderness, they did more than remember the past; they looked forward to the future. The Passover was an act of remembrance and anticipation.

As the people of Israel journeyed through the Sinai desert, they both remembered the past and looked forward to the future. They looked *backwards* to the past, and recalled their period of captivity in Egypt and their glorious liberation through Moses. They also looked *forward* to the final entry into the promised land, the eagerly awaited goal of their long journey. The uncertainties and difficulties of the present were thus sustained by the memory of past events and the hope of future events.

The themes of 'remembering' and 'anticipating' thus played a pivotal role in sustaining the people of Israel in the period between the exodus and the entry into Canaan. Israel was constantly reminded to remember its exile in Egypt, and recall all that God had done for it since then (Psalms 135.5–14; 136.1–26).

A similar theme emerges during the captivity of the people of Jerusalem in Babylon during the sixth century before Christ. After Jerusalem fell to Babylonian armies in 597 BC, many of its population were deported to Babylon. Although some inhabitants remained in Jerusalem and the surrounding region, many of the most prominent Judean families were deported in several waves into captivity in Babylon. Solomon's Temple, widely seen as the emblem of Jewish identity, was destroyed. The Jewish exiles in Babylon were left with no hope of returning to their homeland. The familiar words of Psalm 137 capture the sense of longing felt by those exiles for their distant homeland:

> By the rivers of Babylon we sat and wept
> When we remembered Zion.

The thought of returning to their homeland sustained the exiles throughout the long and harsh years of exile. They remembered Jerusalem, and looked forward to returning there – even though they had no idea when this might happen, if at all. After the final defeat of Babylon by Persian armies in 539 BC, the people of Jerusalem were free to return home. Although some chose to stay in Babylon, others undertook the long walk back to Jerusalem, to rebuild the Temple and reconstruct their national and religious identity. The Old Testament books of Ezra and Nehemiah deal with this formative period in Israel's history, and help us understand the close interconnection of the rebuilding of Jerusalem's Temple and its recovered sense of identity as the people of God.

Thus far, we have explored how sacraments interlink memory of the past and anticipation of the future. So how does this work out in practice? Let's explore this further. We'll begin by thinking about baptism.

Baptism: water and the life of faith

One of the great themes of the history of Israel is that its people were marked by a covenant sign – in this case, circumcision. This was a physical reminder of the relationship between God and Israel. Yet circumcision was limited to males. Women did not bear a sign of the covenant. But from the outset, men and women were baptized. The New Testament presents baptism as the sign of the 'new covenant' between God and believers, bringing to fulfilment the 'old covenant' between God and Israel. This covenant sign of belonging to the people of God affirmed the fundamental equality of men and women before God. 'There is no longer Jew or Greek, there is no longer slave or free, there is no longer male and female; for all of you are one in Christ Jesus' (Galatians 3.28).

The Christian use of baptism can be traced back to Jesus Christ's decision to be baptized by John the Baptist, described in the Gospels. Some find this puzzling. After all, the Nicene Creed speaks of acknowledging 'one baptism for the forgiveness of sins'. Surely Christ did not have sins that needed to be forgiven? The point here, however, is that John the Baptist saw baptism as a sign of humanity's need for purification from sin. In being baptized, Christ was both affirming the need of humanity for redemption, and hinting that he himself would provide the basis for the real forgiveness of real sins.

Christians disagree about whether baptism causes forgiveness, or is a public declaration that forgiveness has been received and accepted. Yet all agree that, in some way, baptism is a means of reaffirming the reality of God's forgiveness of sins in Christ, and of the human need for that forgiveness in the first place. Baptism affirms that our sins need to be washed away, and *can* be washed away on account of the death and resurrection of Jesus Christ.

Yet there is another point here. *Also* Baptism is about connecting up our own individual stories with that of Christ. It's a theme that we can see in Paul's important comments on baptism.

> Do you not know that all of us who have been baptized into Christ Jesus were baptized into his death? Therefore we have been buried with him by baptism into death, so that, just as Christ was raised from the dead by the glory of the Father, so we too might walk in newness of life. For if we have been united with him in a death like his, we will certainly be united with him in a resurrection like his. (Romans 6.3–5)

Through faith, we are united with Jesus Christ. *His* story becomes *our* story. We will share in his death, just as we hope to share in his resurrection – putting to death an older way of being, so that a new one can rise in its place. "Conversion" is about stepping out of our old story and becoming part of a new story.

Yet the symbolism of baptism goes further than this. Early Church writers pointed out how baptism was a reminder of the exodus from Egypt. It established a connection between God's initial act of delivering Israel from bondage in Egypt and God's subsequent act of delivering humanity from bondage to sin. The third-century theologian Tertullian made this point as follows:[1]

> The people of Israel, having been set free from bondage, escaped the violence of the Egyptian king by crossing over through water. Furthermore, it was water that destroyed the king himself, with his entire forces.

Baptism is thus a reminder of this earlier great act of redemption, which is seen as prefiguring the greater act of redemption achieved through the death and resurrection of Christ. Once more, we are connected with a story that is part of our family tree and family heritage.

Remembering and anticipating

As we have seen, the journey of faith is sustained by *memory* on the one hand and *anticipation* on the other. These are like two magnetic poles, constantly drawing us towards them so that our present is constantly nourished by informing memories of our past and inspiring expectations of our future. We must not collapse these different movements, allowing ourselves simply to dream of the future or become nostalgically fixated on the past.

So does one of these movements take priority? In my view, we need to look back before we can look ahead. Let me explain why. To look back on Good Friday is to remind and reassure ourselves that God has dealt with sin. It is, so to speak, finished business; something whose power and lure can be locked into the past, unable to hurt us in the present. We can repent of our sins, knowing that the power of sin itself has been fatally eroded. And being reassured of these things, we can return to the present and anticipate the future, knowing that neither can be destroyed or defaced by the lingering influence of the past. Our past sins are cast into the depths of the sea (Micah 7.19), where they can no longer reach or harm us, allowing us to start all over again.

During its period of wandering in the wilderness of Sinai, Israel looked back to its deliverance from Egypt, and remembered the faithfulness of the God who had called it into being. Yet Israel also looked ahead with an eager hope to the final entry into the land which flowed with milk and honey. As Israel struggled during its long period of wandering through the wilderness, these anchors secured its faith in times of doubt, when some wanted to return to the safety and security of Egypt, fearing uncertainty about their future.

Living between the times, poised in the present in that most delicate interplay of past and future, was no easy matter for Israel, and it remains challenging for Christians today. It is like a trapeze artist who lets go of the security of one bar and soars through the air, poised to catch the next support. Each of the trapeze bars offers security, yet for a moment the artist is not supported by anything. She is suspended in an act of faith. The Christian life on earth is like those mid-air moments – moments of uncertainty and risk which are only finally resolved when we take hold of what lies ahead of us, and grasp it securely and irreversibly.

As Christians, we are invited to remember and anticipate, allowing the past and the future to break into our present life of faith and enwrap it, just as an alpine valley is enfolded by the mountains on either side. In the past, we remember the great act of redemption in which God delivered us from sin, death and despair through the cross and resurrection of Jesus Christ. And in the future, we anticipate our final entry into the new Jerusalem, to be with God for ever and find safety and peace in the presence of the risen Christ.

God's love is demonstrated in God's actions. To speak of the love of God is also to speak of the deeds of God which demonstrate, confirm and embody that love. Remembering and reflecting on God's past actions thus enables us to appreciate that faithfulness, and trust in it for the future. The God to whom both Old and New Testaments bear witness is the same God with whom we have to deal today. *Remembering what God has done allows us to anticipate what God will do.*

We see this pattern also in the Eucharist, Lord's Supper, or Communion service (to note only three of the many ways in which Christians refer to the sacrament of bread and wine). In the first place, this is about remembering something that happened in the past – the Last Supper, in which Christ broke bread and drank wine with his inmost group of disciples:

> While they were eating, Jesus took a loaf of bread, and after blessing it he broke it, gave it to the disciples, and said, 'Take, eat; this is my body.' Then he took a cup, and after giving thanks he gave it to them, saying, 'Drink from it, all of you; for this is my blood of the covenant, which is poured out for many for the forgiveness of sins. I tell you, I will never again drink of this fruit of the vine until that day when I drink it new with you in my Father's kingdom.'   (Matthew 26.26–29)

Paul's letters in the New Testament make it clear that the first Christians maintained this practice, seeing it as something they were commanded to do in memory of Jesus Christ:

> For I received from the Lord what I also handed on to you, that the Lord Jesus on the night when he was betrayed took a loaf of bread, and when he had given thanks, he broke it and said, 'This is my body that is for you. Do this in remembrance of me.' In the same way he took the cup also, after supper, saying, 'This cup is the new covenant in my blood. Do this, as often as you drink it, in remembrance of me.'   (1 Corinthians 11.23–25)

Yet this memory goes back much further. Three of the four Gospels – Matthew, Mark and Luke – represent the Last Supper as a Passover meal. Christ and his disciples were thus recalling the exodus from Egypt, reaffirming their links with a past act of divine deliverance – which Christ would subsequently extend and enrich through his death and resurrection. At several points in the New Testament, Jesus is linked with the Passover lamb. For example, John the Baptist proclaims Jesus to be 'the Lamb of God' (John 1.29), and Peter links the Passover lamb with Jesus, whom he describes as a 'lamb without defect or blemish' (Exodus 12.5; 1 Peter 1.19).

Yet in addition to recalling these rich historical memories and associations, the bread and the wine also invite us to look forward, anticipating being present at the 'marriage supper of the Lamb' (Revelation 19.6–9). We are invited to look both backwards to the foundational events of our faith and forwards to their final consummation in the new Jerusalem. The Lord's Supper is thus an anticipatory meal that we eat on the Road while looking forward to the marriage supper of the Lamb in the place of our final habitation (Revelation 19.9).

The creeds aim to provide us with a series of pegs on which we can hang these memories of the past and allow them to become anticipations of the future. They prevent us from being trapped in the present moment, by inviting us to look backwards and forwards, remembering what has happened and looking ahead to what will happen. Yet paradoxically, the creeds help us to appreciate the *value* of that same present moment. We come to realize that our present is part of a seamless fabric of God's presence in people's lives, not some lifeless point on a map of the history of the universe. Each of us has a role to play now in the continuing 'story of Holy Scripture, which unfolds each day' (Jean-Pierre de Caussade).

The sacraments and the Christian life

So how do the sacraments help us journey on a Road so often shrouded in shadow and mist? How do they speak into the uncertainty we so often experience as wayfarers along this Road, who are unable to stand on the Balcony above and see the bigger picture which makes sense of our journey? I have always found some lines in Matthew Arnold's 'Stanzas from the Grande Chartreuse' helpful in thinking about believers as wayfarers, wandering from one world to another. Arnold sensed that he was[2]

> Wandering between two worlds, one dead,
> the other powerless to be born,
> with nowhere yet to lay my head.

Arnold found himself caught up in the tension between a settled past world of faith and an unknown future, in which faith might seem to be little more than a 'dead time's exploded dream'. The ancient monastery which prompted his thoughts seemed to belong to an alien world, something whose faith might be admired but was no longer shared. Arnold felt he did not really belong anywhere, caught up in the painful tension between a dead past and the uncertainties of the future.

Many Christians feel a similar tension in their lives as they journey on the Road. We seem caught between two worlds – the world that we now know and inhabit, and the unseen world that we believe we will one day enter. We are passing through one world, which is not our home, on our way to another, which is where we truly belong. We are sojourners and pilgrims here on earth, travelling to the new Jerusalem. We travel in faith and hope, believing that our true destiny lies in heaven, where the risen Christ has gone before us.

Yet the sacraments help us cope with this uncertainty. First, they remind us of our family history, and allow us to reach back into our past for encouragement, illumination and inspiration. The people of God – *our* people, *our* family – have been in such situations before. We can learn from them. The people of Israel journeyed through the wilderness on their way from slavery in Egypt to the promised land. We were there too. And as they journeyed, they marked the great event of the Passover, which spoke of their memory of liberation and their hope of settling in a land full of milk and honey. We were there too.

Second, they remind us that our own individual stories are connected with other stories – grander stories – straddling the two maps of history and theology. Receiving bread and wine is a token of something greater, by which we choose to allow our stories to become part of the greater story of God. They become symbols of membership, keys to the gate of a story-shaped world. We gain meaning, value and a sense of location in history by seeing the great events of the exodus and the redemption of the world through Christ as part of our own story.

As we travel on the Road, we are reminded both of where that Road started and where it will finish. Like seasoned travellers, we may carry with us some items that bear witness to our origins, and others that are harbingers of our future destination. Our own story is set in a context of other stories of faith – of those who have travelled this Road before us, and coped with its uncertainties and dilemmas. We are surrounded by a great cloud of witnesses, who have made this journey before us, and whose memory encourages us to anticipate our own arrival into the new Jerusalem. We thus travel in hope.

This naturally leads us to reflect more on this Christian hope, and how this suffuses the life of faith.

17

Eternal life: the hope of the new Jerusalem

———— ◆ ————

Back in the 1960s, I was drawn to Marxism. Why? I think there were two main reasons for this. One of them was that it offered a 'big picture' of reality, which I found intellectually exciting. The philosopher Mary Midgley suggests that Marxism – one of the great secular faiths of our day – is a 'large-scale, ambitious system of thought' which displays 'religious-looking features'. I admired the depth of its engagement with reality. It was only later that I discovered that Christianity rivalled it in terms of its ability to offer an intelligible and coherent account of reality, while offering a deeper level of engagement with questions of human meaning and purpose.

The other thing that attracted me to Marxism was its no-nonsense insistence that we ought to engage with our world, and make it a better place. Marx talked about religion as the 'opium of the people', meaning that it dulled people's interest in doing something about changing the world. Marxists tended to see the reference to 'life everlasting' in the Apostles' Creed as little more than a crass escapist delusion that focused attention on a mythical world, and thus distracted people from the tasks and concerns of the real world.

At the time, I thought Marx was right. Now I think he failed to grasp the all-important point that the Christian vision of heaven gives us both a template and a motivation to change this world. If heaven is a place where there is no more suffering, why should we not try to make earth more like heaven? When rightly understood, the Christian conception of heaven is actually a stimulus to social action, medical research and relief work. 'The Christians who did most for the present world were just those who thought most of the next' (C. S. Lewis).[1]

So how are we meant to think about heaven? Perhaps this is the wrong question. Perhaps we ought to ask how we are meant to *visualize* heaven. The New Testament is more concerned with helping us to *see* heaven in our mind's eye than with understanding it through our reason. We are invited to grasp the reality of heaven through our imagination, by reflecting on biblical images. Two of these are of especial importance: the image of a city, and that of a garden. In what follows, we will explore these two images, and consider how they illuminate the Christian hope.

The new Jerusalem

'I saw the holy city, the new Jerusalem' (Revelation 21.2). These words from the final book of the Bible set out a vision of heaven which has long captivated the Christian imagination. To speak of heaven is to affirm that the human longing to *see* God will one day be fulfilled. One of Israel's greatest psalmists asks to be granted the privilege of being able to gaze upon 'the beauty of the LORD' in the land of the living (Psalm 27.4) – to be able to catch a glimpse of the face of God in the midst of the ambiguities and sorrows of this life. We see God but dimly in this life; yet, as Paul argued in his first letter to the Corinthian Christians, we shall one day see God 'face to face' (1 Corinthians 13.12).

The image of the 'new Jerusalem' has exercised a powerful influence over Christian literature and art down the centuries. It is found towards the end of the book of Revelation, an important and difficult work which is generally agreed to reflect the social exclusion or persecution faced by Christians in the later years of the reign of the emperor Domitian, around the year AD 90.

> Then I saw a new heaven and a new earth; for the first heaven and the first earth had passed away, and the sea was no more. And I saw the holy city, the new Jerusalem, coming down out of heaven from God, prepared as a bride adorned for her husband. And I heard a loud voice from the throne saying, 'See, the home of God is among mortals. He will dwell with them; they will be

his people, and God himself will be with them; he will wipe every tear from their eyes. Death will be no more; mourning and crying and pain will be no more, for the first things have passed away.' And the one who was seated on the throne said, 'See, I am making all things new.' (Revelation 21.1–5)

The consolation of heaven is here contrasted with the suffering, tragedy and pain of life on the Road.

The new Jerusalem does not contain a temple (Revelation 21.22). The cultic hierarchies of the priestly tradition of ancient Israel are no longer needed. All are now priests, and there is no need for a temple, in that God dwells within the city as a whole. In a remarkable transformation of images, the city has itself become a temple, in that God is now all in all. Where Old Testament prophets had yearned for the rebuilding of the Temple, the book of Revelation declares that it has become redundant. What it foreshadowed has now taken place.

This image of heaven resonates strongly with one of the leading themes of Paul's theology, which we touched on earlier – that Christians are to be regarded as 'citizens of heaven' (cf. Philippians 3.19–21). Paul makes a distinction between those who 'set their minds on earthly things' and those whose citizenship is 'in heaven'. Paul himself was a Roman citizen, who knew what privileges this brought – particularly on those occasions when he found himself in conflict with the Roman authorities. For Paul, Christians possessed something greater: the 'citizenship of heaven', which is to be understood as a present possession, not something which is yet to come.

While believers have yet to enter into the full possession of what this citizenship entails, they already possess that status, and have access to the benefits it confers. We have no permanent citizenship in this world, in that our citizenship is in heaven (Philippians 3.20). As the author of the Letter to the Hebrews puts it, 'here we have no lasting city, but we are looking for the city that is to come' (Hebrews 13.14).

The theme of the new Jerusalem is here integrated with motifs drawn from the Genesis creation accounts – such as the presence of the 'tree of life' (Revelation 22.2) – which suggests that heaven can be seen as the restoration of the bliss of Eden, when God dwelt with humanity in harmony. The pain, sorrow and evil of a fallen world have finally passed away, and the creation has been restored to how it was originally intended.

The Christian hope is thus partly framed in terms of the restoration of Eden, inviting us to think of heaven as a renewed paradise. While we usually speak of the 'Garden of Eden', it is perhaps better to think of 'Eden' as the region in which the garden is located, rather than the name of the garden itself. Other biblical passages designate the garden in other manners – such as the 'garden of God' (Ezekiel 28.13) or the 'garden of the LORD' (Isaiah 51.3). The garden rapidly became a symbol of innocence and harmony, a place of peace, rest and fertility. The powerful imagery of the four rivers that permanently watered the rich ground and its opulent plant and animal life served as a stimulus to the imagination of Christian writers.

From the earliest stage, the word 'paradise' came to be associated with a series of qualities which ensured that it became a central theme in the Christian account of heaven. Paradise was seen, like the Garden of Eden, as a place of fertility and harmony, where humanity dwelt in peace with nature and 'walked with God'. That idyllic state had been lost at the dawn of human history, with the expulsion of humanity from paradise. The hope of restoration of this paradisiacal relationship has become a core aspect of Christian understandings of the consequences of the resurrection of Christ.

So how should we respond to the hope of heaven? In what follows, I shall look at two well-known writers who engage this theme – J. R. R. Tolkien and C. S. Lewis. Tolkien is the less explicitly Christian of these two writers, often wearing his faith lightly. But, as we shall see, there are points in his epic fantasy trilogy *The Lord of the Rings* where the theme of the hope of heaven shines through.

J. R. R. Tolkien on hope in a dark world

I was asked to preach at a special service at Merton College, Oxford, to mark its 750th anniversary in 2014. I was a senior scholar at Merton from 1976 to 1978, and was delighted to be asked back to my old college for this landmark event. It is always good to mark special occasions, and think more deeply about their importance. In its long and distinguished history, Merton College had passed through times of light and darkness. The year 2014 marked the centenary of the outbreak of the First World War, an event which called into question the all-too-easy assumption that human beings were essentially rational and good. Those four years of brutal conflict were a dark time for this Oxford college – as they were for the British nation and far beyond. How, many asked, could we keep going in such dark times? What hope was there for us to hold on to?

That need for hope remains important to all of us. At Christmas, many Christians return to a reading from the prophet Isaiah (Isaiah 40.1–8). 'Comfort, O comfort my people, says your God.' They are words familiar to many of us, not least because they open Handel's great oratorio *The Messiah*, widely performed at this time of year. Those words speak to us today, just as they spoke deeply to their original audience – the people of Jerusalem in exile in Babylon, far from their homeland. Would they ever return home? Those too were dark times. And in the midst of that darkness, Isaiah spoke words of comfort and hope. God had not forgotten the people of Jerusalem. They would return home! That hope sustained them as they waited for their liberation. Yes, they were still in exile. But now they had hope for the future.

We still need hope. Not a naïve and shallow optimism, but a robust and secure confidence that there is something good – there is *someone* good – who will triumph over despair and hopelessness. Many felt the need for that hope during the First World War – including J. R. R. Tolkien, then a second lieutenant in the Lancashire Fusiliers, who took part in the Battle of the Somme, and went on to become a fellow of Merton College in 1945. Tolkien's epic work *The Lord of the Rings* was written and published during his time as Merton Professor of English at Oxford University.

The Lord of the Rings is now widely regarded as one of the great works of English literature. One of its most distinctive themes is the reality of evil. Tolkien names evil, thus giving us

permission to challenge the bland and inadequate moral out-
look of our age, which insists we respect everything and criticize
nothing. Like his close friend C. S. Lewis, Tolkien was convinced
that we had lost the moral vocabulary that enabled us to speak
of evil, and thus to fight it.

But that is not the only theme we find so powerfully explored
in Tolkien's epic work. It affirms the role of the weak and power-
less in changing the world for the better. That's why Hobbits –
such as Frodo Baggins and his sidekick Samwise Gamgee, also
known as 'Sam' – are so important in the narrative of *The Lord of
the Rings*. They are the little people, and in the end they are the
ones who make the difference. They may feel they are part of a
story that is too big for them, yet they grow to take up their places
within it. It's easy to feel overwhelmed by a sense of despair and
powerlessness as we contemplate a world that we seem incapable
of redirecting towards the good. Yet, as Tolkien so clearly saw,
we need a vision of the good and a sense of empowerment in
the midst of our weakness if anything is to be changed.

Many feel that one of the most powerful themes affirmed by
Tolkien in *The Lord of the Rings* is the reality of the Christian
hope in the midst of despair and seeming helplessness. We see
this especially in a narrative passage which is found towards the
end of *The Lord of the Rings*, at a moment when the victory of
the forces of darkness seems assured:[2]

> There, peeping among the cloud-wrack above a dark tor high up
> in the mountains, Sam saw a white star twinkle for a while. The
> beauty of it smote his heart, as he looked up out of the forsaken
> land, and hope returned to him. For like a shaft, clear and cold,
> the thought pierced him that in the end the Shadow was only a
> small and passing thing: there was light and high beauty for ever
> beyond its reach.

Tolkien's subtle reworking of the imagery of the 'star of
Bethlehem' affirms the resilience of hope in God in the face
of a darkening world of fading human dreams. That's the kind of
hope that kept the people of Jerusalem going during their time
of exile. Their God was beyond the reach of human tyranny and
oppression, and one day things would change. That's the hope

that keeps many of us going as well – the thought that there is something beyond this world of suffering and pain, which we will one day enter and embrace. This theme is powerfully expressed in the New Testament's vision of the new Jerusalem, a world in which God has made everything anew, and there is no more sorrow, pain or death.

But there is another theme in *The Lord of the Rings* that speaks powerfully to us today as we reflect on the sobering and harsh realities of a world darkened by terror and violence. As the work nears its end, the victory of evil seems inevitable. A dark mood settles over the narrative. And then everything changes. An unexpected event enables the ring to be destroyed, breaking the power of evil. Tolkien called this a *eucatastrophe* – a dramatic, unexpected event that disrupts a narrative of despair, and redirects it towards the good.

For Tolkien, the best and greatest example of this radical upheaval of a story of hopelessness is the resurrection of Christ – a dramatic event that brought first astonishment and then hope; a real hope, grounded in something and someone trustworthy. That is the hope that is to be seized and acted upon, which keeps us going and keeps us growing even in the darkest of times. The Christian hope of heaven raises our horizons and elevates our expectations, inviting us to behave on earth in the light of this greater reality. The true believer is not someone who disengages with this world in order to focus on heaven, but someone who tries to make this world more like heaven.

Tolkien – one of the twentieth century's most subtle Christian writers – needs to be heard here. One of the central themes of the Christian tradition is the need for a warranted hope in a faithful God in sustaining us and inspiring us. 'The grass withers, the flower fades; but the word of our God will stand forever' (Isaiah 40.8). That hope in God, like Sam's vision of 'light and high beauty', can never be taken away from us. The world around us is changing – and not for the better. Many of us feel that the optimism of an earlier generation has now receded. We are facing hard questions, difficult times and uncertainties about the future. But we must not despair. 'The word of our God will stand forever' – and we will stand with it.

C. S. Lewis on the hope of heaven

An American colleague who was visiting Oxford went to see Lewis's grave in the churchyard of Holy Trinity, Headington Quarry, on the outskirts of Oxford. Afterwards, he came to visit me in my Oxford college. Over a cup of tea, we discussed the somewhat forbidding Shakespearean epitaph which adorns Lewis's gravestone: 'Men must endure their going hence.' My friend was puzzled. The inscription seemed to speak of a passive recognition of the inevitability of death. It was an affirmation of human mortality, rather than a celebration of the hope of heaven. Wasn't Lewis meant to be a Christian? So why this melancholy motto, more suggestive of a defiant Stoicism than a joyful Christianity?

Now the text in question was actually chosen by Lewis's elder brother, Warren, who lived with Lewis in Oxford until his death. It had been the 'text for the day' on the family calendar for the day of their mother's death from cancer in 1908, when Lewis was 9 years old. Its grim realism came to express the views of the young Lewis, who became an aggressive atheist as a young man, especially when serving as an infantry officer in the Great War. Where was God in the midst of the carnage he saw all around him?

Yet this proved to be a phase, not a resting place. Lewis's gradual move away from atheism towards Christianity reflected his growing realization that atheism lacked real intellectual substance, and seemed imaginatively impoverished. Lewis had been haunted by a deep intuition that there had to be more to life than what his minimalist atheism allowed. Above all, he found himself reflecting on the implications of a deep and elusive sense of longing, which was heightened rather than satisfied by what he found around him.

Lewis famously termed this experience of yearning 'Joy', and came to the conclusion that it pointed to something beyond the boundaries of human knowledge and experience. 'If I find in myself a desire which no experience in this world can satisfy, the most probable explanation is that I was made for another world.'[3] Lewis concluded that if there were a transcendent realm beyond us – what Christians call 'heaven' – this would make sense of what he experienced within him and observed around him.

For Lewis, heaven was to be thought of as a realm beyond the limits of present human experience, yet which was signposted by our deepest intuitions and experiences. It was like hearing the sound of music faintly, coming from across the distant hills. Or catching the scent of a far-off flower, wafted by a passing breeze. Lewis came to see such experiences as 'arrows of Joy', a wake-up call to discover and experience a deeper vision of reality.

Many scholars think that Lewis's early way of thinking about heaven was perhaps Platonic as much as it was Christian. It was a sense-making device – like Plato's world of ideals – which affirmed the coherence of the world of thought and experience. As Lewis himself put it at that time, 'It matters more that Heaven should exist than that we should ever get there.'[4]

Yet by the 1940s, Lewis had embraced a deeper vision of heaven. While he never lost sight of the idea that the concept of heaven helps us make sense of what we experience and observe on earth, the idea of entering heaven and experiencing its joy became increasingly important to him. For Lewis, this world is God's world, and is to be valued, appreciated and enjoyed. Yet it is studded with clues that it is not our real home; that there is a still better world beyond its frontiers; and that one may dare to hope to enter and inhabit this better place.

Lewis affirms the delight, joy and purposefulness of this present life. Yet he asks us to realize that when this finally comes to an end, something even better awaits us. Lewis believed that the secular world offers people only a hopeless end, and he wanted them to see and grasp the endless hope of the Christian faith, and live in its light. Perhaps some words of Jewel the Unicorn in *The Last Battle*, the concluding novel of the Chronicles of Narnia series, capture this point particularly well. 'I have come home at last! This is my real country! I belong here. This is the land I have been looking for all my life, though I never knew it till now.'[5] For Lewis, the Christian hope is about returning home to where we really belong.

Does this mean that Lewis exults in death? Is he a 'world-denying' writer, who treats this world as devoid of value? No.

2

Like countless spiritual writers before him, Lewis declares that the hope of heaven enables us to see this world in its true perspective. This life is the preparation for that greater realm – the title page of the 'Great Story'.

So how does this way of thinking relate to the Christian story of the death and resurrection of Jesus Christ? While Lewis's writings show him to have had a good grasp of basic Christian theological themes by 1940, his appreciation of their existential depth seems to have emerged later. His *Grief Observed* (1961) incorporates the suffering of Christ on Good Friday into his reflections on his wife's slow and lingering death from cancer, leading him to a deeper grasp of the ability of the Christian faith to support people in times of bewilderment and suffering.

In much the same way, Lewis's later realization that he himself was dying from cancer seems to have prompted a more profound reflection on the meaning of Christ's resurrection. In some of his letters in the final months of his illness, Lewis spoke of the hope that he had in the face of death. He was, he wrote, 'a seed waiting in the good earth: waiting to come up a flower in the Gardener's good time, up into the *real* world, the real waking'.[6] While Lewis's gravestone might speak of our shared mortality, his works and his witness point to something more profound – hope in a greater reality and a better realm, the door to which is thrown open by the death and resurrection of Jesus Christ.

The Christian hope and the life of faith

So how does this Christian vision of hope affect our lives? What difference do these beliefs make to us as we make the journey of faith? Christianity provides us with a map of reality, which helps us to realize that we are sojourners and pilgrims here on earth, whose intended destination is the new Jerusalem. This theological perspective helps us make sense of our deep feeling, sometimes experienced with a heartbreaking intensity, that we really belong somewhere else – even if that place is unknown, and possibly unknowable.

G. K. Chesterton knew this sense of metaphysical disquiet well, and expressed it pithily in one of his neatest aphorisms. 'We have come to the wrong star ... That is what makes life at once so splendid and so strange. The true happiness is that we don't fit. We come from somewhere else. We have lost our way.'[7]

The great missionary theologian Stephen Charles Neill regarded orthodox Christian belief as 'poised on the knife edge of two great errors'. It had to defend and inhabit a narrow region between two positions, each appealing in its own way, yet leading to a loss of a core element of the Christian hope. On the one hand, there are those who think of 'the world as evil' and our bodies as the 'seat of sin'. On the other lies the 'glorification of this world in and for itself'.[8]

For Neill, we have to think of this world as a 'ladder of ascent' through which we gradually make our way towards a world in which the enigmas and riddles of this world are resolved, and we finally come into the presence of God. There is nothing that is intrinsically evil about this world; it is simply that it pales and fades in the light of the greater vision of reality to which we are called and invited, which shows our present world to be but a shadow or echo of this higher realm.

Christians travel in faith and hope, knowing in their hearts (while trusting in their minds) that their true destiny lies where the risen Christ has gone before them. Their earthly lives are but rough sketches of what they shall be. They are in exile on earth, but know they will one day return home. It is a theme familiar to many through the great medieval hymn of Peter Abelard:

> Now, in the meantime, with hearts raised on high,
> We for that country must yearn and must sigh,
> Seeking Jerusalem, dear native land,
> Through the long exile on Babylon's strand.

It is a theme that spoke to many struggling to cope with the ambiguities of life during this bygone age, and is echoed in other writers of that time. In his 'Prayer to Christ', Anselm of Canterbury wrestles with his longing to be with Christ in heaven, which heightens his sense of sadness at not yet being with Christ. He is reduced to tears through the pain of being exiled from his true homeland, while at the same time experiencing hope and encouragement that he will one day be with Christ in heaven.

As Anselm's prayer suggests, one of the great themes of Christian spirituality has been the thought of finally entering heaven, and seeing God face to face (1 Corinthians 13.12). This thought sustains us as we journey on the Road. The psalmist set out his passionate, informed longing to see God in these words (Psalm 27.4, NIV 1984):

> One thing I ask of the LORD,
> This is what I seek:
> That I may dwell in the house of the LORD
> All the days of my life,
> To gaze upon the beauty of the LORD.

The Christian vision of heaven affirms that what the psalmist longed for all his life will one day be the common privilege of the entire people of God – to gaze upon the face of their Lord and Saviour, as they enter into his house to dwell in peace for ever. As John Donne once put it: 'No man ever saw God and lived. And yet, I shall not live till I see God; and when I have seen him, I shall never die.'

Conclusion: journeying in hope in an age of anxiety

None of us ever asked to be born. So, whether we like it or not, we find ourselves living in this strange world of space and time, trying to work out why we are here and what we are meant to be doing. We find ourselves drifting on a misty grey sea of ignorance, hoping that we might discover and inhabit an island of certainty on which all our deepest questions will be answered with total certainty and absolute clarity.

Yet this island does not exist. It is a figment of the human imagination, driven by our relentless longing for simplicity and certainty, and our seeming inability to cope with ambiguity and complexity. It is not as if Christians are alone in feeling uncertain or unsure about their beliefs. Everyone who believes anything worthwhile and takes the trouble to think about things – including atheists, Marxists or secular humanists – will find themselves having to confront the vulnerability of their beliefs. We are all in the same boat. Existentially significant beliefs lie beyond proof, no matter what those beliefs might be.

Some unwisely hoped that the slick and assured slogans of the New Atheism of writers like Richard Dawkins and Christopher Hitchens reflected the certainties of a proven philosophy. Yet the New Atheism turned out to be nothing more than a particularly aggressive form of agnosticism, just as incapable of proving its basic beliefs as everyone else. Its followers unsuccessfully tried to deny and evade this inescapable truth by ridiculing their critics and asserting their beliefs with overwhelming rhetorical force. In the end, however, their supposed certainties merely crumbled, proving incapable of repelling the increasingly confident assaults of sceptics and critics.

Others seek refuge in what they think to be the cultural and social certainties of the past, lamenting their recent erosion. Yet

those certainties are now seen as crystallized cultural conven-
tions, sustained by social forces rather than intellectual necessity.
Others long for a return to the certainties of a religious past, too
easily overlooking the extent to which religion is shaped by its
cultural context.

We journey through life longing for certainty, while slowly
coming to realize that such certainty is only to be had in very
constrained and limited areas of human thought, which stand
at some distance from the realities of everyday life. While hoping to live on the basis of what we can prove, we have to decide
how to live on the basis of what we can trust.

Some simply retreat to what the eighteenth-century 'Age of
Reason' regarded as universal certainties, yet which many now
regard as merely the ethnocentric judgements of dead white
males who ought to have known better. The human situation is
one of having to determine what can be trusted, and living on
that basis. It is a matter of judgement and discernment, not of
demonstration and proof. So roaming the seas, seeking an island
of certainty and failing to find it, we find we have to settle instead
on an island of faith.

Coping with uncertainty, flourishing through faith

The history of Christianity is characterized by periods of crisis
and decay, as well as by periods of reconstruction and renewal.
We cannot freeze some moment in the history of faith, and
declare that it is permanently valid and normative. We do not
know whether we are in an age of decay or renewal; only future
historians can tell us that. We are on the Road, and have to make
our judgements and decisions as we travel, with only limited
perspectives available to us.

We can, however, take some comfort from knowing that
moments of crisis and change produce thinkers capable of opening
up approaches to the Christian faith which remain faithful to their
roots while engaging the present. We might think of Augustine
of Hippo, Blaise Pascal or C. S. Lewis, each of whom rose to the
challenges of the age, and forged a fresh vision of the life of faith,
rooted in history yet adapted to the needs of the moment.

Augustine set out his grand vision of the Christian faith as the civilized world of his day began to implode. The city of Rome – which had stood at the heart of the world's greatest and most stable empire for a thousand years – was on the brink of collapse. Pascal stood in the midst of the intellectual and social changes that ushered in the modern age. Lewis wrote at the end of this modern age, anticipating so much of what we now call post-modernity, but which future historians will probably know by another name.

All three saw the need for the recasting of the Church's theological vision; none saw the need for a loss of confidence, or an abandoning of the core beliefs of their faith. In an age of uncertainty and doubt, they were convinced that the Christian faith was to be trusted, and would bring security in the midst of social and cultural change. It was an island of stability in the midst of a tempestuous sea, offering resources for reconstruction and renewal in the future. We have much to learn from those, such as Marilynne Robinson, who have offered fresh visions of faith, rooted in the past yet open to the uncertainty of the future.

Christianity is not a religious ideology, appealing to the cold logic of reason. It is a vision of reality, a 'big picture', a 'grand story', which captures our imagination and expands our capacity to see and make sense of our world and our lives. It is a way of seeing things which, once grasped, opens up a new landscape of ideas and values. It is this vision that is embraced by the imagination, and percolates into our reason and emotions, as we begin to explore its content and assess its implications. And precisely because this is a vision of reality – not an ideology – it is best expressed and nourished by worship and adoration, which constantly seek to expand and enrich this vision, rather than close it down by reducing it to verbal formulae and dogmatic texts.

Those formulae and texts, however, are necessary. Indeed, this book uses the creeds to frame this vision of faith, even though the creeds themselves are – for entirely understandable reasons – not the most imaginatively or intellectually exciting documents. They are really a checklist for the core themes of faith, assimilated by the mind, not a substitute for the compelling vision of faith itself, which is embraced by the imagination.

Christian doctrine gives us this 'big picture', a way of seeing things that helps us make sense of what we observe around us and experience within us. I was drawn to Christianity partly because I sensed it allowed me to grasp and hold on to the intelligibility of our world, yet increasingly because it affirmed the *coherence* of our world. This point needs to be explored further.

Rediscovering a coherent world in an age of fragmentation

Christianity provides a web of meaning which affirms a deep belief in the fundamental interconnectedness of things. It's like standing on top of a mountain and looking down at a patchwork of villages, fields, streams and forests. We can take snapshots of everything we see. Yet what we really need is to apprehend the panorama that holds the snapshots together – a greater vision of reality that lets us see that there is indeed a single 'big picture', and that each of these little pictures has its place within that greater whole. The fear of many is that reality consists simply of isolated and disconnected episodes, incidents and observations, devoid of meaning.

Our modern age has seen doubts about the coherence of reality, many arising from the 'new philosophy' of the Scientific Revolution. Do new scientific ideas destroy any idea of a meaningful reality? The English poet John Donne articulated this concern in the early seventeenth century, as scientific discoveries seemed to some to erode any sense of connectedness and continuity within the world. ''Tis all in pieces, all coherence gone,' he wrote of this unsettling new world. How could it be held together?

We are not good at doing this joined-up thinking. In his dark poem *The Waste Land*, written in the period of trauma and upheaval following the First World War, T. S. Eliot lamented his incapacity to live out a coherent life in this age of uncertainty. He could connect 'nothing with nothing'. The world seemed to have collapsed into fragments, incapable of being pasted back together again. A framework of meaning was needed, capable of bringing our blurred vision into sharper focus, and allowing us to see the fundamental interconnectedness of all things.

Christians find this theme eloquently engaged in the New Testament, which speaks of all things 'holding together' or being 'knit together' in Christ (Colossians 1.17). There is a hidden web of meaning and connectedness behind the ephemeral and incoherent world that we experience. Christianity provides us with a reassurance of the *coherence of reality* – that however fragmented our world of experience may seem, there is a half-glimpsed 'bigger picture' which holds things together, its threads connecting together in a web of meaning what might otherwise seem incoherent and pointless. As might be expected, this is a major issue in Dante's *Divine Comedy*. As this poem draws to its close, Dante catches a glimpse of the unity of the cosmos, in which its multiple aspects and levels are seen to converge into a single whole.

Conclusion

This volume is an explorer's guide to the landscape of the Christian faith, which has tried to open up some of the great themes of the Christian creeds, considering how they act as signposts to greater truths and help shape the Christian life. We can learn from others who have travelled the Road before us and found these creeds to be helpful frameworks for their living faith. The creeds invite us to explore the landscape of faith, and draw us into a community of discovery and learning which crosses cultures and the centuries. They remind us that our God is not some vague and abstract 'supreme being', but a pilgrim God, who journeys with us on the Road.

We have no fixed place in history, and the cultural certainties of the past, which once seemed so stable and solid, are now seen as shifting sands, a witness to what was believed yesterday without any necessary connection with what will be believed tomorrow. Some Christians may seek security by retreating into the past, looking for an idealized gospel detached from the irritating contingencies of history. Yet it does not need to be like this, and ought not to be like this.

The Christian faith certainly invites us to look backwards – but not to find solace in an idealized past, but to ascertain how that past can offer us insight and wisdom as we contemplate our future. At the dawn of history, we find Abraham being called by God to leave behind his homeland, and journey to an unfamiliar distant land. He left behind his home and homeland, and forged his life of faith afresh in a strange new place, for which his past had left him unprepared. Similarly, Christ called his first disciples to leave behind their homes and their security, and journey with him. Their meaning and identity lay not in what they left behind, but in the one who stood in their midst on the Road.

We live in a time of displacement and exile, in which many feel that their past has lost its capacity to sustain them in the future, degenerating into a sterile nostalgia rather than becoming a generative source of wisdom for the journey. We are tempted to retreat into our places of security, and try to fortify them against future threats. Yet we are called to leave these, and learn to live with insecurity and uncertainty, realizing that the Christian tradition provides us with a rich 'big picture' which sets our situation in its proper context, and opens a gateway to authentic living on the Road.

Yet there is one section of the creeds that has remained unexamined thus far: their final word, 'Amen' – 'may it be so'. The creeds set out, imperfectly and incompletely, a vision of the Christian faith which we are invited to grasp in its fullness, and take delight in its cohesion and brilliance. The final 'Amen' of the creeds is simply a prayer that we might finally behold what is loved, trusted and hoped for, not simply because it confirms our faith, but because we enter into our heart's desire.

Perhaps we might fear that this is simply too good to be true. We cannot know for sure. Like all those who believe anything worthwhile, we are unable to prove this with total certainty to others, or even to ourselves. We nevertheless trust it, for good reasons, and journey in hope through this world of ambiguity and doubt.

We need a compelling vision like this to sustain us as we pass through this perplexing shadowy world. We are given a 'big picture' which affirms that the Road has both a direction and a destination – that it is going *somewhere*. We may be unable to rise above that Road and see the 'big picture' for ourselves – but we can trust that there is such a grander vision of our lives, giving us meaning and purpose as we travel on that Road.

And at this point, I must leave you to explore the landscape of faith further on your own. I have shared some of the ideas and approaches that I have found helpful as I first encountered it and began to make sense of its theological geography. It's time for me to stand back, and allow you to find other travelling companions who can enrich and further develop the basic toolkit I provide in this short work. You can easily work out who my companions have been, in case they might help you as well.

In my view, the best Christian theology always results from respecting and valuing those who have travelled the Road before us and left behind their jottings for the benefit of those who will follow them. They help us get more out of our reading of the Bible, encourage us in the life of faith, and share with us the hope of finally seeing our heart's desire in the new Jerusalem.

Appendix 1: The Apostles' Creed

I believe in God, the Father Almighty,
creator of heaven and earth.
I believe in Jesus Christ, his only Son, our Lord,
who was conceived by the Holy Spirit,
born of the Virgin Mary,
suffered under Pontius Pilate,
was crucified, died, and was buried;
he descended to the dead.
On the third day he rose again;
he ascended into heaven,
and is seated at the right hand of the Father,
and will come to judge the living and the dead.
I believe in the Holy Spirit,
the holy catholic Church,
the communion of saints,
the forgiveness of sins,
the resurrection of the body,
and the life everlasting.
Amen.

Appendix 2: The Nicene Creed

I believe in one God the Father Almighty,
maker of heaven and earth,
and of all things visible and invisible;
and in one Lord Jesus Christ, the only begotten Son of God,
begotten of his Father before all worlds,
God of God, Light of Light,
very God of very God,
begotten, not made,
being of one substance with the Father,
by whom all things were made;
who for us and for our salvation came down from heaven,
and was incarnate by the Holy Spirit of the Virgin Mary,
and was made man,
and was crucified also for us under Pontius Pilate.
He suffered and was buried,
and the third day he rose again according to the Scriptures,
and ascended into heaven,
and sits on the right hand of the Father.
And he shall come again with glory to judge both the quick and
the dead,
whose kingdom shall have no end.
And I believe in the Holy Spirit,
the Lord and giver of life,
who proceeds from the Father and the Son,
who with the Father and the Son together is worshipped and
glorified,
who spoke through the prophets.
And I believe one holy, catholic and apostolic Church.
I acknowledge one baptism for the remission of sins.
And I look for the resurrection of the dead,
and the life of the world to come.
Amen.

Notes

1 The discipleship of the mind: a journey of exploration

1 Bertrand Russell, *A History of Western Philosophy*. London: George Allen & Unwin Ltd, 1946, xiv.
2 Marcel Proust, *La prisonnière*. Paris: Gallimard, 1925, 69.
3 Augustine of Hippo, *Sermon* 38, 4–6.

2 The Christian faith: a map, lens, light and tapestry

1 John Ruskin, *Works*, edited by E. T. Cook and A. Wedderburn. 39 vols. London: Allen, 1903–12, vol. 5, 333.
2 Mary Midgley, *The Myths We Live By*. London: Routledge, 2004, 26–8.
3 C. S. Lewis, 'Is Theology Poetry?', in *C. S. Lewis: Essay Collection*, edited by Lesley Walmsley. London: HarperCollins, 2002, 21.
4 George Herbert, *Works*, edited by F. E. Hutchinson. Oxford: Clarendon Press, 1941, 184.
5 Joy Davidman, *Out of My Bone: The Letters of Joy Davidman*. Grand Rapids, MI: Eerdmans, 2009, 86.
6 Ludwig Wittgenstein, *Notebooks, 1914–1916*. New York: Harper, 1961, 75.
7 Iris Murdoch, *The Sovereignty of Good*. London: Routledge, 2001, 82.
8 Czesław Miłosz, 'The Discreet Charm of Nihilism', *New York Review of Books*, 19 November 1998.

3 A cloud of witnesses: why we need creeds

1 Ambrose of Milan, *An Explanation of the Creed*, 1.
2 C. S. Lewis, *An Experiment in Criticism*. Cambridge: Cambridge University Press, 1992, 137; 140–1.
3 *The Martyrdom of Justin*, 1.
4 John A. Mackay, *A Preface to Christian Theology*. London: Nisbet, 1942, 27–53.

4 What can be trusted? The nature of faith

1 Thomas Hobbes, *English Works*. 11 vols. London: Bohn, 1839–45, vol. 4, 227.
2 Ludwig Wittgenstein, *Tractatus Logico-Philosophicus*, 6.52.

3 G. K. Chesterton, *Autobiography*. New York: Sheed & Ward, 1936, 229.
4 Martin Luther, *Great Catechism* (1529), III.1.
5 C. T. Lewis and C. Short, *A Latin Dictionary*. Oxford: Oxford University Press, 1891, 479.
6 Faustus of Riez, *On the Holy Spirit*, I, 1.
7 Pierre Hadot, *What Is Ancient Philosophy?* Cambridge, MA: Harvard University Press, 2002, 3–4. Pierre Hadot, *Philosophy as a Way of Life: Spiritual Exercises from Socrates to Foucault*. Malden, MA: Blackwell, 1995, 49–70.
8 Emil Brunner, 'Toward a Missionary Theology'. *Christian Century* 66, no. 27 (1949): 816–18; quote at p. 816.
9 John Locke, *The Works of John Locke*. 10 vols. London: Thomas Tegg, 1823, vol. 8, p. 447.
10 John Locke, *Essay Concerning Human Understanding*, IV.3.29.
11 Alexander Pope, *Essay on Man*, II.17–18.
12 Thomas Nagel, *The View from Nowhere*. New York: Oxford University Press, 1986, 67–89.
13 G. K. Chesterton, *The Everlasting Man*. San Francisco, CA: Ignatius Press, 1993, 105.

8 The enigma of humanity: the climax of God's creation

1 Augustine of Hippo, *Expositions of Psalms 99–120*, III, 19.

10 Incarnation: God with us

1 Dorothy L. Sayers, *Creed or Chaos?* London: Methuen, 1947, 32–5.
2 *The Rubáiyát of Omar Khayyám*, translated by Edward Fitzgerald. London: De La Mare Press, 1925, 31.
3 Letter to Arthur Greeves, 18 October, 1931, in *The Collected Letters of C. S. Lewis*, edited by Walter Hooper. 3 vols. San Francisco, CA: HarperOne, 2004–6, vol. 1, 976.
4 C. S. Lewis, 'The Grand Miracle', in *C. S. Lewis: Essay Collection*, edited by Lesley Walmsley. London: Collins, 2000, 3–9.
5 Abraham Pais, *J. Robert Oppenheimer: A Life*. Oxford: Oxford University Press, 2006, 90.
6 Athanasius, *On the Incarnation of the Word of God*, 8.

11 Atonement: putting things right

1 G. K. Chesterton, *The Everlasting Man*. San Francisco, CA: Ignatius Press, 1993, 211.
2 Frederick Buechner, *The Magnificent Defeat*. San Francisco, CA: HarperOne, 1986, 91.

12 Suffering: the shadow of the cross

1 Humphrey Carpenter, *W. H. Auden: A Biography*. Boston, MA: Houghton Mifflin Co., 1981, 282–3.
2 Gabriel Marcel, *Être et avoir*. Paris: Éditions Montaigne, 1935.
3 Tomáš Halík, *Night of the Confessor: Christian Faith in an Age of Uncertainty*. New York: Image Books, 2012, 19.
4 C. S. Lewis, *Mere Christianity*. London: HarperCollins, 2002, 38.
5 Richard Dawkins, *River out of Eden: A Darwinian View of Life*. London: Phoenix, 1995, 133.
6 Friedrich Nietzsche, *Götzen-Dämmerung: oder Wie man mit dem Hammer philosophiert*. Munich: Hanser, 1954, 7.

13 The Spirit of grace: being helped to flourish

1 C. S. Lewis, *Mere Christianity*. London: HarperCollins, 2002, 176–7.
2 John Calvin, *Institutes of the Christian Religion*, III.ii.7.

14 When words fail: exploring the Trinity

1 *The Life and Letters of Charles Darwin*, edited by F. Darwin. 3 vols. London: John Murray, 1887, vol. 2, 155.
2 Marilynne Robinson, *Gilead*. London: Virago, 2005, 203.
3 Werner Heisenberg, *Die Ordnung der Wirklichkeit*. Munich: Piper Verlag, 1989, 44.
4 For what follows, see C. S. Lewis, *Mere Christianity*. London: HarperCollins, 2002, 163.
5 C. S. Lewis, 'The Poison of Subjectivism', in *C. S. Lewis: Essay Collection*, edited by Lesley Walmsley. London: HarperCollins, 2001, 664.
6 I have borrowed this approach from Robert W. Jenson, *The Triune Identity: God According to the Gospel*. Philadelphia: Fortress, 1982.

15 The community of faith: why the Church matters

1 Augustine of Hippo, *Sermon* 88, 5.
2 C. S. Lewis, *Mere Christianity*. London: HarperCollins, 2002, 165.
3 John of Salisbury, *Metalogicon*, III, 4.
4 Cyprian of Carthage, *On the Unity of the Catholic Church*, 6.

16 Signs of God's presence: reassurance and affirmation

1 Tertullian, *On Baptism*, I, 9.
2 Matthew Arnold, *Poems*. London: Macmillan, 1878, 338.

17 Eternal life: the hope of the new Jerusalem

1 C. S. Lewis, *Mere Christianity*. London: HarperCollins, 2002, 134.
2 J. R. R. Tolkien, *The Return of the King*. London: George Allen & Unwin, 1966, 199.
3 C. S. Lewis, *Mere Christianity*. London: HarperCollins, 2002, 136–7.
4 C. S. Lewis, *Surprised by Joy*. London: HarperCollins, 2002, 258.
5 C. S. Lewis, *The Last Battle*. London: HarperCollins, 2004, 171.
6 Letter to Mary Willis Shelburne, 28 June 1963; *Letters*, vol. 3, 1434.
7 G. K. Chesterton, *Tremendous Trifles*. London: Methuen, 1909, 209.
8 Stephen Neill, *Belief: Lectures Delivered at the Kodaikanal Missionary Conference, 1937*. Madras: Christian Literature Society for India, 1939, 85–8.

For further reading

The following are useful studies of the creeds and some of their themes:

Hans Urs von Balthasar, *Credo: Meditations on the Apostles' Creed*. San Francisco: Ignatius Press, 2000.

William Barclay, *The Apostles' Creed for Everyman*. New York: Harper & Row, 1967.

Karl Barth, *Dogmatics in Outline*. London: SCM Press, 1960.

Justo González, *The Apostles' Creed for Today*. Louisville, KY: Westminster John Knox Press, 2007.

Roger van Harn, ed., *Exploring and Proclaiming the Apostles' Creed*. Grand Rapids, MI: Eerdmans, 2004.

Brian Hebblethwaite, *The Essence of Christianity: A Fresh Look at the Nicene Creed*. London: SPCK, 1996.

Luke Timothy Johnson, *The Creed: What Christians Believe and Why It Matters*. New York: Doubleday, 2003.

J. N. D. Kelly, *Early Christian Creeds*. 3rd edn. New York: Continuum, 2006.

Hans Küng, *Credo: The Apostles' Creed Explained for Today*. London: SCM Press, 2000.

C. S. Lewis, *Mere Christianity*. London: Collins, 2002.

Henri de Lubac, *The Christian Faith: An Essay on the Structure of the Apostles' Creed*. San Francisco: Ignatius Press, 1986.

Herbert McCabe, *The Teaching of the Catholic Church: A New Catechism of Christian Doctrine*. London: Darton, Longman, and Todd, 2000.

Oliver C. Quick, *Doctrines of the Creed: Their Basis in Scripture and Their Meaning Today*. London: Nisbet, 1938.

Dorothy L. Sayers, *Creed or Chaos?* London: Methuen, 1947.

J. S. Whale, *Christian Doctrine*. Cambridge: Cambridge University Press, 1941.

Rowan Williams, *Tokens of Trust: An Introduction to Christian Belief*. Norwich: Canterbury Press, 2007.

David Willis, *Clues to the Nicene Creed: A Brief Outline of the Faith*. Grand Rapids, MI: Eerdmans, 2005.

Tom Wright, *Simply Christian*. London: SPCK, 2006.

Frances Young, *The Making of the Creeds*. London: SCM, 2002.

If you would like to study Christian theology as a way of taking the themes of this book further, you might like to try these best-selling introductions, both of which can be used without the need for a teacher:

Alister E. McGrath, *Christian Theology: An Introduction.* 6th edn. Oxford and Malden, MA: Wiley-Blackwell, 2017.
Alister E. McGrath, *The Christian Theology Reader.* 5th edn. Oxford and Malden, MA: Wiley-Blackwell, 2017.

Both these works are long and comprehensive, and you may prefer these two widely used books, which are shorter and more accessible.

Alister E. McGrath, *Theology: The Basics.* 4th edn. Oxford and Malden, MA: Wiley-Blackwell, 2018.
Alister E. McGrath, *Theology: The Basic Readings.* 3rd edn. Oxford and Malden, MA: Wiley-Blackwell, 2018.